Looking at *Agamemnon*

Also available from Bloomsbury

Looking at Ajax, edited by David Stuttard
Looking at Antigone, edited by David Stuttard
Looking at Bacchae, edited by David Stuttard
Looking at Lysistrata, edited by David Stuttard
Looking at Medea, edited by David Stuttard

Looking at *Agamemnon*

Edited by David Stuttard

BLOOMSBURY ACADEMIC
LONDON • NEW YORK • OXFORD • NEW DELHI • SYDNEY

BLOOMSBURY ACADEMIC
Bloomsbury Publishing Plc
50 Bedford Square, London, WC1B 3DP, UK
1385 Broadway, New York, NY 10018, USA
29 Earlsfort Terrace, Dublin 2, Ireland

BLOOMSBURY, BLOOMSBURY ACADEMIC and the Diana logo are trademarks of Bloomsbury Publishing Plc

First published in Great Britain 2021
This paperback edition published 2022

Copyright © David Stuttard & Contributors 2021

David Stuttard has asserted his right under the Copyright, Designs and Patents Act, 1988, to be identified as Editor of this work.

Cover image: Mixing bowl (calyx krater) with the killing of Agamemnon. The Dokimasia Painter, Greek c. 460 BC. Photograph © 2021 Museum of Fine Arts, Boston

All rights reserved. No part of this publication may be reproduced or transmitted in any form or by any means, electronic or mechanical, including photocopying, recording, or any information storage or retrieval system, without prior permission in writing from the publishers.

Bloomsbury Publishing Plc does not have any control over, or responsibility for, any third-party websites referred to or in this book. All internet addresses given in this book were correct at the time of going to press. The author and publisher regret any inconvenience caused if addresses have changed or sites have ceased to exist, but can accept no responsibility for any such changes.

A catalogue record for this book is available from the British Library.

A catalog record for this book is available from the Library of Congress.

ISBN: HB: 978-1-3501-4953-3
       PB: 978-1-3502-1434-7
       ePDF: 978-1-3501-4954-0
       eBook: 978-1-3501-4955-7

Typeset by RefineCatch Limited, Bungay, Suffolk

To find out more about our authors and books visit www.bloomsbury.com and sign up for our newsletters.

Contents

List of Contributors	vi
Foreword	vii
Introduction: *Agamemnon* in Context David Stuttard	1
1 Eating Children Is Bad for You: The Offspring of the Past in Aeschylus' *Agamemnon* Edith Hall	13
2 Agamemnon at Aulis: Hard Choice or No Choice? Alan H. Sommerstein	29
3 The Homecoming of Agamemnon Alex F. Garvie	39
4 Clytemnestra and Cassandra Hanna M. Roisman	49
5 Ritual in *Agamemnon* Richard Seaford	69
6 Let the Good Prevail Sophie Mills	77
7 Agency in *Agamemnon* Robert Garland	89
8 Wealth and Injustice in *Agamemnon* Michael Carroll	105
9 'There is the sea – who can drain it dry?' Natural and Unnatural Cycles in *Agamemnon* Rush Rehm	119
10 Similes and Other Likenesses in Aeschylus' *Agamemnon* Anna Uhlig	135
11 *Agamemnon*, Warfare and Its Aftermath Isabelle Torrance	149
12 Revenge for Murder Seen through Modern Eyes: Recent Reception of Aeschylus' *Oresteia* Betine van Zyl Smit	161
Aeschylus' *Agamemnon* translated by David Stuttard	173
Bibliography	217
Index	223

Contributors

Michael Carroll is Lecturer in Greek Literature at the University of St Andrews.

Robert Garland is Roy D. and Margaret B. Wooster Professor of the Classics Emeritus, Colgate University.

Alex F. Garvie is Emeritus Professor of Greek at the University of Glasgow.

Edith Hall is Professor in the Department of Classics and Centre for Hellenic Studies at King's College.

Sophie Mills is Professor in the Department of Classics, University of North Carolina Asheville.

Rush Rehm is Professor of Theatre and Performance Studies, and of Classics at Stanford University.

Hanna Roisman is Professor of Classics, Arnold Bernhard Professor of Arts and Humanities, Emerita, Colby College.

Richard Seaford is Emeritus Professor of Ancient Greek at the University of Exeter.

Alan H. Sommerstein is Emeritus Professor of Greek at the University of Nottingham.

David Stuttard is a freelance writer, historian and theatre director, and Fellow of Goodenough College, London.

Isabelle Torrance is Professor of Classical Reception at Aarhus University.

Anna Uhlig is Associate Professor of Classics at the University of California, Davis.

Betine van Zyl Smit is former Associate Professor of Classics at the University of Nottingham.

Foreword

Aeschylus' *Agamemnon* is the first play in the only extant Greek tragic trilogy, the *Oresteia*, and while it is tempting to consider the three plays as a unity it is equally valid to discuss them on their own. After all, every other surviving tragedy was once part of a trilogy, and the loss of its companion pieces is not considered an insuperable impediment to our studying it. In the case of *Agamemnon*, of course, the presence 'in the background' of the other two plays enhances our knowledge, and our awareness of how the trilogy develops and ends adds to our appreciation of its beginning.

I first translated *Agamemnon* for performance (as a stand-alone play), which I directed for Actors of Dionysus in 1999. I directed a subsequent, very different production for the same company in 2003. Since then I have been fortunate to work on several of the speeches with Sian Philips, Stephen Greif and the late Fenella Fielding. Every actor who has performed my words has enhanced my understanding of the text, and my personal thanks go to them all.

Every chapter in this volume, too, has deepened my understanding and appreciation of the text and context of *Agamemnon*. The collection was assembled during the Covid-19 crisis of 2020, and my sincere thanks go to every contributor who, despite the many demands imposed upon them by having to revise courses for distance-learning, managed so determinedly to submit their chapters – especially Edith Hall and Richard Seaford who, when two of their colleagues were forced to drop out because of illness or bereavement, stepped into the breach, adapting and updating material from lectures they had given in association with one of my productions of the play.

As with other volumes in this series, I have allowed authors to choose those aspects of the play on which they wished to focus. Inevitably there is the occasional small overlap between some chapters, with which I have not interfered, and, while I suggested that authors use the forms 'BC' and 'AD', I respected the wishes of those for whom it was important to use 'BCE' and 'CE'. Equally, I have respected contributors' choices with regard to transliteration from the Greek and spelling of names, e.g. Clytemnestra / Clytaemestra.

Many of the quotations from *Agamemnon* are taken from my own translation (a slightly revised version of my 1999 version), which is printed after the chapters. Readers wishing to use it for productions of their own should contact me through my website, www.davidstuttard.com, where applications for performance should be made before the commencement of any rehearsals.

Finally, I would like to thank all those who have been involved in the production of this book, especially the twelve Olympian contributors, who have given so generously of their time, and with whom it has been such a pleasure to work. At Bloomsbury, my thanks go to Alice Wright, who commissioned it, her maternity-leave replacement, Georgina Leighton, and her assistant Lily MacMahon; also to Rachel Walker, the Senior Production Editor, Dave Cummings, who edited the text and Terry Woodley, who designed the cover; also to the ever-efficient Merv Honeywood, the Client Manager at RefineCatch. A very big thank you, too, to the home team, my wife Emily Jane (not yet quite so frustrated by my endless forays into the classical world that she has been driven to emulate Clytemnestra) and my research assistants, our two cats, Stanley and Oliver, lion-cubs 'reared in the palace', but thankfully (so far) with a better outcome than that imagined by the chorus in *Agamemnon*.

Introduction: *Agamemnon* in Context

David Stuttard

Agamemnon is at heart a revenge play. On the face of it the plot is simple: it tells how Queen Clytemnestra of Argos murders her husband, Agamemnon, leader of the Greek army in the Trojan War, in vengeance because he killed their daughter. But there is nothing simple in how Aeschylus handles his material. As the drama unfolds and we delve deeper into the circumstances that have led to this moment, the reasons why Agamemnon apparently must die become increasingly more complex: motive piles on motive as more and more characters, both human and divine, become implicated in the litany of savagery that plagues the royal palace, until the very building appears to assume a malignant life of its own. Yet this is no mere horror story. While Agamemnon's palace, with its slaughtered children, gushing blood and vengeful furies that at times seem to possess Clytemnestra, may share similarities with the Overlook Hotel in Stanley Kubrick's film, *The Shining*, in Aeschylus' hands the atrocities perpetrated by its inhabitants become the starting point for a profound meditation on the nature of crime and punishment, innocence and guilt, vengeance, justice, good government and the relationship between humankind, the gods and the world around them, overarching themes that will permeate the whole of the *Oresteia* trilogy of which *Agamemnon* forms the first part.

However, while the themes are universal and the tragedy may in many ways be timeless, *Agamemnon* was very much a product of its age, so to begin to appreciate it fully we must be aware of the social, cultural and political conditions familiar to Aeschylus and his audience in the Athens of 458 BC, when it was first staged. Not that this was its only performance: so popular was the *Oresteia* that it was often revived – including by Aeschylus himself in Sicily, and after his death by his successors in Athens and elsewhere – while today it enjoys the distinction of being the only classical Greek trilogy to survive (almost) complete. Considerations of context as well as of why *Agamemnon* has intrigued so many for so long are the subject of many of the chapters in this book. But before we begin to examine the play in depth, it might perhaps be useful not only to set it in its historical and cultural context but to consider briefly the process of translating the text into English. And, because the first audience was more familiar with the mythological background to the play than many of us are today, it is with this that we shall begin.

The myth of Agamemnon and the House of Atreus

According to most versions of the myth, the Anatolian King Tantalus invited the gods to a feast, where unbeknownst to them the menu included his own son Pelops, whom he had killed and cooked in a stew. Only Demeter was tricked into eating a tiny portion. When the other gods saw what had happened, they cursed Tantalus to eternal punishment, while Pelops, reassembled and restored to life (complete with a prosthetic shoulder, the only part consumed), travelled to Greece, where he fathered two children, Atreus and Thyestes.

The brothers were quarrelsome. Both believed that they should rule Mycenae, the wealthy city in the Argolid, and, while Atreus (the elder) took the throne, Thyestes plotted to unseat him. Seducing Atreus' wife, Aerope, he stole his brother's golden lamb, which symbolized his right to kingship, and, as Atreus fled for sanctuary to Sparta, Thyestes proclaimed that he would abdicate only when the sun moved backwards in the sky (something he believed to be a cosmic impossibility).

But Zeus was angry with Thyestes for stealing Aerope and usurping the throne. He reversed the sun's path, and Atreus returned in triumph. Although he took revenge upon the faithless Aerope by drowning her, he pretended to forgive his brother and organized a banquet in his honour. Only when it was over did Atreus reveal the truth: in true family tradition, he had served up to Thyestes his own children. Horrified, Thyestes cursed his brother and his family (called by Aeschylus the 'House of Pleisthenes' but more usually the 'House of Atreus') before fleeing into exile where, advised by an oracle that he would achieve vengeance only if he had a child by his own (surviving) daughter, Pelopia, he raped her. Soon afterwards, Atreus married Pelopia, but when she gave birth to a son, she abandoned her baby on the hillside, where he was reared by goats – hence his name, Aegisthus (*aix, aegos*, from which it is derived, means 'goat') – until Atreus rescued him and brought him up in his palace along with his two older sons by Aerope, Agamemnon and Menelaus. When Aegisthus came of age, however, he discovered his true identity, killed Atreus and restored his father, Thyestes, to the throne.

Now it was the turn of Agamemnon and Menelaus to flee to Sparta, where the king arranged for Menelaus to marry his daughter, Helen. As for Agamemnon, his heart was set on Helen's twin sister, Clytemnestra. That she was already married was no impediment to Agamemnon – he murdered her husband and her infant son, and forced Clytemnestra to become his bride. Then the two sons of Atreus (known as the 'Atreidae') marched on Mycenae and drove out Thyestes and Aegisthus.

For some years all went well. In Mycenae, Agamemnon and Clytemnestra had three children: a son, Orestes; and two daughters, Iphigenia and Electra. But, when Paris, Prince of Troy, abducted Helen from Sparta, Menelaus asked Agamemnon to lead a Greek army to bring her back. The troops assembled at the Bay of Aulis on the east coast of the Greek mainland opposite the island of Euboea, but while there Agamemnon somehow angered the gods – specifically Artemis, goddess of both hunting and young animals, who subsequently sent strong winds that prevented the ships from sailing. With no end to the storm in sight Calchas, the military prophet, announced that only one thing would appease Artemis: Agamemnon must sacrifice to her his daughter, Iphigenia. He duly did. And ten years later he and his army captured Troy, the starting point for our present play.

Meanwhile, however, Aegisthus had returned to Mycenae, where he found a sympathetic ally in Clytemnestra (who was furious with Agamemnon for yet again killing one of her children). The two began an affair. Plotting Agamemnon's death, they sent Orestes to far-off Phocis. When Agamemnon at last came home, Clytemnestra coaxed him into a warm bath, threw a net across him (to constrain him) and either stabbed him repeatedly with a knife or hacked him to pieces with an axe before declaring herself Aegisthus' queen.

The plot of *Agamemnon* ends here, but the first audience knew what happened next (and would soon see it in the remainder of the *Oresteia*). For the cycle of vengeance was not yet over. Some years later, when Orestes reached manhood, he returned to Mycenae, where he took revenge for his father by killing both Aegisthus and Clytemnestra. Yet, although he had been instructed by the god Apollo, he could not escape retribution. With no family member left to punish him, the Erinyes (or 'Furies') took over. Grim, ghastly female monsters, they pursued him first to Delphi, then to Athens, where on Areopagus Hill opposite the Acropolis the goddess Athena set up a court of law with Athenian citizens as jurors to try Orestes for matricide. With Apollo acting as counsel for the defence against the prosecuting Erinyes, Athena (the judge) conceded that, since the father is the dominant parent (the mother being simply the seed-bed and incubator of his sperm), Orestes had been right to prioritize avenging Agamemnon, even if it did mean killing his mother, Clytemnestra. This is the climax of the *Oresteia* trilogy, which ends with the Erinyes (grudgingly reconciled to the verdict) being offered a home in Athens and a role protecting the city for as long as the Athenians should behave piously.

The *Oresteia*

As already mentioned, *Agamemnon* is the first tragedy in a thematically connected trilogy, the *Oresteia* (named from Orestes the protagonist of the second and third plays) that explores how the primeval *lex talionis*, the 'eye-for-an-eye' law of personal retaliatory revenge, evolves into a civic system of judicial trial and punishment administered by a court of law. *Agamemnon* and *Choephoroi* ('Libation Bearers', or 'Grave Gifts' in my translation), the middle play, pose the problem: once we embark upon a cycle of vengeance, how can we ever escape it, especially if (as is the case with the murky House of Atreus) it becomes increasingly unclear precisely whose crime we are avenging – in *Agamemnon*, Clytemnestra's primary motivation is her husband's sacrifice of their daughter, Iphigenia, while her paramour, Aegisthus, is seeking vengeance for his butchered siblings. Further problems arise, too, when we realize that some of those involved have been provoked to kill through the direct or indirect intervention of a god. In Agamemnon's case this is Artemis (her will communicated through the human agency of the seer, Calchas); in Orestes' case it is Apollo (speaking through the Delphic oracle).

In addition to these questions of motivation and agency, by the time that the reluctant Orestes (abetted by Electra) kills his mother, Clytemnestra, the cycle of revenge has proved so efficient that there is no family member left alive to continue it, but by the beginning of *Eumenides* ('The Kindly Ones'), the final play, the solution to this problem becomes shockingly clear. Orestes is being pursued by Erinyes, known sometimes as Furies, horrific goddesses with snaky hair and suppurating eyes, one of whose *raisons d'être* is to exact retribution for familial murder. Like supernatural bloodhounds, they track Orestes first to Delphi, then to Athens, whose patron goddess Athena (representative of a younger generation than the Erinyes) finds a fine civilizing solution, establishing a law-court, enlisting Athenian citizens as jurors and inviting each side, prosecution and defence, to set out their case. With the jury split evenly, Athena casts the deciding vote in favour of Orestes, who is free (once he has ritually purified himself) to return to normal life. As for the Erinyes, they are offered a new home in Athens and a new role as benign protecting goddesses (hence their new name, 'Eumenides'), while the trilogy that began in darkness with a Watchman searching for a spark of firelight ends in a blaze of celebration.

This was not the end of the *Oresteia*, however. In the first production, *Eumenides* was followed by a satyr play, a coda in which material from the myth was treated in a more light-hearted manner, its chorus formed of actors dressed in costumes representing rowdy half-human, half-horse satyrs, followers of Dionysus, patron god of drama. Sadly *Proteus*, the *Oresteia*'s satyr play, does not survive, but its *dramatis personae* may have included Helen, a counterpart to her sister Clytemnestra whose constant presence dominates *the Oresteia*.

In *Agamemnon* (despite the title) Clytemnestra is the undisputed protagonist, the palace chatelaine, the spider lurking at the centre of a grim web, 'the one' (as the chauvinistic Watchman puts it) 'who has a man's brain in a woman's body', next to whom the briefly seen Agamemnon seems weak, and the oleaginous Aegisthus venal. In *Choephoroi*, however, where she appears less often, she seems to have subtly changed as she expresses not only her need to defer to her new husband but her mother-love for the returnee, Orestes. But it is simply an act. At the start of *Eumenides* her ghost materializes in a terrifying scene to goad the awakening Erinyes into pursuing her son. Even here, however, she trumps Agamemnon: in *Choephoroi*, when Orestes and Electra try to summon his spirit from the Underworld, it is too weak or too unwilling to appear.

Clytemnestra's prominence within the trilogy is far from accidental: it highlights the ultimate horror of Orestes' matricide, the killing of the one who gave him birth and – as she graphically reminds him – suckled him (though in *Choephoroi* his wet-nurse Cilissa claims that the responsibility for this was hers). Her inescapable presence makes Orestes' acquittal all the more powerful – his trial switches the focus away from the act of killing even such a dominating character as Clytemnestra to a cool, rational balancing of the circumstances of the deed.

The law-court of the Areopagus becomes the cradle of civilizing justice, with the Athenian jurors as its representatives on earth, which must have delighted the original Athenian audience no end, not least because the drama was in effect legitimizing a political move just four years earlier, when, having had many of its old aristocratic powers removed, the ancient aristocratic Council of the Areopagus became in effect a democratic court judging certain cases of homicide. No wonder that the People's representatives awarded the *Oresteia* first prize in the dramatic competition (though, even without its two competitors' survival, we may be pretty certain that it deserved its place thanks to the dazzling quality of its writing alone).

Life of Aeschylus

When Aeschylus, in 458 BC already in his mid-sixties, wrote the *Oresteia*, he was the darling of the Athenian audience. Born around 525 BC to a wealthy family from the Attic coastal town, Eleusis, the site of annual initiation ceremonies promising a blessed afterlife, he entered history in 490 BC fighting for his city against the Persians in the pivotal Battle of Marathon. Ten years later, he probably fought as a marine at the naval battle of Salamis, an encounter that he describes vividly in *Persians*, his earliest extant play, performed in 472 BC in a production paid for by the rising politician, Pericles. The trilogy (or tetralogy, if we include the satyr play) of which it formed a part won first prize at the Festival of Dionysus, a feat that Aeschylus repeated on no less than twelve other occasions, meaning that fifty-two out of a total output of roughly seventy to ninety plays were awarded the top prize.

Like other contemporary tragedians, Aeschylus is said to have performed as an actor – perhaps taking the role of Clytemnestra in the *Oresteia*. He was reportedly stunningly innovative in his stagecraft, too, dressing his cast in long-sleeved flowing robes and platform-soled boots, and at one performance of *Eumenides* (though probably not the premiere) supposedly shocking the audience so much with his chorus of Erinyes that sensitive young men fainted and pregnant women went into premature labour. Whereas tragedies had previously involved a chorus and just one actor, Aeschylus reputedly transformed drama by introducing a second actor, allowing characters to enter into dialogue and debate. The *Oresteia* skilfully utilizes a third actor, too (supposedly introduced by his rival, Sophocles), in unexpected ways: in *Agamemnon* the foreign and previously silent Cassandra suddenly bursts into incomprehensible babbling that soon transitions into rational, if terrifying speech; while in *Choephoroi* a crucial three lines reminding Orestes of Apollo's order to kill his mother are given to the otherwise non-speaking third actor, Pylades.

Despite his good democratic credentials, Aeschylus also wrote for the courts of Sicilian tyrants (or potentates) and it was in Sicily at Gela that he died while supervising a production of the *Oresteia*. According to legend, hoping to crack its shell, an eagle dropped a tortoise onto Aeschylus' bald head, mistaking it for a rock. One inscription on his tomb read, 'I died, struck by a missile from an eagle's claws', but the patriotic Aeschylus had already composed another, more noble epitaph for himself: 'Beneath this marker lies Aeschylus, son of Euphorion, an Athenian who died in Gela, rich in wheat fields. The groves of Marathon tell of his courage, and the long-haired Persians know it well.'

Staging *Agamemnon*

We have no information about the first production of *Agamemnon*, but some details may be inferred. It was performed in the open-air Theatre of Dionysus on the south-east slope of the Athenian Acropolis, whose temples were still in ruins, having been burned by the Persians prior to their defeat at Salamis some twenty-two years earlier. The theatre itself probably consisted of a flat-roofed wooden stage-building, the *skēnē*, which in *Agamemnon* represented the palace, furnished with one wide central doorway (jealously guarded by Clytemnestra). Immediately in front of the *skēnē* was the *orkhēstra* (dancing floor), the area occupied predominately by the chorus. While we are familiar with the Classical Greek circular *orkhēstra* and the Roman horseshoe version, in 458 BC it was probably rectangular. Embracing the *orkhēstra* on the three sides not occupied by the *skēnē* was the *theatron* (the Greek word derives from a word meaning 'to see', whereas our equivalent, 'auditorium', comes from the Latin for 'to hear'), with temporary wooden benches arranged (probably in straight rows) up the rake of the hill, sufficient to seat around 5,000 spectators.

If the performing space was rudimentary, it is clear that Aeschylus used it with imaginative panache. Whereas most plays begin with the entry on foot of an actor or actors, *Agamemnon* starts with what might at first have seemed a disembodied voice issuing not from the stage or the *orkhēstra* but from the *skēnē* roof, where the Watchman, who had perhaps lain muffled in his blanket as the audience took its seats in the twilight hour before the dawn, crouched 'like a watch-dog' waiting for the beacon's light. Immediately his *prologue* speech was over, the members of the chorus (probably fifteen in number, though perhaps twelve) entered through one of the two *parodoi* (singular = *parodos*), passages between the *skēnē* and the *theatron*. As they did so, they performed an entrance song (also known, somewhat confusingly, as the *parodos*). From now on they would remain in view throughout the play (though in *Eumenides* they exit temporarily), interacting with the main characters and occasionally dancing while singing odes (*stasima*; singular = *stasimon*), between which (in so-called *episodes*, literally 'between odes') the solo actors delivered speeches and dialogues, usually declaiming their lines but occasionally – at times of heightened emotion – singing them.

Like the chorus (and probably like the audience, too), the actors were all male. Their performances were likely to have been relatively stylized – necessarily so, not simply because of their relatively cumbersome costumes, but because they all wore masks, those of the actors individualized to suit their characters, those of the chorus probably identical to convey a sense of anonymity or group-identity. The reason behind the masks is still unclear but, given the acoustics of an open-air space, their use must have meant that speeches were delivered 'up and out', directly to the audience. Performances were not static, however. Choruses danced – or at least moved rhythmically – to the music of an *aulos* (a wind instrument rather like the modern oboe or the Armenian duduk), their gestures choreographed to suit the metre of the poetry they were singing, the ode divided into metrically matching *strophes* (literally 'turns') and *antistrophes* (literally 'turnings back') rounded off with an independent *epode*.

Today we are used to Aristotle's notion that Greek drama observed the three 'tragic unities' of time, space and action. Luckily, Aeschylus had never heard of them. While the plot of *Eumenides* takes us from Delphi to Athens, the action of *Agamemnon* telescopes days into minutes, for within half an hour of hearing by means of a beacon relay that the Greeks are in the process of taking Troy, first the Herald and then Agamemnon appear on stage having completed the perilous voyage home. Agamemnon's entrance is another of Aeschylus' *coups de théâtre*, for it is clear from the text that he arrived in a vehicle (a wagon or chariot), which it is not unreasonable to suppose was drawn by live horses. But he was not alone. Beside him stood an exotic female figure clad in robes perhaps recognizable as the vestments of a priestess of Apollo – the Trojan princess, Cassandra. Yet Aeschylus' staging was about to become even more spectacular. Rather than allow her husband to walk into the palace on bare earth, Clytemnestra has her attendants spread red fabrics from the *skēnē* door to Agamemnon's vehicle, creating a powerful image that suggests a river of blood flowing from the house, up which the king must walk.

More drama is to come. With Agamemnon now offstage, first the chorus, and then Clytemnestra crowd round the silent Cassandra, whom the audience imagines is a non-speaking supernumerary – until, in a shocking outburst, she screams out the first of her unearthly cries, '*otototoi popoi da!* Apollo! Apollo!' This is soon to be replaced by an all-too-understandable flood of speech as the prophetess describes what she sees before her very eyes (although the audience cannot see it) – the murdered children of Thyestes, 'clutching in their hands their flesh, their guts, their entrails, sweetmeats in a feast for their own father'. It is an extraordinary scene: the prophetess at times whipped into unearthly speech by a forceful Apollo, at times left limp to converse in her own voice, finally rejecting her role of priestess altogether, discarding her robes and trampling them on the ground (just as Agamemnon has trampled the red fabrics) before going into the palace and what she knows must be her death.

And then, more disembodied voices – Agamemnon's screams as he is murdered – and the chorus, disunified now as they panic, speaking not as a group but individually, the only time in extant Greek tragedy that this happens, before the *skēnē*'s doors swing open and the final dramatic coup gets underway. From inside the building, a low platform is wheeled out, the *ekkuklēma*, with, standing on it, Clytemnestra, bloodied, holding in one hand a knife or sword, and in the other the hunting net that she has thrown over Agamemnon before murdering him in his bath. And with the corpses of her husband and Cassandra slumped at her feet, she delivers a speech of intense, triumphant power.

How could Aeschylus top such high tension? He did not try. Instead, the subsequent bickering between Clytemnestra and the chorus is deliberately anticlimactic, while even Aegisthus' thwarted attempts to get his henchmen to attack the chorus seem deliberately bathetic. When the play ended not with a concluding choral summation but with performers exiting in silence, the first audience must have sat back in stunned admiration. They had just been privileged to witness one of the most remarkable productions ever staged in the history of world drama.

Translating *Agamemnon*

As Michael Evans writes in his entry, 'Translations (English) of/Translating Aeschylus', in *The Encyclopaedia of Greek Tragedy*:[1] 'Aeschylus created his dramas at the same time as highly patterned, syntactically complex and allusive odes to celebrate victories at the Olympic and other games made Pindar the equivalent of a modern millionaire.' He goes on, however: 'Accordingly, one of the first imperatives when translating Aeschylus' often complex verse is to be clear and transparent, preserving the imagery wherever possible. I propose two fundamental criteria for a good modern translation of Aeschylus, to which all others should be subordinate. These two criteria, which necessarily are in a creative tension with each other, are that the translation should be *accurate* and that it should be *actable*.'

What, though, might we mean by 'accurate' and 'actable'? Given the right performer, the telephone book can be 'actable', while 'accurate' can cover a multitude of sins. For me, a translation must do three things: first, it must be a faithful transposition of *meaning* from one language into another; second, it must try as far as possible to reproduce the *style* of the original in the new language; and third, it must *flow* as if it was originally written in the language into which it has been translated. If all three of these criteria are met, a script composed by a brilliant dramatist such as Aeschylus will cry out to be acted.

My translation of *Agamemnon* in this volume is a slightly modified version of one written for performance in 1999, subsequently revived in 2003 and adopted the same year by The Open University as part of their course, *AA(ZX)300, Europe: Culture and Identities in a Contested Continent*. For the accompanying Study Guide, I was interviewed by Lorna Hardwick about the translation process, and the observations that I made then remain pertinent, not least that 'I took some comfort in a footnote in the edition I was using by E. Fraenkel,[2] where he says "*I cannot understand this passage.*"' I went on:

> I wanted my translation to convey the monumentality of Aeschylus, with all the richness of his imagery and poetic vocabulary, without losing the dramatic momentum ... Given the obscurity of some of Aeschylus' language, and my need to produce a speakable acting script, I tended towards conveying the spirit rather than the letter of the original. This does not mean 'making it up', but occasionally expanding the denser images, developing passages or images so that their full impact might be felt ... [Some] images are woven through the text like the warp and weft of the net, the 'drag-net of destiny', which Agamemnon first casts over the vanquished Troy, and which in the end is used to capture him. Like much in Aeschylus, the net is at the same time both symbol and reality, and the challenge for the translator is to preserve this inner tension.

Later, responding to a question about how the translator bridges the cultural divide between ancient and modern, I addressed the question of a prose versus a poetic (or metrical) translation:

> Ancient performances were more akin to opera or musicals than to conventional modern theatre: significant passages were sung and danced; and whereas spoken passages were characterized by iambic metre, these musical set-pieces could be in any of a number of metres, ranging from slow and stately to fast and frantic. I made no attempt to replicate the exact metres, though I did take the intention of each into account, modulating the language used so that it reflected the original metrical context. For example, readers may notice how, in the Cassandra scene, there is a high degree of metrical writing. This prolonged episode was one of the musical highlights of Aeschylus' production, an extended scene mirroring Agamemnon's brief entry into the palace, but much more elegiac, and using Cassandra's knowledge of past, present and future to create a scene of devastatingly tragic inevitability. Interestingly, the first words Cassandra speaks are '*otototoi popoi da! Apollo! Apollo!*', a jumble of non-verbal sounds, crystallizing at the end into the name of the god Apollo, put into her mouth by Aeschylus deliberately to reinforce her foreignness. Like the Chorus we think 'our friend needs a translator'. Like the Chorus, we're wrong.

However, as Michael Evans implies in his article, a translation of a drama must be written in the assumption that it might be performed. Addressing Lorna Hardwick's question about translating for the stage, I summed the process up like this:

In the end, theatre can often convey more through actions than through words. We are fortunate enough still to possess the words of many of the plays of antiquity and, in translation, they should be treated with care. But once they have been turned into a modern script, they are precisely that: a script. Aeschylus was not a classicist. He was not an academic. He was a man of the theatre, and a modern production must bring the drama gloriously to life – for this *is* drama, and the production is the final link in the translation.

Agamemnon, then, is not just a classical text of profound significance but a script that can still affect an audience today – and it is as both that the twelve scholars, whose essays follow, will consider it.

Notes

1 Roisman (2014).
2 Fraenkel (1950).

1

Eating Children Is Bad for You: The Offspring of the Past in Aeschylus' *Agamemnon*

Edith Hall

Our deeds are like children that are born to us; they live and act apart from our will; nay, children may be strangled, but deeds never; they have an indestructible life, both in and out of our consciousness.

George Eliot

The infancy of humankind

In one of the most extraordinary ghost scenes in world literature, the clairvoyant Cassandra of *Agamemnon* sees the spectres of the little children served up at the Thyestean feast, diminutive ghosts who died in and haunt the house forming the scenic background to the tragedy. 'Do you see those young creatures', she demands of the Chorus, 'beside the house, like figures in dreams? They are the children, slaughtered by their own kindred; their hands are full of the meat of their own flesh; they are clear to me, holding their vitals and entrails, which their father tasted' (1217–22). As if to emphasize her isolation, Aeschylus has designed the scene so that only Cassandra can see these very special spirits of the untimely dead – pitiful, butchered, roasted and disembowelled.[1] In Cassandra's vision, the themes of kin-murder, flesh-eating and cannibalism, which are recurrent throughout the entirety of *Agamemnon*, are realized visually, albeit only in the audience's imagination, to shocking effect. This chapter aims to illuminate these themes by exploring (1) their relationship to the idea of the family curse afflicting the Argive royal family and the parallel curse afflicting the original divine family in Hesiod's *Theogony*, at the precise moment when the Erinyes were born, and (2) their interactions with images drawn from the animal world and human as well as other mammalian reproduction.

Intermingling with Cassandra's vision of the ghostly, cannibalized sons of Thyestes, numerous metaphorical and symbolic children haunt the imagery and figures of speech characterizing the tragedy as a whole.[2] The Chorus complain about growing old; they are as weak and ineffectual as children (75; 81). At Troy, says Clytemnestra, children are being thrown onto the corpses of the very men who begot them (327–28). Temptation, state the Chorus, is a domineering child who incites a man to arrogant behaviour (385–86); such an arrogant man is, in his delusion, like a child who chases a bird (394).[3] Clytemnestra complains about being addressed as if she were a child of no understanding (277); childishness is equated with a lack of sense of comprehension (479). When the Chorus can finally understand unambiguously something that Cassandra says (i.e. that she is about to die), they reply that 'even a newborn infant' could understand her words (1163). Aegisthus also contributes to the repertoire of infancy images: he describes how he was sent into exile by Atreus when he was still only in swaddling-bands (1606).

It is not easy to understand the pervasive equation of imperfect powers of comprehension with those of children in isolation from the other plays in the *Oresteia*. In the course of the tragedies, Aeschylus uses the analogy of the life of a human being to symbolize the progress of humankind from barbarism to civilization. In terms of the advance of civilization, the people in *Agamemnon* remain in their infancy. In *Libation Bearers* Orestes is at the point of leaving adolescence; by the stage of human development portrayed in *Eumenides* the Argive prince, who now represents a new level of social evolution, has himself become an adult and can be tried as a morally competent and autonomous agent in a civic criminal court. The court is of course in Athens, which in Aeschylus' vision has no king, and is beginning to construct the community institutions that would eventually coalesce, when Aeschylus was a teenager, and take the form of the state apparatus of the Cleisthenic democracy. The course of a human life – from birth through babyhood, infancy, childhood and adolescence to adulthood – is thus used as a paradigm of the progress of Greek society from the moral toy box of simple, reciprocal blood-feuds under monarchy and tyranny to the complexities of 'grown-up', publicly administered justice in democratic, fifth-century Athens. But it also interacts in several ways with the ancient Greeks' account of the origins of conflict amongst the earliest gods, their violent, vindictive family, and their struggle for control of the cosmic political order as played out in Hesiod's *Theogony*.[4]

The Erinyes and the family curse

For the ancient Greeks of Aeschylus' time, the legacy of past deeds was conceptualized more concretely, more extremely and more physically than it is in our modern notions of internal guilt which torments the malefactor.

Murderers (and there was no crime more serious than murder within the family, outlawed by an ancient and grave taboo) were tormented not so much by their own consciences as by the Erinyes, or vengeance-spirits, of the murdered victim. The Erinyes could only be appeased by the blood of the murderer, or vicariously by the blood of his or her children. When this blood was spilt on the ground, they drank it voraciously from their subterranean home beneath it.[5] In drinking human blood, and their association with hunting, blood-hounds and tearing flesh, which will receive such an emphasis when they physically appear in *Eumenides*, they have their own cannibalistic qualities.

The centrality of the Erinyes to the entire *Oresteia* is, however, set up by several important passages in *Agamemnon*. In a vivid passage, the Chorus imagine eagles wheeling, mourning and seeking vengeance for the loss of their young, as an *Erinys* that brings punishment (55–59); although the context implies a comparison with the vengeful Atridae, the simile also reminds the audience of Clytemnestra, awaiting revenge for the loss of her daughter Iphigenia.[6] Later, they reflect that 'the gods are not unaware of murderers. Eventually, the black Erinyes bring to oblivion the man who has succeeded by unjust means, and reverse his fortunes by wearing him down' (461–66). Helen herself is seen as a bride whose effect on Troy (and consequently on the Argives) was that of an Erinys who brings tears (748–49). And Cassandra describes another group of terrifying spirits haunting the palace, reminiscent of the cannibalized children, but associated rather with the crime of adultery which had resulted in the Thyestean feast, because Thyestes seduced his brother's wife, Aerope (1186–93): 'For a cacophonous chorus, singing in unison, never leaves this roof, for it speaks only of ill. And so, glutted with human blood, and thus emboldened, a revel-procession of kindred Erinyes haunts the house, and can't be driven away.'

The Erinyes bring with them the story of their own strange genesis, as members of the primordial family in Greek myth, as disseminated in Hesiod's *Theogony*, one of the Greeks' oldest narratives and part of their core identity and cultural curriculum. The Erinyes are some of the youngest in the long line of siblings produced in the first sexual mating, between Gaia and the son she has produced alone, Ouranos. They are thus primeval, but also low-status among this primordial generation; they are framed, forever, as the junior, little sisters of mighty beings. But several of the core themes and images in Hesiod's account of the original, conflicted, family in the universe reverberate within Aeschylus' account of the later, conflicted royal family at Argos in the Peloponnese.

In the *Theogony*, the Erinyes are said to have originated materially in the blood falling on Gaia, and socially within a phenomenally dysfunctional family *already* encompassing patriarchal privilege, incest, inter-generational violence, conflict between sexual partners and co-parents, mother-child collusion, castration and child abuse. Its complexity in terms of both ethics and gender ideology – a complexity that helps us understand why it was the Greeks who invented their household-focused genre of tragedy – can be seen from a brief comparison with its Hittite/Hurrian precursor. Kumarbi did bite off and swallow his father Anu's genitals, before spitting out the blood. Earth was inseminated. She gave birth to male god Tasmisu (connected with the important male Weather-God) and a female, a rather straightforward personification of the river Tigris. There is no sense of a conflicted nuclear family and the engendering of the cosmic principle of retribution for kinship-group crimes.[7] Similarly, when Enkidu returns from below after his katabasis in the Sumerian text *Bilgames and the Netherworld*, he reports the eternal punishment of groups whom the Greeks certainly saw later as the responsibility of the Erinyes – those who disrespected or were cursed by a parent, and oath-breakers.[8] But there is no sense that the punishment in the Mesopotamian underworld was carried on by any supernatural females born into a fundamentally dysfunctional divine family.

To summarize Hesiod's account of the background to the arrival of retributive justice – the fundamental theme of *Agamemnon* – in the universe (132–92): Gaia lay with Ouranos and gave birth to several children, including 'Cronos of the crooked counsel', who 'hated his vigorous father'. Then she gave birth to a series of monstrous sons including the Cyclopes, and they were all 'hated by their own father from the first'. He stuffed them back inside their mother, so she persuaded Cronos to castrate him. When Cronos threw his father's genitals on the ground, Gaia received the 'bloody droplets' and gave birth to the Erinyes. From the white foam that issued from bits of the genitals thrown into the sea, there was born Aphrodite.

In this primal scene of crime and counter-crime, the first felon is the patriarch. Ouranos represses all except one of his younger group of children and their mother. The oldest of this group, although not himself oppressed by his father, castrates him. It is at this pivotal moment that the Erinyes are born: between the second and third acts of violence in what is to become an infinite cycle. They somehow mark the very instant when the process, rather than finding a solution in the form of a doublet, a punishment to fit a crime (which is what Clytemnestra at the end of Agamemnon fervently wishes the day's murders comprise, as we shall see), forever loses all possibility of being limited and indeed becomes triple and escalates. It is also the moment when reciprocal violence is no longer a matter of straightforward tit for tat. Cronos' intervention, and the genesis of the unlimited, plural Erinyes, underline the potential for revenge to be redirected, for collateral damage, and for confusion about who is guilty of what, to spiral out of control.

Moreover, just after the birth of the Erinyes, the upshot of the castration of Ouranos is the first, primordial curse. The wounded patriarch declares that on Cronos and the hidden-away sons, there will late come vengeance (*tisis*) for their evil deed. This, as the Greeks knew, would expand in significance beyond the family to become the first great *political* struggle for power in the universe, when Zeus overcomes Cronos and the Olympians wrest supremacy from the Titans and Giants; in *Agamemnon*, where a similar curse operates, the revenge wreaked by Clytemnestra, with an unknowable amount of assistance from Aegisthus, is not only an act of personal and domestic revenge but part of a life-and-death struggle for absolute sovereign power, which she turns into a tyranny in *Libation Bearers*, in Argos.

The symbolic importance of this threefold movement establishing an irreversible process of crime and counter-crime, which is marked in Hesiod by the birth of the Erinyes and the first curse, is dazzlingly dramatized in the *Oresteia*.[9] The Hesiodic situation resembles that in *Agamemnon*. Here, too, there is a family curse, although the details of its genesis and first effects amidst earlier generations are not clearly spelled out. There is a frustratingly uninformative reference to another ancestor somehow embroiled in the saga of the family curse, Pleisthenes (1569); he was a mysterious son of Tantalus,[10] the founder of the Argive royal house and murderer of Pleisthenes' much more famous son, Pelops. Tantalus sacrificed Pelops and cannibalized him, serving him up in a banquet for the gods (Pindar, *Ol.* 1.58–65). In *Agamemnon*, however, just as there were different reasons why Ouranos and Cronos were hated, the reasons for the killing of Agamemnon are plural and confused, and the audience is reminded of shocking collateral damage in the deaths of the innocent Iphigenia and Cassandra. There is another similarity between the dysfunctional families of Hesiod and Aeschylus, and that is the centrality of the theme of the curse.

A range of images and vocabulary is applied to the curse on the House of Atreus in *Agamemnon* in addition to the choruses of murdered children and Erinyes whom Cassandra can perceive. The Chorus recall Calchas' prophetic description of the Clytemnestra-shaped Wrath (*Mēnis*) which would be the legacy of the sacrifice to Artemis (a sacrifice that would 'cause the wife to stop respecting the husband'): 'terrible, irrepressible, a treacherous housekeeper, a remembering Wrath, child-avenging' (153–55). Cassandra sings of the 'insatiable civil war' (*stasis*) that afflicts the Argive royal clan (1117). There is a notion that some fiend or malevolent spirit (*daimōn*) has occupied the household and ravens for blood like an Erinys. The Chorus accuse the '*daimōn* who has befallen on the house and the two descendants of Tantalus' (i.e. Agamemnon and Aegisthus) of operating through Clytemnestra (1469). Clytemnestra responds that they are correct to name 'the thrice-gorged *daimōn* of this race'; it is through him that 'the lust for lapping blood is fostered in the belly, so that before the ancient wound is healed, there is new bloodshed' (1475–80). It is interesting that she semi-eroticises the fiend's lust for blood to drink by calling it an *erōs*. But Clytemnestra hopes – in vain – that in killing Agamemnon she has stopped the cycle of reciprocal violence and wants to 'make a compact with the *daimōn* of the Pleisthenids' (1568–70). She later prays that the suffering the family has endured already will prove sufficient, visualizing the fiend as a horse or bull: 'kicked as we have been by the heavy hoof of the *daimōn*' (1660).

The Athenian audience in 458 BCE were also well accustomed to the idea of a family curse, arising from a sacrilegious killing, which afflicted prominent citizens at the top of the political ladder. Two of the most distinguished aristocrats and statesmen in the half-century history of the democracy, Pericles and his great-uncle Cleisthenes, both belonged to the Alcmaeonid family, which had fallen under a curse in the seventh century BCE. Their ancestor Megacles had authorized the killing of the followers of Cylon of Athens during an attempted coup, even though Cylon had taken refuge as a suppliant in Athena's temple (Herodotus 5.71; Thucydides 1.126). Although the family had eventually been rehabilitated, the old curse was still a live issue in Athenian memory and public rhetoric.

In Hesiod, the Erinyes' position within the first ever dysfunctional, strife-ridden family is precise. They are generated immediately before the curse – the threat of the *counter*-counter-crime – is delivered. This critical moment establishes a law of cosmic penology which is played out in every Greek mythical cycle. The law is re-enacted in Agamemnon, where Clytemnestra, who (as we shall see below) describes herself as a semi-supernatural embodiment of vengeance, kills her husband in a counter-crime for the sacrifice of Iphigenia just before Orestes must return to murder his mother and Aegisthus in the third swing of the pendulum, the counter-counter-crime.

The Erinyes' younger half-sister Aphrodite, conceived at the same time as them, is the goddess of sexual impulses. The Hesiodic genealogy this implies is the alliance between the destructive feelings engendered in the soul by sexual infatuation with another person and the desire to inflict reciprocal damage. This psychosomatic alliance is mirrored in Agamemnon's relationship with Cassandra and in Clytemnestra's with Aegisthus. But where Aphrodite is born from the semen-like 'white foam' emitted by the genitals (190–91), the Erinyes are born from their 'bloody droplets' from their father's groin (183). The word 'droplets' (*rhathaminges*) is used in the *Iliad* for drops of blood which issue from wounds which have nothing to do with genitals (e.g. 11.536). Their deviant conception may explain why they are females, but defective ones who do not themselves give birth. They are barren, distorted females, born from earth and blood rather than semen, who destroy rather than foster. They are like the snakes they brandish on vases; they inject venom into bodies of criminals but also drain their victims of blood. Their breasts, so often prominent in the iconography, are not breasts that will ever produce milk and nurture young.

Yet, like most monstrous collectives in Greek myth, the Erinyes are indeed female. Gruesome depictions of them are available in the last play of the trilogy, *Eumenides*: they are wingless, black, bloodsucking, polluting, snort awful blasts from their nostrils, ooze filthy mucus from their eyes, and wear disgusting clothes. Apollo says that they belong to the torture chamber, like those rumoured to be operated by the barbaric despots of Persia, 'where men are beheaded, have their eyes gouged out, are castrated, mutilated, are stoned to death, and impaled beneath the spine, moan long and piteously' (186–90).[11] In this last play of the trilogy the Erinyes, who act on behalf of the dead Clytemnestra (who has also been suggestively associated with non-Greek, barbarous conduct in *Agamemnon* when she prostrates herself before her husband),[12] actually appear to the audience in the form of the Chorus; they have to be appeased by Athena when she takes away their right to avenge murder, replacing them jurisprudentially with the gods' new invention – a state-administered homicide court. Aeschylus' Erinyes were so frightening in appearance that the ancient *Life of Aeschylus* 9 claimed that pregnant women in the original audience suffered spontaneous miscarriages. This biographical anecdote is probably not true, but the emergence of the story in later antiquity reveals another kind of truth: it preserves an authentic response to the emphasis in the *Oresteia* of dead infants and on the process of mammalian reproduction.

The offspring of the past

The 'offspring of the past', whose deaths eventually all operate as sacrifices to appease the Erinyes, form the central Argive triangle of *Agamemnon*: Agamemnon, his wife Clytemnestra, and his cousin (and her lover) Aegisthus. None of them can eradicate past deeds; their actions in the play are direct results of the past actions (especially infanticide) committed by themselves, their parents, or in Clytemnestra's case, her husband. Agamemnon's father has murdered his brother Thyestes' children, which Aegisthus cannot forgive, since they were his own brothers. Thyestes had seduced his brother's wife; Agamemnon had slaughtered his own daughter, Iphigenia. The deaths of both Thyestes' children and of the young Iphigenia have left a horrific legacy of Erinyes thirsting for blood.

Aeschylus, in composing a tragedy about the death of Agamemnon, chose a particular day, a period of hours between dawn and dusk, in which he is murdered. But in the compass of that single day Aeschylus conveys to his audience a panoramic transhistorical vision, delving into the past through the successive crimes in the family descending from Atreus, and also envisioning its equally miserable future: Cassandra predicts explicitly the deaths of 'another woman' and 'another man' (1317–18). The architecture of the tragedy's temporal scheme allows Aeschylus to unfold the story of the House of Atreus across three blighted generations. The three central characters have little sense of the large wheeled mechanisms in which they are but small cogs. But by careful use of the Chorus, of the seer Cassandra, and of the imagery of human and animal reproduction, Aeschylus allows his audience a much more comprehensive and transhistorical grasp of the endlessly self-replicating revenge murders blighting Argos.

Eating children

Eating children is not just bad for the children and the consumer's digestion. In ancient Greek myth it is bad for the entire extended family, affecting them down the generations. In the *Theogony*, the curse with which Ouranos blights his son Cronos' future plays out in a new, shocking twist in the divine family saga when Cronos not only oppresses his own children, but actually devours them. In this narrative (*Theogony* 403–506), Hesiod tells us that Cronos' wife Rhea bore him splendid children – Hestia, Demeter, Hera, Hades, Poseidon and Zeus. Cronos, in an attempt to maintain his mastery of the universe in the face of these mighty children, because he had been told by his parents that he was destined to be displaced by a son, swallowed the first five of them when they were born. Rhea succeeded in protecting the youngest, Zeus, by hiding him and substituting a great stone wrapped in swaddling clothes, which she presented to Cronos and he swallowed. But when Zeus grew up, he gave his father an emetic, and both the stone (which became the navel-stone at Delphi) and the other ingested children were vomited up. Zeus acquired cosmic supremacy.

A similar dynastic struggle and devouring of children had featured in the family of Agamemnon just one generation before. Kin-killing was one of the most serious offences Greek ethics could imagine. But compounding it with the eating of human flesh outraged every religious sensibility. The two fathers of Agamemnon and Aegisthus had between them contrived to do both at the same time: they had compounded kin-killing with cannibalism. Cannibalism (which in this instance, since Thyestes was unaware of what he was eating, would more correctly be termed 'anthropophagy'), was presented in even the earliest Greek literature as a sign of the utmost barbarism: Achilles imagines devouring part of Hector raw in the *Iliad* (22.346–48), but even in his wildest fits of anger, and despite the close connection between the alimentary and the retaliatory evidenced in the story of Cronos, he stops short of such an atrocity. Human flesh-eating in Greek thought is only practised by such cultural outlaws as the Cyclopes of the *Odyssey*, and remote savages located by ethnographers beyond the margins of civilization. The eating of humans by humans is explicitly proscribed in Hesiod (*Works and Days* 276–80), for consuming members of your own species is regarded as the way of beasts. If humans are to preserve that important boundary between themselves and animals, they must absolutely abjure the consumption of human flesh.

Agamemnon is concerned with an incident but a generation before when human flesh – indeed human *infant* flesh – was undeniably eaten. This incident is one of the most repellent episodes in Greek myth; it is portrayed in the tragedy as an outrage which threatened to annihilate all distinctions between humanity and bestiality. It was planned by Agamemnon's father Atreus as a personal assault on his brother, Thyestes, who also happened to be Aegisthus' father. Aegisthus escaped ending up in a saucepan with his brothers, an escape he seems to explain by saying that he had at the time been just a tiny baby, not yet out of swaddling-clothes (1606). The two leading men in the tragedy, Agamemnon and Aegisthus, are thus bound together not only by their shared woman, Clytemnestra, but by the horrible knowledge of what had happened on that unspeakable day when the father of one had served up to the father of the other his very own children's flesh.

Aeschylus' poetry in *Agamemnon* is not gentle on the audience's sensibilities. It contains some of the bloodiest language and imagery in Greek tragedy. Even though something has happened to shorten or distort the transmission of the Greek text of Aegisthus' description of the Thyestean feast, and even though it does not approach the nauseating extension and detail of the equivalent passage in Seneca (the messenger speech of *Thyestes*), it certainly conveys the physical reality of the occasion when, just inside the walls the audience can see, the tiny bodies were literally 'butchered', devoured and regurgitated. In Aegisthus' embittered account, Atreus could not forgive Thyestes for trying to appropriate his throne, and so he summoned him to a festival. But first he killed his nephews, broke off their fingers and toes in order to disguise the nature of the flesh, and then served them up to his brother. When Thyestes realized what he had eaten, 'he let forth a great cry, reeled back, vomited forth the slaughtered flesh', and cursed the entire family line of Atreus, all his descendants in perpetuity (1590–1602), kicking over the banqueting table to underline the curse as he did so.

The Thyestean feast, which happened when Aegisthus and (presumably) Agamemnon were still tiny, is important to the understanding of the tragedy because the murders it enacts, and those to follow in the other plays, are the direct result of the child-killing, the cannibalism and the curse. This becomes transparently clear in the great Cassandra scene, where her supernatural powers allow her to intuit the entire criminal history of the palace to which she has been brought. What she has to say to the audience, who know her visions are truthful, is horrific. She says that she has come to a house loathed by heaven, a house which has witnessed the butchering of family members, the slaughter of men, and whose floor is swimming with blood (1090–92). Then she points to the roof of the house, at something unseeable by our eyes or those of the Chorus, and screams, 'behold those children bewailing their slaughter and their roasted flesh, eaten by their father' (1095–97). Shortly afterwards Cassandra returns once again to the theme of the ghostly children clutching their own entrails, and delivers the terrible words quoted in the opening paragraph of this chapter.

The imagery of reproduction

The tragedy extends the imagery of human genesis and reproduction (sometimes called by academics 'paedogonic' imagery) to encompass its cosmic and ethical themes. Even the alternation of day and night is conceptualized in terms of childbirth: Clytemnestra, shortly after her entrance, speaks of the morning which is 'born from its mother', night (264–50), and subsequently says that the night has 'given birth' to the sun (279). The cosmos is conceptualized by the same images of childbirth and reproduction we find elsewhere in the play; but this is particularly appropriate language for a woman whose own role as mother is a crucial issue, and who offers as one ground for her murder of Agamemnon the fact that he had sacrificed her daughter Iphigenia 'as if she were an animal', the daughter to whom Clytemnestra recalls giving birth 'with the sweetest labour pains' (1415–18). Much earlier in the play mammalian gestation has been central to the Chorus's sung account of the omen which precipitated the sacrifice of Iphigenia: two eagles had appeared near the palace, and had devoured a pregnant hare, including her unborn brood (114–20). This disgusting picture of two birds devouring another creature's foetuses, while obviously relevant to the theme of infant-flesh-eating, also introduces the god Artemis. It is she who is angered, as the deity responsible for lion cubs and suckling young (140–45), and who demands the sacrifice of *human* young before the Greeks can leave for Troy.

One of the most illuminating animal images occurs in the Chorus's actual description of the sacrifice of Iphigenia. The play throughout implies that Agamemnon has inherited his infanticidal tendencies from his father Atreus, who blurred that vital distinction between animals and beasts by forcing his brother into anthropophagy. Agamemnon similarly blurs this distinction by offering a human sacrifice instead of an animal one. Greek literature universally presents human sacrifice as an abomination, practised only by Carthaginians and other barbarians on the margins of the civilized world. Yet Agamemnon chose to have his daughter Iphigenia sacrificed 'like a kid' (231–38); she has a bit in her mouth to gag her, like a young animal, and is substituted for the fawn or other wild sacrificial beast which would have been the customary offering to Artemis.

Thus the omen of the eagles and the pregnant hare thematically prefigures the death of Iphigenia. It also makes concrete the overarching theme of the child-destroying family curse, a curse which affects children born to the household even before their birth. Agamemnon was once the innocent little child of Atreus; the stage building representing Atreus' physical house, a psychoanalytical critic might suggest, becomes itself an enormous, toxic, lethal womb. It disgorges the bloodied corpse of Agamemnon, killed like a defenceless baby in amniotic fluid of his homecoming bath; he is dragged alongside Cassandra, stillborn or aborted in a sinister parody of a multiple birth, through the vulva-like doors of the palace into the harsh daylight of Argos. In the polysemic world of Aeschylean poetry it is not too outrageous to see the killing of Agamemnon and Cassandra, enclosed within the stage doors, as prefigured by the omen where the eagles killed the unborn children of the hare, still embryos in the mother's womb.

Yet the most important dimension of the child-producing imagery, the most informative use of the Greek terminology of begetting, conception and engendering, is the way it formulates the ethical ideas which lie at the heart of the play's conception of human action. Half-way through the play the Chorus await the return of their king and try to sort out their thoughts about the Argive crisis. 'It is', they assert trenchantly, 'the evil deed which thereafter begets more evil deeds, in breed like itself' (758–60). In *Agamemnon*, the king's downfall is caused specifically by the working out of the curse, sworn by Thyestes at the Thyestean feast, against the offspring of Atreus. The Chorus believe that it is not prosperity itself which causes the destruction of a household (a traditional and widespread view), but a single iniquitous deed. The evil deed begets more evil deeds, in breed like itself (758–60). The criminal act spawns more criminal acts. The Chorus's metaphorical family of parent crimes and child crimes then almost imperceptibly mutates into the physical reality of a human family: the doer of the evil deed begets further doers of evil deeds. With another slide between concrete and metaphorical families the doer then becomes the deed again: an act of hubris in the past, the Chorus continue, 'begets' an act of hubris in the present; the 'children' of hubris curse the household, but are in fact replicas of their hubristic parents (763–66).

There can be no clearer statement that the miseries of a household are the direct result of former crimes in the past. Bad behaviour begets bad behaviour, inherited by each child of a cursed family from its cursed parents. While the idea of an inheritable curse may seem alien and primitive to us, it is worth thinking in terms of modern theories about the adverse effects on children of bad parenting and of poor parental examples. Dysfunctional families do often produce dysfunctional children, who reproduce, when they become parents themselves, the maladjusted behaviours of their own bad parents. Taken from this perspective, the archaic concept of the inheritable curse may not seem so bizarre after all. What is extraordinarily striking is that Clytemnestra, the murderous mother from whose body sprang both the victim Iphigenia and the future avenger Orestes, claims that she is the vehicle through which this family curse is working. In her dialogue with the Chorus over the corpses she claims that the person they see before them is not Agamemnon's wife: no, she is an avenger (a fine strong word in Greek, *alastōr*), wreaking revenge upon Atreus, in offering up his son Agamemnon as a sacrifice to appease the children of Thyestes. She is the spirit of the very curse, she says, delivered by Thyestes at the fatal banquet (1500–4).

The notion of the curse, doomed to work itself out in repeated patterns of behaviour down the generations, is subtly developed in Aeschylus' handling of the traditional material in the case of the two brothers, Atreus and Thyestes. They were rivals for the throne of Argos: their two sons, the cousins Agamemnon and Aegisthus, repeat this rivalry over the throne. Thyestes had once, before the fatal feast, been driven into exile by his brother; his baby son Aegisthus was doomed to be similarly exiled, as he tells us on his entrance; and the third-generation male, Orestes, is also in exile throughout the duration of this play. Again, the brothers Atreus and Thyestes had fallen out over a woman: Thyestes had seduced Atreus' wife, Aerope, indeed eventually married her. Atreus and Thyestes' two sons, Agamemnon and Aegisthus, follow the identical course in their respective relationships with Clytemnestra. Lastly, the destruction of innocent children has already shown itself to be a recurrent element in the family's dysfunctional activities: Atreus killed his brother's sons; Agamemnon kills his own daughter. It seems that there is no way out of this vicious cycle of recurring violence in the House of Atreus. The past produces offspring in breed like itself.

Natural law and jungle law

But what is the philosophical result of all this astonishing reproductive imagery, imagery which connects dead children across generations through inheritable curses themselves configured linguistically as human infants? Aeschylus' decision to frame the ethical choice as reproductive biological imperative implies that the 'system' of reciprocal killing is embedded deep within nature. The implication is that humans can only escape the bloody 'natural order' with the dawning of a new enlightened age of reason, in which they can demarcate themselves off from animals, and create a higher system of law administered by communities (like democratic Athens) which transcend biological ties. Here the imagery of reproduction becomes inseparable from the proliferation of animal imagery (which has been much more carefully studied by scholars in the past than the repertoire of reproductive terms).[13]

The humans at the infantile stage of social development depicted in *Agamemnon* find it almost impossible to conceptualize the universe they inhabit without resorting to analogies with the law of the jungle, or at the very least to the law of the farmyard and of the hunt. The Watchman who delivers the prologue already describes himself as a 'hound', who must place the 'ox' of silence on his tongue (3; 36). The Argive battle-cry was like the scream of eagles who have lost their babies, and wheel in lonely bereavement over their empty nest (48-54); the Argives were like a ravening lion who drank the blood of Troy (824-28). Clytemnestra complains that buzzing mosquitoes awoke her from her dreams (891-94); but she herself strikes one speaker or another as a hound, a snake, a lioness (1258-59), a croaking raven (1473), and twice as a spider in whose web Agamemnon dies (1115; 1492). Mere nature seems inadequate to furnish beasts adequate to compare her with: she is likened to two supernatural monsters, the amphisbaena (1233), the serpent born from the blood shed by the decapitated Medusa, and the human-devouring Scylla (1233-36). At the end of the play the Chorus insultingly refer to her and Aegisthus as a hen and a cock (1671), but Cassandra has previously called Aegisthus a 'cowardly lion' (1223-25).[14] Agamemnon comes to be equated with a bull, a hound and a lion (1125-26). Cassandra is variously likened to a swallow (1050), a newly captured wild animal (1063), a hound (1093), a nightingale (1141-42), a sacrificial ox (1298) and a swan (1445-46), who saves its last song for the moment of its death. The nightingale is a particularly appropriate example, for the mythical precursor of the nightingale was an Athenian princess called Procne, who slaughtered her own son Itys, and vengefully served him up in a casserole to Tereus, the murdered child's sadistic rapist of a father. Sophocles wrote a famous tragedy on this theme, the *Tereus*, which is extensively parodied in

Aristophanes' *Birds*.[15] The song of the nightingale was explained by Greek mythology as the infanticidal Procne's unceasing lament for her son.

All these images suggest that in the primitive mythical world of Argos, before the invention of civic justice in the evolving Athenian democracy, humans were social and psychological infants, who still behaved like bloodthirsty animals. The images also imply that they could only think about one another in the images of the bestiary, like insults thrown around a playground, or the animal figures in children's fables and nursery rhymes.[16] It is perhaps in Helen that the connection between the reproductive imagery and the imagery of the jungle is most brilliantly wedded. Helen, who arrived in Troy as the beautiful bride of Paris, yet who acted like an *Erinys* and caused the annihilation of the city, is associated with the potent idea of a lion cub fostered in a household. At first the cub is an adorable, gentle companion, allowed to play with children, and nursed in the arms like a newborn baby; as it grows up, however, it turns fierce and violent, causing carnage and destruction (717–36).[17] It is striking that not only Helen but also Aegisthus, Clytemnestra and Agamemnon are connected through imagery with lions. It is tempting to speculate that Aeschylus was perfectly aware that lions were not only an important symbol of power encoded in the art and architecture of the Bronze-Age palaces of kings such as Agamemnon, but – like his tragic humans – are one of the very few mammalian creatures capable of eating their own children.[18]

Notes

1. Schein (1982) provides a fascinating account of this scene.
2. Well discussed, from a different angle, in Tyrrell (1976).
3. See Potamiti (2015).
4. There are some excellent points on the relationship between Hesiod and Aeschylus' *Eumenides*, although less so on *Agamemnon*, in the final chapter of Solmsen (1949).
5. The Erinyes are discussed at length in Hall (2018).
6. See below and Hall (1998); for the impact of the avenging Clytemnestra of Aeschylus on subsequent adaptations, see Hall (2005).
7. Güterbock (1948).
8. George (2003), 776–77.
9. On the importance of the number three in Aeschylus' presentation of revenge cycles, see Clay (1969).
10. For the little we know about him, see Dalzell (1970) and Kakridis (1978).
11. See Hall (1989), 205.
12. 918–22: see Hall (1989), 206–8.

13 See, for example, Heath (1999) with further refences.
14 S. West (2003).
15 Hall (2020), esp. 193–96.
16 Well brought out in M. L. West (1979).
17 See further Knox (1952) and Nappa (1994).
18 See Younger (1978) and Hall (2019), 272–77 on the lion-similes in relation to filicide in Euripides' *Medea*.

2

Agamemnon at Aulis: Hard Choice or No Choice?

Alan H. Sommerstein

The sacrifice by Agamemnon of his daughter Iphigeneia, when his fleet bound for Troy lay at Aulis in Boeotia imprisoned by adverse winds, is not technically part of the action of Aeschylus' *Oresteia*. But it is certainly made one of the most important elements of the back-story, and is presented as providing the largest share of the motivation for Clytaemestra's murder of her husband.[1] The main, lyric section of the first choral song (the *parodos*), occupying nearly one-tenth of the whole length of *Agamemnon* (104–257),[2] is as narrative entirely devoted to the sacrifice and how it came about. After Agamemnon's death, Clytaemestra refers to the sacrifice repeatedly and very bitterly (1414–20, 1432, 1523–29, 1555–59); later even Agamemnon's surviving daughter Electra will speak of 'the sister who was pitilessly sacrificed' (*LB* 242), though that, almost exactly at the midpoint of the trilogy, is the last clear reference to Iphigeneia.

Agamemnon killed his daughter. What was even worse, the sacrifice was made possible by a cruel deception (1523–24); Aeschylus gives no details, probably assuming the story to be very well known of how Iphigeneia was summoned to Aulis in order – so she and her mother were told – to be married to Achilles. But the sacrifice was declared to be necessary by the prophet Calchas, as the only way to put an end to the adverse winds which had been brought upon the fleet by an angry Artemis. How great, morally speaking, was Agamemnon's responsibility? Could he have avoided the sacrifice? If so, would there have been a price to pay, and should he have been willing to pay it? And had he been responsible for the trouble arising in the first place, by angering Artemis? We know that different tellers of the story, especially if they were dramatists anxious to find a new angle on it, often modified it in quite important respects, so we must be very cautious about using elements from other versions of the myth to help us interpret Aeschylus' version, unless we can point to evidence positively indicating that Aeschylus presupposed these elements, as we can in the case of the bogus marriage to Achilles discussed above.

Let us take a journey through this song. We may note, in the first place, that for quite a long time there is nothing to tell us that its main subject will be the sacrifice of Iphigeneia. There is no mention of her, or of Aulis, or even of Artemis until nearly the end of the long second stanza (134), thirty lines into the song by the current numbering. After a somewhat enigmatic introduction (104–7), the Chorus sing of an omen which appeared to 'the twin-throned rulers of the Achaeans' – Agamemnon and Menelaus – as they left their palace in Argos to join their army bound for Troy.[3]

Two eagles of different species appeared on the right-hand side (a good sign), swooped down on a hare and ate it (114–20); the hare was in the last stages of pregnancy (119, 136). The prophet Calchas identified the two eagles, with their contrasting plumage, as representing the two kings of contrasting character (Agamemnon tougher, Menelaus gentler), and predicted that their expedition would conquer Troy (122–27). But he also said that there was a risk of 'divine resentment' (131), specifically from Artemis, who as a goddess of childbirth, and protectress of all young creatures, 'bears a grudge against the winged hounds of her Father' (140) – a grudge which she may choose to activate by forcing Agamemnon's fleet to remain in harbour (147–50); and he talked obscurely about 'another sacrificial slaughter' (151) and a 'fearsome guileful keeper of the house ... that ... will avenge a child' (153–55). Obscure to the Chorus, but not to the audience!

The cause of Artemis' anger, at any rate, is stated clearly enough, and it is not what we probably expected. Her resentment is directed not at Agamemnon, who so far as we are told has not himself wronged her at all, but at the two eagles, and therefore at Zeus who sent them. Why then does she act upon this grudge in a way that will harm Agamemnon? Well, what else can she do? She cannot hope to hurt Zeus directly, but since Zeus is among many other things the divine patron of kings, she can damage Zeus by damaging a king. And Agamemnon is particularly vulnerable just now, because he is about to sail against Troy, the most difficult and perilous mission that he could have undertaken – and it is a job that Zeus particularly wants done, as witness the omen itself. Artemis will not prevent him from undertaking, and from accomplishing, the mission; but she will ensure that if he does, it will be at the cost of his life.

At this point the narrative is interrupted by the so-called Hymn to Zeus (160–83). When it resumes, it is in a different metre, which implies different patterns of music and dance – the same patterns, in fact, as those of the Hymn. It soon becomes clear that wherever the Atreidae and Calchas were located before, they and the whole vast army and fleet are now at Aulis, and stuck there because of the adverse winds (188–98). The Chorus's syntax gets stuck too. Their first sentence begins firmly enough with its subject ('And then the senior leader of the Achaean fleet ...', 184–85), but it soon loses its way in a jungle of subordinate clauses, and the main verb is never reached. Instead a fresh start is made at 205 ('And the senior king spoke, and said this...'); but there is a good case for holding that when that unwieldy sentence began at 184, the word that the Chorus, or rather the poet, had in mind for its main verb was one that does not turn up until 224, where it is accompanied by the 'resumptive' sentence-particle combination *d'oun*, which means something like 'well, anyway' or 'end of digression' or 'to cut a long story short'. Agamemnon is still the subject, and we learn that 'he brought himself to become the sacrificer of his daughter'.

The forty lines, four stanzas, that come between these points are our best evidence for the process by which Agamemnon reached this terrible decision. What can they tell us about that process? Is Agamemnon portrayed as weighing up alternatives, and if so, does he do it well or badly? Were there, in fact, any alternatives? Or was there never really anything for Agamemnon to do except resign himself to the inevitable?

We should remember one or two things which the Chorus do not mention explicitly but which an audience familiar with the story will have taken for granted.

1. The expedition against Troy, comprising contingents from almost the whole of Greece, had been summoned to Aulis by Agamemnon.
2. They would be fighting, however, at least professedly, not in his cause but in that of Menelaus, to secure the return of his wife and/or the punishment of the Trojans for her abduction.
3. When the crisis first arises, Iphigeneia is not at Aulis; there was no reason for Agamemnon to bring his teenage daughter there – not, that is, until Calchas announced that Artemis demanded her sacrifice as a condition of allowing the fleet to sail. In order to fulfil that demand, Agamemnon would first have to have her brought to Aulis; that is why he had to pretend that she was to be married to Achilles. If he refused to summon her, there was no way the sacrifice could take place – unless indeed the army under its other leaders were to march on Argos and take Iphigeneia by force, something that is not threatened even in Euripides' *Iphigeneia at Aulis*.[4]

This is what we are told about the run-up to Agamemnon's final decision.

> And then the senior leader of the Achaean fleet, not criticizing any prophet, blowing together with the blast[5] of fortune that struck him, when the Achaean host was grievously afflicted by foul weather which emptied their stomachs, while it stayed on the mainland opposite Chalcis, in the place where the waters surge back and forth, at Aulis;

and winds coming from the Strymon[6] bringing unwelcome leisure, hunger, and bad anchorage, making men wander,[7] unsparing of ships and cables, making time seem twice as long, wore down and shredded the flower of the Argives; and when the prophet also cried forth another remedy for the hateful storms, one more grievous for the leaders, declaring Artemis as their cause, so that the Atreidae struck the ground with their staffs and could not hold back their tears –

and the senior king spoke, and said this: 'It is a grievous doom not to comply, and a grievous one if I am to slay my child, the delight of my house, polluting a father's hands with streams of a slaughtered maiden's blood close by the altar. Which of these options is free from evil? How can I become a deserter of the fleet, *xummakhias hamartōn*?[8] That they should long with intense passion for a sacrifice to end the winds, and for the blood of a maiden, is quite natural. May all be well!'

And when he put on the yoke-strap of necessity, his mental wind veering in a direction that was impious, impure, unholy, from that point he turned to a mindset that would stop at nothing; for men are emboldened by miserable Infatuation, whose shameful schemes are the beginning of their sufferings. In short, he brought himself to become the sacrificer of his daughter, to further a war of revenge over a woman and as a preliminary rite to the fleet's departure.

The first stanza and a half (184–98) vividly sketch the crisis caused by the foul winds. A thousand ships and their crews have assembled at the little port of Aulis, and have been detained there for many days (and it feels like even more, 196). They are starving (188, 194), reduced to roaming the countryside foraging for anything they can find that is edible (195). Their ships are riding at anchor (194); normally a ship staying in port for more than a night or two would be beached, but there would be no room for this at Aulis, and even the anchorages, in or close to the stormy Euripus, would not be all that safe. The ships are moored to the shore by cables (195), but the gusty winds, alternately stretching and relaxing these, are steadily weakening them. Something needs to be done about it, and soon. It has been correctly assumed that all this is the work of a hostile god or gods, and attempts have been made to win them over; we know this because Calchas speaks of 'another remedy' (199), i.e. a remedy different from those previously tried. All these efforts have failed. We are not told immediately what Calchas's 'remedy' is; we do not need to be, especially once we have heard that it involves Artemis (202) and is 'grievous for the leaders' (200), specifically Agamemnon and Menelaus who both burst into tears (204). *Both*, that is important. Agamemnon is never normally the weeping sort, and Menelaus has more to gain than anyone from the war if it goes ahead, and more to lose if it is called off; but both are equally repelled by the idea of making Iphigeneia a sacrificial victim.

And Agamemnon does not mince words in describing the horror of such a sacrifice (207–11), though it may be of some concern that he apparently rates it only equal in gravity with the consequences of non-compliance (206, 211). Then he raises another consideration, or a closely connected pair of considerations, which apparently turn the scale. First, he asks rhetorically (212), 'How can I become a deserter of the fleet (*liponaus*)?' Military desertion (*lipotaxion* or *lipostration*) was a serious crime in Athenian law, attracting heavy penalties. But that is when a private citizen ignores a call-up notice issued by or under the authority of a democratic organ of government. Who called Agamemnon up to serve on the Trojan expedition? Why, Agamemnon himself. And for whose benefit? For the benefit of Menelaus. Somebody needs to say to Agamemnon, 'Look here, you can't desert yourself, and you can't desert an expedition mounted in the name of your brother if your brother doesn't want you to go through with it.'

But Agamemnon's thoughts have gone further. He is the leader of a great alliance of Greek states. If he abandons the expedition, he will be *xummakhias hamartōn*. What does this mean? Most translators and commentators take the meaning to be something like 'defaulting on my obligations to my allies'. But nowhere else does Agamemnon recognize the existence of any such obligations. More to the point might be a recognition of what we may call *de facto* duties or practical expectations. A community that joined a league of which Athens, say, or Sparta was the head, knew it would normally be expected to contribute ships, or men, or money towards the league leader's campaigns; but if it fulfilled these responsibilities loyally, it could also expect – or at least it *would* expect – the leader to come to its assistance if it came under attack itself.

Yet this is hardly relevant. None of Agamemnon's allies has come under military attack. One has been the victim of an attack on his honour, but he is, to say the least, very doubtful whether he would be right to seek revenge at the terrible price that has been demanded. None of the others have been attacked at all – but they want a fight, they are *philomakhoi* (230), lovers of battle, and they 'long with intense passion for a sacrifice to end the winds' (214–17). And that phrase *xummakhias hamartōn* can have another meaning. At line 535 of this play it is said of Paris that 'having been found guilty of abduction and theft, *tou rhusiou . . . hēmarte*' – that is, 'he lost his booty'. And Hugh Lloyd-Jones (1979), almost alone,[9] was right to translate *xummakhias hamartōn* as 'losing my allies'.

Before he raised this issue, Agamemnon was unable to decide between two alternatives which seemed to him equally bad. But now the scale has been tipped. He has recruited a great army – the greatest that Greece had ever brought together – for a campaign in which Zeus himself, through the omen, has assured him of success, against a wealthy city whose capture promises ample booty. If he succeeds, he may well establish for himself and his heirs a lasting hegemony in the Aegean region. But what may happen if, having brought his allies to the port of embarkation and made them endure several weeks of privation, he now tells them there will be no war after all and sends them home? Such an inglorious climb-down may well deal a fatal blow to his prestige, and the grand alliance under his leadership will have been stillborn. And this danger, a matter of pure power politics, is the consideration that tips the scale.

Agamemnon adds that it is *themis* that his colleagues are so eager for the sacrifice. This word is usually understood to mean 'right in the eyes of heaven' (Lloyd-Jones). But that does not make much sense. Greek gods are frequently pleased or offended by human actions and words; they are not normally pleased or offended by human thoughts. And *themis* too has another meaning which would work better here.

In Book 9 of the *Iliad*, when the Greek leaders are debating what to do about Achilles, Agamemnon announces a series of lavish promises, including the return of the captive Briseis whom he had seized from Achilles; 'and on top of that', he adds, 'I will swear a great oath that I have never gone up to her bed and had intercourse with her, which is *themis* for humans male and female' (9.132-24). In Book 14 of the *Odyssey*, the disguised Odysseus asks if anything is known in Ithaca about Odysseus' fate, and is told that they hear only rumours which regularly prove to be false – but Penelope listens carefully to all these visitors; 'and as she lamented for him the tears fell from her eyes, which is *themis* for a woman whose husband has died abroad' (14.128-30). In both these passages 'right in the eyes of heaven', or anything like it, just will not do. Many kinds of sexual activity are pleasing or at least acceptable to the gods, but not all kinds – not, for instance, adultery or incest (except when practised by gods themselves). The natural translation of *themis* in passages like these is, well, 'natural'. Human beings, by their nature, have sexual desires. Women, by their nature, grieve for the loss of a good husband, particularly when they have not been able to take part in his funeral (if he even had one). And alpha males, such as these leaders certainly are, by their nature are eager for the glory and profit of war, and may not be too interested in whether that war is made possible by the murder of someone else's daughter.

In the course of these reflections Agamemnon repeats the phrase 'maiden blood' from 209-10. There, however, the phrase highlighted the abhorrence with which he regarded the proposed sacrifice. Now, by contrast, it is something for which it is perfectly natural to long with intense passion. Agamemnon ends with a wish that recurs over and over again in tragedy and especially in the *Oresteia*: 'may all be well'. Needless to say, all hardly ever is.

Agamemnon has made up his mind, and there can be no doubt that the Chorus think he has made it up in the wrong way. 'Impious, impure, unholy ... a mindset that would stop at nothing ... miserable infatuation [and her] shameful schemes' – the words of condemnation pour like a stream. And we are reminded, too, of what the whole thing was about in the first place – 'to further a war of revenge over a woman' (225–26), and an adulterous woman at that (62). The sacrifice is also called a '*proteleia* of the ships': *proteleia* were properly sacrifices offered before a *marriage*, and many will remember the dreadful deception by which Iphigeneia was brought to Aulis. It is in the light of this context that we need to interpret the difficult phrase 'put on the yoke-strap of necessity' (218).

Sir Denys Page, in an edition of *Agamemnon* which after sixty-two years is still in print,[10] argued, almost entirely on the basis of this phrase, *that Agamemnon has no choice but to do what he does* (original emphasis). He forgot that Iphigeneia was not at Aulis until she was summoned, and he also seems to have assumed that Agamemnon knew he was the agent of Zeus for punishing Paris and the Trojans (in which case why isn't he made to mention this in his soliloquy?). He did, however, perceive one possible weakness in his case, and he covered it up with bluster:

> It hardly needs adding that nobody can seriously believe that the reference in *anankē* [necessity] here is not to the action which he now undertakes but to *the inevitable consequences* of that action.

To which the only possible response is 'why on earth not?' Agamemnon has allowed himself to be metaphorically placed under a yoke. The thing about a yoke, from the animal's point of view, is that once you are under it, it is very difficult to get out until the farmer, or charioteer, or whatever, releases you. In other words, a yoke, whether literal or metaphorical, binds for the future as well as the present; and we have already heard from Calchas, if we did not know it already, what the 'inevitable consequences' of sacrificing Iphigeneia will be for Agamemnon. To most people they will seem a good deal worse than the consequences of not sacrificing her.

With Agamemnon's decision the action moves on immediately to the preparations for the sacrifice itself. Here too the horror of the act is repeatedly emphasized. We hear Iphigeneia pleading for her life, crying out 'daddy, daddy' (228); daddy's response is to order six or eight of his attendants to hoist her up 'like a yearling goat' (232) – twice (231, 239) we are invited to see the flash of colour as her bright yellow dress unfolds itself – while others put a gag on her 'to restrain speech that might be a curse on his house' (235–37). She can thus 'speak' only with her eyes, and she gives each of the men around her 'a glance to stir pity'; it is added that she is personally acquainted with all of them, having been called in to sing a paean to go with the third libation (243–47). No doubt she was smiling then, and so were they.

And there the film, as it were, is abruptly cut off – as on that day at Aulis was the life of a teenage girl, by the sword of her father. Or was it? 'What followed', sing the Chorus, 'I did not see and do not say' (248). We may reflect that they didn't see what preceded either (there was no reason why at their age they should have gone all the way to Aulis); we quite understand that they don't want to sing about the actual slaying – what they did sing about was harrowing enough. The Chorus's reticence may possibly remind us that there existed versions of the myth in which Iphigeneia was not killed at all – Artemis snatched her away and substituted a hind; if so, it will not become clear till after Agamemnon's death (1414–18) that Clytaemestra knows nothing of any such substitution.

There follow some rather vague thoughts about the possible outcome of the war, and then for the fifth time we hear that futile wish that all may be well (255) followed by a clause that effectively nullifies it:

> May the sequel produce a good outcome, as is the wish of this closest guardian, this sole bulwark of the land of Apia.
>
> 255–57

By 'this closest guardian' the Chorus have sometimes been thought to mean themselves, but that would involve them in a tautology; a good outcome, from my point of view, *means* an outcome in accordance with my wishes. No, the closest guardian, the sole bulwark, is Clytaemestra, and the irony is acute. We know that she has received news of the fall of Troy at the earliest possible moment – and we know why she arranged to get it; but no one in the Argos of the play knows that, except for one man whom we will not see till line 1577.

When Calchas declared that Artemis required the sacrifice of Iphigeneia or else the fleet could not sail, Agamemnon had two options: perform the sacrifice, or abandon the expedition against Troy. If he had chosen the second option, he might or might not have lost his allies, as he feared he would, but he would have saved not only his own life but many thousands of others.

And, of course, the purpose of Zeus (to punish Paris) would have failed. But Zeus's purposes do not fail. When he decided to make Agamemnon the instrument of his plans, he knew well enough what manner of man Agamemnon was: the man we will see later in the play, a man devoted to power and prestige, who in his speech at homecoming (810–54) does not mention the casualties and has nothing to say to or about their grieving relatives, while devoting some twenty lines to alleged political malcontents and the measures he will take ('by cutting or burning', 849) to render them harmless; a man who would rather accept honours fit only for a god than forgo any of the glory due to a conqueror (905–57); a man who, having resolved on a war, will allow nothing, nothing at all, to stand between him and the waging of it. In that sense it was inevitable that Agamemnon would sacrifice his daughter. But that does not mean he had no choice. It only means that Zeus chose the right man for his job.

From the same perspective we need not be alarmed to discover that, as Page[11] puts it, 'it is the will of Zeus that Troy shall be taken … but also that anybody responsible for many deaths (as the taker of Troy must be) shall be severely punished' (cf. 461–74). To be an agent of the will of Zeus is not a guarantee of moral rectitude or divine favour. Clytaemestra, after all, was also an agent of the will of Zeus. The sack of Troy is the greatest of a series of acts spread out through the *Oresteia* which are both just punishments and terrible crimes. Such, in the *Oresteia*, is the nature of vengeance. Such therefore also are the gods who preside over and direct it.

Notes

1. The only other motive to which Clytaemestra admits is resentment of Agamemnon's extramarital affairs during the war (*Ag.* 1439; *Libation Bearers* 918) and especially of his having brought Cassandra home presumably as a concubine (*Ag.* 1440–47); but a further motive, which she never explicitly avows, arises from her own adulterous relationship with Aegisthus. Aegisthus himself is motivated mainly by the desire to avenge his father Thyestes and his brothers (cf. 1577–1611); the two boys had been murdered and butchered by Atreus, who then tricked Thyestes into eating their flesh. Clytaemestra seems to allude to this crime by speaking at 1504 of the slaying of 'the young ones' (masculine plural).
2. Henceforth, references to passages of *Agamemnon* will be by line number(s) only. The other two parts of the Oresteian trilogy, *Libation Bearers* and *Eumenides*, will be cited as *LB* and *Eum.* respectively.
3. The omen is said to have appeared to the two kings (this is stated three times: 108, 114, 125), not to the army as a whole, and it appeared 'near the house' (116), which to any non-clairvoyant listener must refer to the home of the two kings, the house which forms the backdrop to the Chorus's dance and song, the only house of which mention has yet been made in the play. See Sommerstein (2010), 171–77.

4 Or rather, the play of that name which has come down to us – left unfinished by Euripides at his death, completed and produced by his nephew (?) of the same name, and considerably tinkered with by later actor-directors. One line of that play (413, where Menelaus says that if Agamemnon refuses to sacrifice his daughter, 'I will go to other plans and other friends') may remotely hint at such a threat, but this is at once forgotten (not least by Menelaus himself) when the brothers are told of the imminent arrival of Iphigeneia *and her mother.*
5 Or, to use a metaphor more familiar in English, 'swimming with the tide'.
6 That is, northerly winds blowing from Thrace.
7 In search of whatever food they could find, the army's stocks being exhausted; cf. *Odyssey* 4.368–89, 12.330–32.
8 I have left this phrase untranslated; its meaning is controversial, and crucial for the understanding of Agamemnon's 'dilemma'.
9 H. Lloyd-Jones (1979) 28; see also Winnington-Ingram (1980), 83–84, and Raeburn and Thomas (2011), 91.
10 Denniston and Page (1957), xxiii–xxviii.
11 Ibid., xvi n1.

3

The Homecoming of Agamemnon[*]

Alex F. Garvie

In *The Stagecraft of Aeschylus*,[1] Oliver Taplin classified a small group of Greek tragedies as *nostos* plays, in that they all presented the story of the return home of a hero after a long absence abroad. The group comprised Aeschylus' *Persae* and *Agamemnon*, Sophocles' *Trachiniae*, and Euripides' *Heracles*, while several others, in which, Taplin judged, the return home was not so central to the plot, nevertheless displayed elements of the theme (for example, *Choephori* and the Electra plays of Sophocles and Euripides). I would add Euripides' *Andromache*, the only one in which the hero returns home as a corpse. Behind all this lay a long tradition of *nostos* poetry, which is represented for us, and no doubt principally for a fifth-century audience, by Homer's *Odyssey*. But it is certainly older than Homer, in whose poem the bard Phemius sings of the return of the heroes from the Trojan War, and the tradition was maintained after him, with the *Nostoi* of the poet Agias, in which, we are told, the only heroes who had an uneventful and safe return from Troy were Nestor and Diomedes. *They* are unlikely to have provided material for exciting narrative poetry. The lyric poet Stesichorus also wrote a poem entitled *Nostoi*. Homer himself, through the mouth of Nestor and Menelaus, provides Telemachus and us with tantalisingly brief accounts of the journeys home of the major heroes from Troy. They cover almost every possible variation of the theme, from the Lesser Ajax who dies on the journey, to Odysseus who arrives home safely after ten years of adventures, largely in an exotic world, to Menelaus whose adventures are in the real world, and to Agamemnon who arrives after a largely uneventful journey, but only to be murdered on his arrival. With the exception of Nestor and Diomedes, the common factor linking the *nostos* of all the heroes, as my former student Marigo Alexopoulou has made clear,[2] is that it is never what the hero expects. He himself has changed in his absence, and so too has the home to which he returns. Similar poetry was studied by A.B. Lord in the South Slavic tradition, and is still found in modern Greece.

---

[*] This chapter is based on a paper given in Rome on 28th March 2014 to the Istituto Nazionale del Dramma Antico (INDA)

Such is the tradition which Aeschylus adapts to fit the very different requirements of a performance before an audience in the theatre. Perhaps he was the first tragedian to do so; certainly we do not hear of any earlier attempt. We can be sure that his audience of *Persae* and *Agamemnon* was thoroughly familiar with the traditional themes and their conventions, and that, far more than modern audiences, it would be alert to the way in which Aeschylus uses, manipulates and departs from those conventions, to suit his own dramatic purposes. Given the nature of tragedy, we should expect its homecomings to be generally unhappy. In a forthcoming publication I have tried to demonstrate this for *Persae*, arguing that scholars have been too concerned to quarrel about the historical veracity of Aeschylus' presentation of the battle of Salamis, and not concerned enough to appreciate the structure of the play in the light of the narrative conventions which lie behind it, that is to say the conventions of *nostos* poetry. Today I wish to consider *Agamemnon* from this point of view.

One of the conventions of a *nostos* poem is that it regularly pays as much attention to the people at home, anxiously awaiting the arrival of a loved one, as it does to the absent hero. In the *Odyssey* it is not until Book 5 that we meet the hero himself. The first four books, after the proem, are entirely concerned with the situation on Ithaca, with the behaviour of the Suitors, which will mean that the homeland to which Odysseus will return will be different from the peaceful one he left twenty years ago. Regularly, too, the principal waiting character is female – the wife in the *Odyssey* and in *Trachiniae*, the sister in *Choephori* and the Electra plays, the mother in *Persae*, and two women with different emotions, wife and concubine, in *Andromache*. In the *Odyssey* the political situation of the *basileus* (usually translated as king) in Ithaca is far from clear, but Penelope is at least potentially a powerful woman. So, certainly, is Arete, Odysseus' hostess in Scheria, in the last stage of his travels.

Nor is there any doubt about the authority of Clytaemestra in *Agamemnon*. Just as the proem of the *Odyssey* announces that this is to be a *nostos* poem that will end with the safe arrival home of its hero, so Aeschylus begins his play with the Watchman, who, having begun with his complaint about the long period of waiting for Agamemnon to return, suddenly sees the beacon and rejoices that the waiting is now over and that it is time to rejoice; this is to be a *nostos* play, and Agamemnon will soon be home. The audience, like modern scholars, would recognize that the Watchman himself is borrowed from the *Odyssey* (4.524–28), in which a watchman is appointed by Aegisthus to warn him of the approach of Agamemnon. Aeschylus could hardly have made it clearer that it is specifically the *Odyssey* that we are to have in mind. In Aeschylus he is appointed by Clytaemestra, but he is evidently loyal to Agamemnon. He might suppose that as a loving wife she longs to have the first news of her husband's imminent arrival. But his uneasiness is betrayed by his notorious description of her 'man-counselling heart', and by his cryptic allusion to a dark secret inside the house which he is unwilling to divulge. It is probably a convention of *nostos* poetry in general that the returning husband has doubts about the chastity of his wife. Even Penelope, in the second half of the *Odyssey*, can behave rather surprisingly in front of the Suitors, so that for some scholars Homer is deliberately suggesting alternative endings to the story. But for the most part Aeschylus' audience is well aware that in the *Odyssey*, as well no doubt as in the post-Homeric tradition, it is the contrast between the faithfulness of Penelope and the unfaithfulness of Clytaemestra that is a vital theme. Unless the audience makes these connections it will fail to understand the role of the Watchman and the nature of his suspicions. Agamemnon is not going to receive the welcome that he expects.

The Agamemnon, however, who returns from Troy will also be a different man from the great king who departed for Troy ten years ago. In the proem of the *Odyssey* Homer makes it clear that it was not Odysseus but his men who were responsible for their own deaths. Perhaps this kind of question was regularly raised in *nostos* poetry when a hero returned home from war, especially if the casualties had been high and if he returns alone or virtually alone. In *Persae* it is an important part of the chorus's complaint against Xerxes (918–30), who is thus contrasted unfavourably with his father Darius, whose expeditions always led to νόστοι ἀπαθεῖς (*nostoi apatheis*), 'painless homecomings', for his men (861–62). Even Odysseus does not completely escape censure from his enemies for the loss of his men (*Od.* 24.427–28, the father of one of the Suitors; cf. Eurylochus at 10.437). And he was certainly foolish to reveal his identity to Polyphemus at the end of Book 9. But for the most part we are meant to admire and take the part of Odysseus as the hero of the poem. It is different with Agamemnon in Aeschylus' play, and it is the chorus, a dramatic device not available to the epic poet, that Aeschylus uses to raise doubts about his behaviour in the long *parodos* of the play. Agamemnon's daughter, who in happier days used to sing with her pure voice at her father's dinner parties, will not be on the beach to welcome her father home, because he had to sacrifice her at Aulis on the outward journey, to enable the fleet to sail to Troy. As the chorus sing, he 'went under the yoke of necessity' (218). Whether he was free *not* to do so is a question that will for ever be debated by modern scholars and set for university examinations, but there can be no doubt that the chorus disapprove of his action. Nor are they happy with the suffering that befell Trojans and Greeks alike in the course of the war (63–67), a war fought for the sake of Helen, a mere woman. If the Prologue raised questions about the reception that Agamemnon is likely to receive, the *parodos* makes us wonder what reception he *deserves* to receive.

Aeschylus keeps us waiting for the answers to these questions. First, he introduces us to Clytaemestra herself. She is given a respectful welcome by the chorus, and she gives no hint of what she is planning. In her celebrated Beacon speech she convinces an unbelieving chorus that Agamemnon is indeed on his way home, as she describes the course of the beacon-fires that have brought the news all the way from Troy to Argos. Later we shall hear about his voyage. In the account of Odysseus' travels in the *Odyssey* the verb πέμπω (*pempō*), the noun πομπή (*pompē*) and their cognates play a strikingly large part, as at every stage of his journey he finds an escort or someone to send him on his way. He is fortunate indeed to meet with the Phaeacians who have much experience in this activity, and who will bring him finally home to Ithaca. His travels are mirrored by those of Telemachus, who too finds escorts or people to send him on his way when he visits Nestor and Menelaus. The same words play an important part also in *Persae*, in which Xerxes, having arrived home γυμνὸς προπομπῶν (*gumnos propompōn*), 'without escort' (1036), at the end of the play will have only the old men of the chorus to escort him on his sad return to his palace: πέμψω τοί σε δυσθρόοις γόοις (*pempsō toi se dusthroois*), 'I shall escort you with ill-sounding lamentation' (1077, the last line of the play). In *Agamemnon* the Herald who arrives on stage in advance of his master will pray that the heroes who have escorted (πέμψαντας, *pempsantas*, 516) the army on its outward journey to Troy will bring the remnant safely home again. Agamemnon himself, in the last line of his first speech will thank the gods who have escorted him on his way and brought him back again (οἵπερ πρόσω πέμψαντες ἤγαγον πάλιν, *hoiper prosō pempsantes ēgagon palin*, 853). These terms, so characteristic of *nostos* poetry, are, however, strangely absent from the rest of the arrival scene in *Agamemnon*, which makes it all the more striking that in the Beacon speech (281–316) five of them, a veritable cluster, are to be found, as Clytaemestra describes the passage of the light from one beacon-fire to the next. Would it be too fanciful to suggest that the Beacon speech serves as a kind of substitute for the journey of Agamemnon himself from Troy to Argos? The fire which began on Mount Ida to signal the happy news of the destruction of Troy ends by crashing down (σκήπτω, *skēptō*, 308 and 310, a violent word) on the Arachnaeon mountain at Argos and finally on Agamemnon's palace. The first fire, says Clytaemestra, is the grandfather of the last. In the recurring imagery of the trilogy, light ought to symbolize joy and salvation. Agamemnon's journey began with the joy of victory, but it will end with the consequence of that victory, his humiliating defeat by a woman and his murder in his bath. In the first two plays of this trilogy joy always gives way to foreboding and fear.

In her second speech the Queen imagines, with apparent sympathy, the suffering of the army at Troy, and expresses the hope that, now that it has won the victory, it will not do anything to anger the gods and thus endanger its homeward journey. This naturally increases the foreboding of the audience, which will shortly learn from the Herald that this is exactly what Agamemnon has done; he has destroyed the Trojan temples and, like Odysseus in the *Odyssey*, has become the enemy of the gods. Some scholars have found all this inappropriate to the character of Clytaemestra, who should surely welcome any suggestion that Agamemnon does not have divine protection. It is usually explained as a sign of her hypocrisy; she really wants her husband to return safely, so that she can have the pleasure of killing him herself. More important perhaps is that by reminding the audience of the proper attitude and behaviour of the waiting wife in a traditional *nostos* story, she will clarify for the audience the difference between the faithful wife whom she claims to be and her real self.

The first *stasimon* begins as a joyful song of victory, but, as the chorus reflect on the deaths of too many men at Troy (it is only their ashes that Ares has escorted home – πέμπει, *pempei*, 441), the mood gradually changes, and the ode ends with the chorus reluctant to face the consequences of the victory, so they hope that Agamemnon is not after all about to return. It is only a woman who has given them the news of the beacons, and women are of course unreliable. In the *Odyssey* it is the woman Penelope, who in Books 17 and 19 refuses to believe the various reports which she receives of her husband's imminent arrival, and who distrusts even the dream which would seem to confirm them (19.535–69). In our play the arrival of the Herald shatters the chorus's wishful thinking, as he confirms that Agamemnon will be close behind him. The homecoming of the hero in *nostos* poetry seems regularly to have been preceded by a herald or messenger. In the *Odyssey* a herald and Eumaeus together report to Penelope that Telemachus has returned safely to Ithaca (16.130–33, 328–40), while before Xerxes can return in *Persae* the Messenger has a major part to play. In *Trachiniae* both the Messenger and Lichas report to Deianeira that Heracles' arrival is imminent. In *Agamemnon* the Herald rejoices at his own return, but goes on to reveal the fulfilment of Clytaemestra's warning: Agamemnon is hated by the gods, and he has come home with only a single ship; the rest have been lost in a storm. In a *nostos* poem in which the hero has to face troubles on his arrival it is essential that some way must be found for him to lose all or most of his companions, so that he is left to prove, or fail to prove, his heroism by facing those troubles alone. The narrative of Odysseus' wanderings presents a process by which he gradually loses all his ships and men until he arrives alone on Calypso's island. In *Persae* Xerxes loses almost all his men in the homeward journey, especially in the crossing of the Strymon, so that he too will have to confront the chorus alone on his arrival, and will not receive the welcome which he expects. Even Telemachus, on his return from his travels, sends off his companions before proceeding alone to Eumaeus' house. The easiest way for the poet to eliminate the companions is by means of a storm at sea. In the *Odyssey* little is said about Agamemnon's voyage home, but in one passage (4.514–37), which for various reasons is considered by some modern scholars to be an interpolation, a storm drives him off his course. In that version, but also in other passages, Agamemnon has companions who are killed with him in Aegisthus' house by Aegisthus' men. In Aeschylus, however, possibly following an unknown variant version of the story, Agamemnon arrives on stage alone, apart from Cassandra. The Herald's speculation that Menelaus may still be alive prepares us for his appearance in the satyr-play, but at this stage what matters is that he is not present to protect him against the dangers waiting for him at home, and the feeble old men of the chorus will turn out to be incapable of helping him.

On the other hand, Agamemnon does arrive on a carriage, as befits a successful king and general on his return from war. Contrast the failure Xerxes, whose arrival on foot, instead of on the luxurious vehicle on which he left for Troy, is explicitly mentioned in the text, as was the second entry of Atossa which contrasted with her first entry on a chariot. The audience may think of another form of the *nostos* poem, the epinikian ode which was sung at the return home of a victorious athlete from the Games, riding on a carriage (Pind. *Ol.* 4.8–13). Agamemnon is not at all dismayed by the somewhat muted reception that he receives from the chorus, and when they warn him to beware of those who are not well-disposed to him, he assures them of his competence to distinguish the good from the bad, and his readiness to put right all that is wrong in the city. In the *Odyssey* Athena gives a similar warning to Odysseus when he wakes up on Ithaca, and no doubt it was a regular element in the return of the hero. Enrico Medda has shown how the same theme is used by Aristophanes with comic effect in his *Plutus*.[3] Odysseus heeds Athena's warning and takes the appropriate steps to deal with the threat, whereas Agamemnon completely misses the point. So the great victor of Troy will fall victim to a mere woman. Before she persuades him, against his will, to walk on the crimson fabrics, she has continued to play the role of the wife who has yearned for her absent husband's return, and in the last words that her defeated husband hears her speak before he enters the palace, she lavishes on him the praise that is appropriate only to a victor, whether in war or the Games. Incidentally she explains the absence of Orestes, who is not yet available to play the part of Telemachus in supporting his father, and at the same time prepares us for Orestes' homecoming in the next play of the trilogy.

Agamemnon of course is not entirely alone; he has brought Cassandra with him. She is part of his homecoming story already in the *Odyssey*, but it seems likely, though we cannot be sure, that Aeschylus was the first to develop her role, so that she becomes the only character in the play to defeat Clytaemestra, if only temporarily, in her attempt to force her to enter the palace. And, as the inspired prophetess of Agamemnon's murder, she may be the first to relate it all to the family curse. Perhaps Aeschylus borrowed something from the much less important prophet in the *Odyssey*, Theoclymenus, the companion of Telemachus on his voyage home to Ithaca.

The exact staging of the original production is uncertain, and it is a problem for every modern producer of the play. Like most scholars I have till now assumed that there is only one carriage, which Cassandra shares with Agamemnon, and I have supposed that the audience will detect yet another form of *nostos*, that in which the bridegroom conveys his bride on a carriage or wagon to his old and her new home. In this case, however, she is met at the door, not by her mother-in-law, but by her husband's existing, and no doubt jealous, wife. The perversion of what ought to be a happy occasion is just one of the many perversions in this trilogy. The situation was to be exploited by Sophocles in *Trachiniae*, and one may think also of Euripides' *Andromache*. However, Oliver Thomas has recently made an interesting case for two carriages. The first, bearing Agamemnon alone, stops immediately in front of the great central door, and it is removed by attendants immediately after he has walked over the crimson fabrics into the palace. The second, carrying Cassandra and the rest of the spoils that Agamemnon has brought back from Troy, remains 'not central, though in a position which can become focal when Clytemnestra re-emerges'.[4] This would be consistent with the homecoming of Agamemnon as a successful general, and the spoils *are* mentioned by the Herald at 578–79. One might add that it would also recall the rich gifts of the Phaeacians, which Odysseus brings home with him to Ithaca (5.33–42, 13.134–38), and which, in his case, have to be hidden for a while in the Cave of the Nymphs. Either way, the producer has to decide whether, before Cassandra enters the palace the red fabrics have already been removed, as scholars generally assume, which would indicate her inferior status, or whether she too walks over them, which would emphasize her sharing in Agamemnon's fate. If the *skēnē* was, as most scholars believe, a very recent addition to the theatre of Dionysus, *Agamemnon* is likely to have been the first play in which the death-cries are heard from behind the door. I myself, however, believe that the *skēnē* may have been there as early as *Persae*, fourteen years before.

I would like to think that it was Aeschylus himself who conceived the murder of Agamemnon in his bath, trapped in a net-like robe. But at least the robe seems to appear in one or two representations of the murder in art. Whether the bath too can be identified in art is more dubious. In a kalyx krater by the Dokimasia Painter a robe envelops Agamemnon, who stands naked as if he has just emerged from a bath. Emily Vermeule thought that this must derive from Aeschylus' play.[5] However, there the king dies *in*, and not *after*, his bath. In any case the krater is now dated to *c*. 470 BC, long before the production of the play. Whether or not the setting for the murder is entirely original, there can be no doubt about the powerful use that Aeschylus makes of it. Both bath and clothes may be essential elements in a *nostos* story. The arrival on Scheria of the naked shipwrecked Odysseus is one of the lowest moments in his adventures, and the beginning of his restitution to his status as a hero is marked first by his bath in the river and secondly by his putting on of the clothes lent to him by Nausicaa. He is not yet home, but he has returned at last to a civilized, if still semi-fantastic, society. When he does reach Ithaca, he is dressed as a beggar in rags, and it is only when he is bathed and dressed in Book 23 that he is reinstated in his real identity, and can lay claim to his proper place in Penelope's marriage-bed. In *Persae* Xerxes too arrives in rags, and the ghost of Darius instructs Atossa to meet him with clothes appropriate to his status. Her failure to do so means that for Xerxes there is to be no rehabilitation. Normally, as one would expect, the bath precedes the donning of the ceremonial robe in preparation for the banquet that will follow it. In *Agamemnon*, however, the two stages are combined into one. Clytaemestra puts the robe on her husband *in* the bath, and instead of a symbol of rehabilitation it has become an instrument of murder. In effect Agamemnon is still naked when he dies. The bath has become his coffin, and the robe has become his shroud. In both *Agamemnon* (1540) and *Choephori* (999) the bath is described as a δροίτη (*droitē*), which can also, at least in later Greek, mean a coffin. At *Choephori* 1011 the robe is a φᾶρος (or φάρος, *pharos*), which can also mean a shroud. Both words occur in successive lines at *Eumenides* 633–34. In *Trachiniae*, when the long-awaited Heracles is on his way home, the robe sent to him by Deianeira, as a token of her love, causes his death, but, unlike Clytaemestra, she certainly did not intend it.

In the remainder of the play Aeschylus explores the ethical implications of the murder – not the least of his contributions to the development of the story – and looks ahead to the homecoming of Orestes in the next play of the trilogy (1646–48, 1667). Already in the *Odyssey* Orestes' role as the avenger of his father is presented as a model for that of Telemachus in his support of Odysseus (1.298–302, 3.195–200, 11.448–53). In *Choephori* Orestes will arrive home in disguise, like Odysseus in the *Odyssey*, and like so many of the characters in South Slavic poetry, and he will be greeted by his hostess with the promise of a hot bath. She still understands how a proper hostess *ought* to behave. The play will end with no rehabilitation for Orestes, as he is forced to set off once again on his journey to Delphi and finally Athens. One may recall that even Odysseus will have to depart again on his travels before he can finally settle down peacefully in his own home. After his acquittal by the Areopagus in *Eumenides* Orestes leaves finally for Argos, and we hardly notice him go. The dramatic interest has moved to the Erinyes, who now depart, not back to their old home in Agamemnon's palace, from which it was impossible then to shift them, a κῶμος δύσπεμπτος (*kōmos duspemptos*) (*Ag.* 1189–90), but to their new home in Athens, 'under the kindly escort' (ὑπ' εὔφρονι πομπᾶι, *hup' euphroni pompai*, 1034) of their προπομποί (*propompoi*). So the whole trilogy ends with a kind of homecoming. I doubt whether it was the one expected by the audience at the beginning of the first play.

Notes

1 Taplin (1977), 123–27.
2 Alexopoulou (2009).
3 Medda (2013), 391–93.
4 Thomas (2013), 494–5.
5 Vermeule (1966), 1–22.

4

Clytemnestra and Cassandra

Hanna M. Roisman

Clytemnestra and Cassandra differ in age, status, and vitality, yet Aeschylus uses a similar dramatic strategy to present the manipulative queen and the captive concubine. The sequence of their experiences is similar, as are their reasons to wish Agamemnon dead. The playwright's choice to create this kind of symmetry between two women of such seemingly different types gives the audience the opportunity to consider the broad repercussions of masculine actions.

The Cassandra scene

Overview

Cassandra spends an uninterrupted 549 lines on stage, 50 per cent more time than Clytemnestra until she re-enters after the murders.[1] Up until Cassandra alights from the chariot, Clytemnestra has been on the stage for only 276 lines, during which she intermittently speaks 215 lines.[2] Cassandra dismounts from the chariot in line 1072, after 291 lines of silence and immobility and exits the stage at 1330. During these 258 lines, usually referred to as 'the Cassandra scene', Cassandra erupts in song and dance. For about half of her stage presence (47 per cent to be exact), the audience see her move, sing, dance, and speak for 180 lines, only 35 lines fewer than Clytemnestra. That is to say, the two women have had roughly equal time to express themselves while on stage up to the point when Cassandra enters the palace.[3] Therefore Cassandra's scene is significant based on the number of lines, as well as on her contribution to the plot. It is true that after Cassandra's murder, Clytemnestra resurfaces for another 301 lines, but during these lines she speaks only 127 lines, less than 50 per cent of her presence, in exchanges with the Chorus and Aegisthus.[4] Once Aegisthus enters in line 1576, her speech is minimal, amounting to 12 lines out of 97, in which Aegisthus dominates the stage in preparation for his ascendance in power in the second part of the trilogy. In sum, Clytemnestra is onstage for a total of 577 lines and Cassandra for 549 lines. While the audience see the two figures on the stage for almost the same number of lines, Cassandra's presence is continuous. She enters the stage on a chariot with Agamemnon around or at line 783, but is not alluded to until line 950, and there only as 'foreign woman' (*xenē*). For 170 lines, then, the spectators must wonder about her role and significance, and even afterwards her continuing silence must have aroused their curiosity further. They are left guessing whether she is a mute character or a third speaking character recently introduced to the theatre.[5]

Cassandra's motionlessness in the chariot parallels Clytemnestra's stasis at the gates of the palace. Until Cassandra dismounts from the chariot, there is a kind of 'draw' in physical dramatic effect between the queen and the Trojan princess. This performative balance between the two characters shifts when Cassandra refuses to answer the queen's brusque injunctions to descend from the chariot.[6] Insulted by the captive's silence, Clytemnestra withdraws abruptly into the palace. The scene now changes dramatically: bursting into words and dance, Cassandra takes complete control of the stage.[7] With her youthful vitality, both frantic and surprising, she dominates the stage.

Cassandra's refusal to obey Clytemnestra's bidding to enter the palace or engage in any discussion deprives Clytemnestra of the rhetorical power in which her superiority resides; the younger woman, who embodies the threat any concubine poses to a wife, symbolically undermines Clytemnestra's status as the mistress of the house. In everything she does, Cassandra draws attention to the contrast between Clytemnestra's control over Agamemnon in the tapestries scene and the queen's lack of control over her, Cassandra, who maintains her free-will. Agamemnon, the victorious hero, walks into the palace deceived, ensnared, and defeated by Clytemnestra. Cassandra, a female captive, eventually goes inside but in her own time, fully aware of her fate.

Cassandra's song and frenzied activity are not unrelated to her former silent, motionless presence. On the contrary, her sudden transition is the epitome of her presence. Her prolonged silence must have intrigued the audience, as they waited for her to dismount from the carriage, just as they waited for Clytemnestra's re-entry from the palace. The usual assumption that the scene has no effect on the story unfolding in the play and could be omitted is patently mistaken.[8] Cassandra's scene adds dynamism and depth to the play, and is important both in the immediate context of her appearance, but also to the arc of the three tragedies as a whole. Her resistance signals trouble ahead for Clytemnestra; she is the first person to suggest that Clytemnestra's power may be undermined. The Chorus tried but failed. When Cassandra refuses to immediately follow Clytemnestra's commands, the imperiousness of the queen is crippled. Indeed, she never recovers her former dominance. Cassandra's silence and inertia in the face of Clytemnestra's orders give the younger woman a potent grandeur. From this moment on, Clytemnestra's power wanes.[9]

Aegisthus will shortly appear with his guard and tell the Chorus how he used Clytemnestra for his own interest (see below). Her power will gradually diminish, to the point that in *Libation Bearers* she is relegated to the position of any wife who takes care of the household proper, but is not involved in matters of the *polis*. She offers bountiful hospitality to Orestes and Pylades: hot baths and good bedding to assuage their fatigue, but 'if anything else needs to be done that calls for more deliberation (*bouliōteron*), then it is a job for men, and we will communicate it to them' (*LB* 672–73, Sommerstein), she tells them. She is no longer the woman of 'hopeful heart which plans like a man' (*androboulon elpizon kear*, *Ag.* 11, Sommerstein). Clytemnestra will soon be murdered. Even after her death she will be further diminished when Athena allows the acquittal of Orestes by not contesting Apollo's contention that a mother is no more than a receptacle for the father's seed, and that there is no blood relationship between mother and child (*Eu.* 734–40). This diminution of a woman's role in the creation of a child, sanctioned by a female goddess, robs Clytemnestra of her greatest justification for murdering Agamemnon, his sacrifice of their daughter. Clytemnestra's powers are thus deleted by a female goddess, as they were weakened in the first part of the trilogy by the quintessentially feminine Cassandra.

Cause and effect

Cassandra's scene elucidates the causality behind the events in this part of the trilogy and also in the remaining plays. Without this scene, the subsequent murder of Agamemnon and Orestes' later vengeful slaying of Clytemnestra seem to result from the occurrences of the last ten years. Cassandra provides a much fuller history for these crimes, as well as some hope for an end to the chain of retribution.

Up until this scene, the audience have watched Clytemnestra's rhetorical battle with the Chorus; her greetings to the Herald; and her welcome to Agamemnon, when she subdues his will to her own. In these early scenes the temporal context of the play is defined as the ten years between the Greeks' departure for Troy and the city's fall. The causation of the events is thus initially only explored within that ten-year time period. The Watchman hints that something is not right with the house, where he has been keeping watch on the roof, but he is referring only to the last ten years during Agamemnon's absence. Hinting obscurely at Clytemnestra's affair with Aegisthus, he complains that 'a bull lolls leaden on my tongue'. The Chorus introduce the sacrifice of Iphigenia and make a veiled reference to the earlier history of the house when they report Calchas' words: 'It has not died, no, *it breaks out afresh, the terror and the treachery, the governess that guards the house*, the child-avenging Fury which will not forget' (150–55). They do not, however, connect these events to any repercussions. It is only Cassandra who links the atrocities which took place in earlier generations to what is about to happen. She also intimates that the curse of the house will not end with this round of violence, but that Agamemnon's and her deaths will be avenged in the future, thus introducing the thematic arc for the next two parts of the trilogy. Her visions of past and future (see below) connect the murders about to take place with the gruesome deeds which have occurred in the House of Atreus long before the sacrifice of Iphigenia.

While Cassandra's scene introduces the theme of cause and effect informing the remainder of the trilogy, it also looks performatively and thematically backwards to the tapestries scene.[10] In that scene Clytemnestra convinced Agamemnon to walk on expensive tapestries, thereby committing *hybris* in plain sight: 'The sacrilege of which he is already guilty is acted out before our eyes', says Lebeck.[11] Previously Clytemnestra has said nothing about Agamemnon's sacrifice of Iphigenia, which she will claim as the main cause of her vengeance. Without directly mentioning the events at Aulis, she tricks Agamemnon into re-enacting his *hybris*, and revealing what he is capable of. Just as he was persuaded by Calchas and the army to sacrifice his daughter, he is persuaded by Clytemnestra to trample the rich, blood-coloured tapestries, even though, fearing the jealousy of the gods (946–49), he feels it is wrong to do. It is important for the audience to experience Agamemnon's *hybris* first hand in view of the looming punishment. Cassandra's visions, however, show the audience that Agamemnon's past and present failings are not independent of the curse on the House of Atreus. Agamemnon's murder is not an isolated act, but only one link in a long chain of events, going far back to the crimes of Pelops; Thyestes' seduction of his brother Atreus's wife; Atreus's vengeful murder of Thyestes' children, whom he served to Thyestes at a banquet; Thyestes' subsequent curse on Atreus; and so on. However, this hereditary curse does not exonerate Agamemnon from responsibility; he makes his own mistakes that lead to his doom.

As with Agamemnon, Cassandra's lot follows the sequence of cause and effect. At the end of the scene, Aeschylus has Cassandra relive her rejection of Apollo when explaining the source of her prophetic visions to the Chorus, as he had Agamemnon recapitulate his bad judgement. Cassandra accuses Apollo of destroying her for 'the second time' (1082). She tells the Chorus that having promised herself to Apollo in exchange for the gift of prophecy, she then rejected his advances.[12] Apollo retaliated by rendering his gift void, ensuring no-one would believe her. We know that her prophecies about Paris were ignored, and as a result she was unable to prevent the Trojan War. Now she is reaping the fruit of her deception: she is going to die because of this war: 'And she'll kill me ... Like a witch, who works her poison, she will stir my wage, my wormwood! And she revels as she whets the sword and boasts that it's because he brought me home that she will kill him with my slaughter as his payment' (1260–63). This is her ruin by Apollo for the 'second time'.[13] Seeing her death approach simply because she was forced to accompany Agamemnon as a captive, Cassandra rebels. She symbolically rejects the gift of prophecy Apollo gave her. She strips off all her prophetic trappings: her staff, the woollen bands about her neck, and finally her garment; as they fall to the ground, she tramples on them as Agamemnon stepped on the tapestries. Sider[14] has already called attention to the parallel in the scenes by noticing her use of the verb *ploutizete* in her rejection address to Apollo: 'Go, *give* some other girl your *wealth* of ruin [i.e. prophecy] – not me' (1268), which recalls the noun *ploutos*, 'wealth' used for the robes trampled by Agamemnon (949).

Just as the audience needed to see a repeat of Agamemnon's *hybris* before his death, so they needed to witness a reprise of Cassandra's former sexual rebuff of Apollo. The transgression which leads to her death is not tied to any misdoing of the city of Troy, as claimed by Leahy,[15] but to her rejection of Apollo. In a circuitous way, this trickery of hers led to the war that ultimately is going to kill her. Her casting off of her prophetic garb is a symbolic gesture reiterating this rejection, after having initially accepted both his advances and his gift of prophecy.[16] The Cassandra scene therefore reinforces the theme of cause and effect presented in her visions of past, present, and future regarding the House of Atreus, and also in terms of her personal responsibility in an analogous way to Agamemnon's hubristic act of trampling on the tapestries.

In terms of performance, the tapestries scene presented a tremendous spectacle. The many lengths of luxuriant, blood-coloured fabrics are slowly laid down before the carriage in full view of the spectators. Although Cassandra's garb and prophetic emblems are less spectacular, her singing and frantic dancing are as attention-catching as the tapestries. The scene is traumatic enough to impress upon the spectators that while Agamemnon trampled on the abundant wealth of his household, Cassandra, a seemingly powerless captive, is nevertheless casting away the little she has. Secondly, while Agamemnon was persuaded by Clytemnestra to commit an act he fundamentally disagreed with, as he did at Aulis, Cassandra retains her own agency, as she did years ago when she dared to reject a god.

How do the two women engage?

The two heroines do not engage dramatically. After Agamemnon enters the palace, Clytemnestra comes back to fetch Cassandra and addresses her haughtily. She makes sure Cassandra knows who the mistress of this house is. Cassandra ought to accept her slave status, she tells her. Cassandra should be happy to have come to a house of established old wealth. *Nouveaux riches* would treat her cruelly, but this house will treat her according to custom (1035–46). Cassandra's recalcitrance insults the queen. Cassandra remains silent. Ignoring Clytemnestra's goading and the Chorus's call for an interpreter, she bursts into a whirlwind of activity after Clytemnestra leaves the stage. After her murder, Clytemnestra ignores Cassandra, other than calling her a whore of the ships' benches. Cassandra, however, has already prophesied Clytemnestra's death, and she goes to her own death knowing that her murderess won't live long either.

Why does Clytemnestra kill Cassandra? Cassandra poses no danger to her. Is she motivated by jealousy, by the feeling of being scorned? Is she driven by emotion or maddened by power? Cassandra sees her murder by Clytemnestra as 'an extra ingredient in Clytemnestra's wrathful retribution'.[17] She knows she is not the main target for Clytemnestra's wrath, but she symbolizes an additional transgression by Agamemnon (1137). In all of her predictions and explications, Cassandra never mentions Iphigenia. For her it is the fall of Troy that justifies Agamemnon's murder. She accepts her death as an intrinsic part of Troy's suffering and as part of the revenge on the man who brought that suffering about: 'Why such self-pity? Why these tears? I saw my city, I saw Troy endure all it endured; I saw the men who raped my city taken as the gods decreed in retribution. And so I shall go. I too shall die. This house – it is as if it is the house of death, of Hades' (1285–89).

Cassandra has correctly interpreted the reason for her death by the hand of Clytemnestra. Iphigenia was the main reason for Clytemnestra's revenge on Agamemnon, but his sexual activities clearly served as the catalyst. After the murders, we hear Clytemnestra exclaim: 'But *Agamemnon* – I have laid him sprawling on the ground, my ruin, my ... my Casanova with his harem and his whores at Troy, and she his bondage-slave, so good with crystal balls, his faithful little bed-mate, tugging on his oar, kneeling by his bench below the main mast' (1438–43). If she knows about Chryseis and Cassandra's prophetic powers, she must have also heard of the predilection of Agamemnon for Cassandra. Of course, he would present Cassandra as merely war booty, a gift from the army (955), but in a later play by Euripides we also learn that there was a version of the story including Agamemnon's fondness for Cassandra. In this version it was for Cassandra's sake that he tacitly collaborated with Hecuba's plan to avenge herself on Polymestor (*Hec.* 824–32, 850–57). Aeschylus probably relied on the audience's assumption that Clytemnestra was aware of Agamemnon's feelings for the Trojan princess. It is difficult not to recognize jealousy in her words. Should we seek a metaphorical explanation? If the two heroines form a composite of Agamemnon's ideal wife, would the killing of Cassandra symbolize the eradication of any vestige of loyalty Clytemnestra might still have felt towards her husband? Cassandra has good reason to ignore Clytemnestra's bidding to dismount and enter the palace. Knowing what to expect, she has no reason to converse with her executioner.

Myth and image commonalities

On the face of it, the play capitalizes on the contrast between Clytemnestra and Cassandra. One is a lawful wife, the other a concubine; one is old, the other young. One has given birth multiple times; the other is a virgin.[18] One is static; the other, once she dismounts, resembles a whirlwind. However, the two heroines share several mythical commonalities, and the playwright clearly wished the audience to notice what they do have in common.

Aeschylus doubtless presupposed the existence of a broad pool of mythic material known to the ancient audience. All of the tragedians mined this resource, adapting it as needed. According to some versions of this myth, Agamemnon forced himself on both of the women. In the later play *Iphigenia at Aulis* by Euripides, Clytemnestra recalls that Agamemnon coerced her into marrying him after he killed her first husband and her baby boy. Cassandra was awarded to him as a gift by the army, 'the choice flower of its rich booty' (*Ag.* 954–55, Sommerstein), according to Agamemnon. Both women plan his demise, although for different reasons. Clytemnestra avenges the murder of her eldest daughter, Iphigenia, and as a side-effect of the war, his bringing home a beautiful younger woman as his concubine. Cassandra is aware that her death will occur as a result of Agamemnon bringing her to Argos, a homecoming made possible by his sacking of Troy. In an odd way, both women want him dead for bringing Cassandra to Argos. Euripides' *Trojan Women*, albeit a later play, presents Cassandra explicitly wishing to bring about Agamemnon's death as revenge for her fallen brothers and murdered father. 'For I shall kill him and plunder his house, exacting revenge for my brothers and my father!' (*TW* 359–60, Kovacs) she exclaims after learning that she has been allotted to him as a concubine.

Both women also deceive the male. Pretending to be a faithful wife, Clytemnestra tricks Agamemnon into entering the palace, while Cassandra reneged on her promise to have sex with Apollo. Both also conceal and reveal information, as they please. However, while the concealment serves Clytemnestra, for Cassandra it is irrelevant since Apollo has seen to it that she is never believed. Both women are also criticized by the Chorus of Argive Elders. Cassandra ignores them more than Clytemnestra, probably because she knows they don't matter in terms of her fate. They do, however, pose a threat to Clytemnestra since they know of her affair with Aegisthus. Finally, both go to their death knowingly. Cassandra enters the palace after having visualized her death. Clytemnestra in *Libation Bearers* follows Orestes to the palace, where she knows she will be killed (903–7).

In text of the play, the playwright connects the two figures through words and imagery, a strategy found in the *Odyssey*, where certain formulas are used only for Odysseus and Penelope or the extended family of Odysseus.[19] Both women use canine imagery for themselves. Clytemnestra's referral to herself as the watchdog of the house (*dōmatōn kyna*, 606) is replicated by Cassandra in her explanatory iambs, where she calls Clytemnestra a 'hateful bitch' (*misētēs kynos*, 1228).[20] It is also paralleled by the Chorus's comparison of Cassandra to a hunting-dog, after the first proof of her prophetic abilities: 'This girl is like a hunting-dog, keen-scented, casting for the spoor of slaughter and she will find it' (1093–94). Cassandra repeats this image of herself to the Chorus when she says: 'Join me in the hunt, track down the scent, the spoor of all these horrors done so long ago' (1184–85), focusing on her 'scent-tracking abilities'.[21]

Both heroines are also sensitive to sounds emitted by those who suffer or cause suffering. In her imagined picture of the fall of Troy, Clytemnestra describes to the Argive Elders the voices one can hear when a city is overrun by enemies (321–25). Cassandra too in her visions focuses on sounds and voices. She sees the slaughtered children of Thyestes wailing (1096–97); she wishes she had the fate of the clear-voiced nightingale rather than dying by two-edged sword (1146–49). In her vision, she also hears the chorus of Erinyes who haunt the House of Atreus, 'chanting its cabbala in unison, cacophonous, words so diabolic ... they're haunting all the house now with their ghostly tarantella' (1186–87). The two women also use similar vocabulary for the sounds they describe. Clytemnestra says she *shouted of victory* (*anōlolyxa*, 587) when she saw the beacons, and when boasting about the carrying out of the thanksgivings she ordered, she says: 'they sacrificed, like old-women, here and here and everywhere throughout the city, *croaked their cries of victory, "may all turn out well"*' (*ololygmon*, 594–96), which is paralleled by Cassandra's vocabulary when she paints the image of the net of death enveloping Agamemnon: 'So let the strife insatiate *raise for the family the triumph of victory* (*katalolyxatō*), where death comes by stoning' (1116–18). She also describes Clytemnestra as raising a 'cry of victory' (*epōlolyxatō*, 1236), a monster waging war against her nearest and dearest.

Thematic commonalities

Encounters with the Chorus

Both women face off with the Chorus, and both fail to communicate their realities to the Elders. In the first encounter between the Chorus and Clytemnestra, the Chorus repeatedly criticize Clytemnestra's order of thanksgiving sacrifices all around the city, claiming that her rash behaviour reflects a womanly tendency to believe in rumour and gossip rather than to base decisions on solid facts. They demand proof for the fall of Troy. However, when she tells them that she has learned that Troy has been taken from the beacon-signal Agamemnon has sent her, giving them an accurate and precise geographical account of the fire transmission, they cannot digest the information and call on her to repeat it 'from beginning to end' (317–19). Clytemnestra must have understood their cognitive difficulty and chooses to present them not with a further factual account, but with one completely fabricated by her. She provides them with an imaginary, heartrending description of a city falling into the hands of enemies (320–50). As if in a cinematic rendering, she depicts the sounds. In the fallen city it is easy to distinguish between the conquerors and the conquered by sound alone, she tells them, so distinct are the cries and shouts of the conquerors and the conquered. As if in a reply to their constant denigration of her as a woman, she draws them to the kitchen, the world of women: the variant sounds do not mix as vinegar and oil fail to mix even when in the same vessel. She briefly depicts the anguish and grief of those who have lost their dear ones, to whose corpses they cling. She moves then back to the conquerors, and in a womanly fashion observes their physical comfort and discomfort: they are hungry after a night of fighting and are looking for breakfast. Having found shelter in the houses of the Trojans, however, they do not suffer anymore from the cold and feel more relaxed. She follows with a warning that there is still danger lurking for the successful victors: they should not plunder or offend the gods (330–50).[22]

Clytemnestra's ploy of drawing the Elders into her imaginary scene and giving the impression that her sole interest lies with the well-being of the army shows how she can take advantage of their credulity with a baseless tale. By convincing the Chorus through a description created by her, she actually feminizes them since now they behave 'like a woman does' (485–87, cf. 272–77), the same charge they brought against her when she told them of the beacon-signal. Clytemnestra's poignant description is labelled by the Chorus as 'sure evidence' (*tekmēria*, 352) and earns her the Chorus's highest commendation: 'your words were like a man's' (351). However, in spite of this compliment, only 123 lines later they not only doubt the beacon-signal, but revert to their misogynistic selves: 'A rumour proclaimed by a woman vanishes' (478, 487), they claim. Clytemnestra is perfectly aware of their gender-based suspicions of her, and after the Herald has proven that her announcement about the fall of Troy was correct, she taunts the Chorus: 'I raised the shout of victory long since when first the fire shot through the night to bring its news to me, to tell of Troy, how it was taken ... Yet there were those who sneered at me' (587–91).

Cassandra's experience with the Chorus is similar. Her prophetic revelations are divided in two. The first part is purely lyrical and of great emotional intensity but enigmatic. In the second part she mostly recapitulates in spoken iambic trimeter what she presented previously in her lyrics presenting her prophesy in terms of cause and effect. In both she sees visions relating to past events in the House of Atreus, tying them to her visions of the future. In the lyrical part she first cries out in horror at her visions of the crimes that have occurred in the past (1090-91,1095-97). In four enigmatic outcries she also bewails the evil scheme taking place in the house at present: a woman who is planning to cause evil to her husband in the bath. She sees the future moment in which the woman reaches to pick up the robe she will throw over her victim as a net to immobilize him in the bath, and predicts a crime worthy of stoning, which translates into kin-killing, and calls out to keep the cow from the bull (1100-4, 1107-11, 1114-18, 1125-29). In her vision the cow will ensnare the bull: 'she's snaring him fast in the webs of her weaving, the black horns are goring, the weapon sinks home. And he's sliding back in the bath, in the water, the purifying bowl of adulterous death' (1126-28). She does not name the woman or the husband, and her animalistic imagery is unclear.

The Elders recognize Cassandra's accurate divination of the past, and say they have heard about her fame as seer, *but* 'we don't look for any clairvoyants here' (1098). They have already stated in the very beginning of the play that one cannot know the future, thus eliminating the whole function of prophecy:

> What will be will be, and you will know it. Face it now, or (rather) weep.
> For it will come as clear as any dawn, which slices through the mists that rise with morning.
>
> 251–54, cf. 1132–35

They admit Cassandra has pinpointed the past accurately, but they say that the whole city resounds with this information: one does not need a seer for this (1105–6). However, when she launches into her vision of the future, they are lost: 'What good ever comes of an oracle anyway?' (1132–33, cf. 112–13).

This assumption that one cannot know the future will prevent them from listening to Cassandra just as their assumption that a woman is unable to make fact-based decisions prevented them from believing Clytemnestra when Troy had been taken. Nevertheless, Aeschylus suggests that in spite of their claims of misunderstanding and dismissal, there is an increasing anxiety in the Chorus. While in the first four stanzas they respond to her song in spoken iambic trimeter, in the fifth of the seven stanzas they change from trimeters to dochmiacs and liken their fear to death (1121-22). They do realize that what she claims is bad (1130-31), but cannot figure out the entire picture. In the remaining stanzas, however, the reverse is happening. The Chorus, who previously answered Cassandra's lyrics with spoken iambs, take the lyric part, showing their growing stress, while Cassandra, grown calmer, closes each of her statements with trimeter, before moving to her clarifying restatements, in which she repeats in spoken iambic trimeter what she has previously revealed in lyrics and more (1178-97, 1215-45). Is she coming to terms with her imminent death?

A similar scenario happens in the iambic exegeses in which she repeats the information she gave in the lyrical part but more clearly. When she speaks of the past horrors, the Chorus agree that she is as informed as if she were an Argive (1198-201), but when she launches into the present and future events in the palace, i.e. the murder of Agamemnon by Clytemnestra and Aegisthus, they are again unable to grasp her words: 'Thyestes' feasting on his own sons' flesh – I follow you ... But all the rest – I heard it but I'm wide of understanding' (1242-45), they state. Even when she unequivocally states: 'I tell you: you will look on Agamemnon dead' (1246), they shy away from bad news: 'No malediction, no, talaina! Hush what you're saying now' (1247). When she claims that even though she speaks plain Greek, they fail to follow her, the Chorus's reply is: 'So does the oracle of Delphi – it's still hard to understand' (1255). At the end of the scene, Cassandra is so discouraged by her inability to burst the barrier of the Chorus's addled mind and their failure to grasp the immediate danger to Agamemnon and herself, that she tears her prophetess's robes as an attack on Apollo, whom she blames for the Chorus's failure to understand her prophesy, and shakily but courageously approaches the palace's doors, knowing she will be killed upon entrance.

Clytemnestra and Cassandra's encounters with the Chorus follow a similar pattern. First, they disbelieve Clytemnestra's news, then believe her fictional story of the fall of Troy, then go back on their acceptance of the news. With Cassandra the path is a little more circuitous but similar. They fail to understand her lyrical prophesies, accept her account of the past, but fail to grasp her warning about the upcoming murders. While Clytemnestra reacts to their disbelief in her news by mocking them later, Cassandra's reaction is more extreme. She casts off her prophetic clothing and tramples on it, blaming Apollo for her life of misery: being mocked as a deranged prophetess while she was prophesying the truth. Both heroines fail to communicate with the Elders. In both cases their previous assumptions prevent the Elders from absorbing new information. They do not believe Clytemnestra because she is a woman. They do not believe Cassandra because no one can know the future. Yet their presuppositions are at odds with the very nature of the two women. Clytemnestra prides herself on being a woman and yet able to make fact-based decisions the way a man would. Cassandra's essence lies in her prophetic powers that are truthful, despite being cursed to be unbelievable. Aeschylus duplicated the theme of information transmission in the scene of Cassandra's face-off with the Chorus. However, unlike Clytemnestra, whose spurious account convinces the Chorus, Cassandra's true account fails to do so.

Hiding and revealing

The duality of hiding and revealing is another characteristic that connects the two heroines. Each of them is engaged in concealing and elucidating. Clytemnestra first hides her true intentions towards the homecoming king, and then reveals them by the act of murder and her boasts over Agamemnon's corpse. A similar strategy is followed by Cassandra, who first hides her prophecies in complicated phraseology which even she knows is incomprehensible. 'I will tell you now, and no more riddles' (1183), she tells the Chorus when she moves from the lyrics to spoken iambic trimeter, and plainly explains what has happened in the past in the House of Atreus, what is happening in the present, and what will happen in the near and far future (1177–97, 1214–45).

Clytemnestra's strategic obfuscation is expertly achieved through the formidable rhetorical powers with which she assures Agamemnon of her fidelity, while coldly planning her revenge. Her speech to the Herald is a masterpiece of a wife hiding her pernicious intentions through ambiguous phraseology, as is her admiring speech to Agamemnon himself. The best example of the former is Clytemnestra's bidding the Herald to report to Agamemnon: 'may he find his wife at home as faithful (*pistē*) as she was the day he left' (*Ag.* 606–7). Her self-description as *gynē pistē*, 'loyal/faithful wife' (606), is a rhetorical *tour de force*. She uses the military concepts of 'fidelity' or 'loyalty', familiar to Agamemnon from ten years spent with his army. The use of language from his comfort zone creates a false sense of security. The phrase itself is triply odd. *Pistos*, 'loyal', is a rare personal epithet found previously only in Homer and limited to a military context, but Clytemnestra transports it into a domestic environment, where being a 'loyal wife' becomes the heart of her wifely identity. Secondly, it is used formulaically and only for Homeric heroes who have proven their loyalty in death.[23] That Clytemnestra is attuned to this original meaning of the epithet becomes clear in her reference later to the slaughtered Cassandra, whom she calls Agamemnon's 'loyal (*pistē*) bedfellow', meaning that she was so loyal to her master that she died for him (1442).[24] Thirdly, her use of the epithet for herself is unique: there is no other extant case in epic or the tragedies where a person uses this epithet to describe himself/herself.[25] There is also the possibility of a semantic ambiguity in the phrase as it appears in the text. When the two words *gynaika pistēn* are pronounced fluidly and emphatically together, they can be heard and understood as *gynaik'apistēn* meaning the exact opposite: 'unfaithful/disloyal wife'.[26] In terms of performance the text gives latitude to an actor to pronounce Clytemnestra's phrase as he pleases.

She is also cautious enough to claim that 'I know no more of finding pleasure with another man or earning bad repute than I know how to plunge brute bronze into an icy bath to harden it' (*Ag.* 611–12). The spectators surely knew that the claim is patently untrue. The puzzling allusion to 'tempering bronze' might be her attempt to say that she knows nothing of masculine matters. All 'real' men know that steel is tempered, not bronze. In other words, she is a helpless woman who doesn't understand the world of men. There is no reason to fear her. On the other hand, this *double entendre* might suggest that fidelity is as foreign to her as tempering bronze would be.[27] It is unclear whether this is another attempt at downplaying her ability, an intentional 'slip of the tongue', as may befit a woman displaying her femininity, or is she making a mistake any man would spot to eliminate suspicion that she could handle a weapon?[28]

She aimed a similar disingenuous message at Agamemnon when in his presence she addressed the Elders of the Chorus declaring: 'I'll feel no shame to speak before you as a loving wife' (856–57). She follows with the description of her suffering during Agamemnon's absence, casting herself in the Penelope mould when she sought news about her husband from passers-by (*Od.* 14.121–31). She listened to one frightening report after another about her husband. In her description of Agamemnon's possible death, she equates his wounds to the number of holes in a fishing net. Having embarked on the description of Agamemnon wounded in battle, she then pictures him as triple-bodied, killed once for every shape, and describes the triple cloak of earth needed for his burial. As if suddenly aware of revealing too much of what she desires, she describes her own attempts at suicide.

Once Clytemnestra has murdered both Agamemnon and Cassandra, she shamelessly appears before the Chorus boasting of her achievement (see below). She has no intention of presenting herself as innocent, until the

Elders mention the *daimōn* and the evil spirit (*alastōr*) haunting the house (see below). Even then, however, she does not claim innocence but sees herself as the victim of the curse plaguing the House of Atreus, and offers to strike a deal with the *daimōn*: her possessions in exchange for having the *daimōn* go to another house (1567–76).

Cassandra's scene contains similar thematic obfuscation and clarification. As she climbs down from the chariot, she bursts into inarticulate lament, and for seven strophic and antistrophic stanzas she utters incomprehensible prophecies to the Elders of the Chorus. She bewails the slaughter of the children of Thyestes, and their roasted flesh served to their father to devour (1096–97). She sings of the current great evil being schemed in the palace (1100–4). She predicts the crime of 'a wretched woman' against her husband, and of the net with which she is going to trap him with (see above). She moves to her own suffering, envisioning her own impending death. She wishes she had the fate of Procne, whom gods turned into a clear-voiced nightingale in order to save her from the revenge of her husband Tereus (1136–39, 1146–49). While continuing the lament for herself, she recalls Paris's fatal marriage and her childhood home in Troy, soon to be replaced by one in the Netherworld (1156–61). Other than her depictions of the past sufferings of the House of Atreus, all these 'revelations' are lost on the Chorus, who cannot grasp either her claims about the dangers a wife poses to her husband or her claims of her own impending death, and obviously they do nothing to prevent it, as Cassandra has just predicted.

When Cassandra switches from lyric to iambic trimeters, her insights gain more fluency and clarity, and link together the chain of crime and retribution more logically. In two speeches (1178–97, 1215–41) and a brief stichomythia with the Chorus (1202–13), she refers to the previous riddling language in which her insights were sung as a veil, which now will be pierced and her visions clearly expressed. She does this in order to have the Chorus testify to the truth of what she is saying, as she smells out the trail of past crimes. The picture is discordant. She speaks of a chorus of revellers that haunt the house perpetually and sing about crimes in unison, but in ugly and ill-omened strains. Normally, a band of drunken revellers goes from house to house where they drink wine, but this one is not leaving the house, and is not drunk on wine but on human blood. The band consists of 'kindred' Erinyes, whose task is usually avenging crimes committed among kinsmen. They show their abhorrence at Thyestes' adultery with Atreus's wife, which resulted in the horrific vengeance of the banquet in which Atreus served Thyestes' children to their father.

In the following brief stichomythic exchange Cassandra explains to the Chorus that her knowledge was a gift from Apollo, who wished to sleep with her and promised her the gift of prophecy in return. She learned how to prophesize truthfully but then refused to sleep with him, so Apollo removed the persuasiveness of her prophecies. The Chorus surprisingly reply: 'But *we* believe you. *We* believe your prophecies' (1213), not realizing that not believing her in full is just the curse that has been imposed on her by Apollo. Cassandra ventures then into her second and last speech, where she predicts her own death at the hands of Clytemnestra. At least as far as Cassandra is concerned, everything is now completely revealed.

Knowledge and ignorance

The play capitalizes on the duality of ignorance and knowledge, truth and deception as related to both women. However, the reality of their situations is not equally available to each of them; their own perspectives and grasp of their situations is quite different. One knows the truth and what awaits her; the other acts under the mistaken impression that she knows her reality.

Clytemnestra is sure she knows the reality surrounding her. On the face of it, her confidence is justified. She either interprets reality by signs agreed by her and Agamemnon, or meticulously strategizes and plans it. She is confident Troy has fallen, because the beacons have signalled this. She deplores and shames the Chorus of Elders who doubt her as a credulous woman. Her meticulous plan for her husband's murder includes a deceptive message boasting of her fidelity during the ten years of his absence. She lures him into trampling on expensive tapestries as he enters the palace so he will be guilty of present *hybris* as well as exhibiting this flaw in the past. She seems in control of the events surrounding Agamemnon's arrival, is sure of her victory, and is certain that Zeus is on her side, desiring the death of Agamemnon (973–74). However, she is in fact mistaken at almost at every turn save the fall of Troy. She was originally misled by Agamemnon's pretence that Iphigenia was to be married to Achilles when he demanded that she send her daughter to Aulis (*Ag.* 1524).[29] Aegisthus shamelessly misleads her for his own agenda. While giving her the impression that she would stay in power in Argos, he is coveting both the power and the wealth for himself, using her as means to an end. Failing to respect Cassandra's prophetic powers, Clytemnestra misreads Cassandra's lack of response to her as Cassandra's not understanding her language. She will also be deceived by the alleged messengers from Phocis in *Libation Bearers* (and by Electra in Euripides' *Electra*, who summoned her mother to perform the customary ritual for her newborn, while in reality setting a death-trap for the older woman).

Clytemnestra's biggest self-deception in *Agamemnon*, however, is her confidence that her murder of Agamemnon was an independent act of revenge, completely unaware that she is merely a link in the chain of disasters emanating from the curse on the House of Atreus. She brashly announces to the Elders her responsibility for the murder of her husband and his concubine. She declares that she alone killed him: '*I* stand where *I* struck. *I*'ve achieved *my* purpose. What *I* have done, is done, and *I* shall not disown it ... *I* cast its [the net's] fabric and its wealth of cruelty around him. *I* strike two blows ... on his fallen body *I* bestow a third' (1379-86). The gruesome imagery describes her joy at Agamemnon's death, comparing her delight at being covered in the spurt of his blood to an ear of corn glad in Zeus's gift of rain. 'No other speech in Greek tragedy contains so many (ten in all) and such insistent references to the speaker's responsibility for a deed', says Conacher.[30] After the Chorus' outburst criticizing the way she dares to speak about her husband, Clytemnestra is even more defiant in her claim of murdering him: 'This is Agamemnon; this is my husband; this is the corpse created by my hand; and this is how things are' (1404-5), a vaunt reminiscent of heroic narrative and casting Clytemnestra as an even more masculine woman than the Watchman declared her to be (*Ag.* 10-11).[31] She goes on, claiming that she has carried out the act for Justice (*Dikē*), Ruin (*Atē*), and Fury (*Erinys*). She even refers to Agamemnon as a '*lumēntarios*' (1438), a Greek word which is usually used for a rapist, and heaps lurid insults upon the young woman she has just murdered in cold blood (1440-43), whom the audience has just seen as intelligent, vital, and courageous. However, once the Chorus bring up the idea that what has just happened must be due to the intervention of a *daimōn* (evil spirit), Zeus, and the avenging spirit (*alastōr*),[32] Clytemnestra backtracks. First, she relinquishes her sole responsibility for the act, accepting the intervention of the *daimōn* as the source of her deed. Next, she claims to be the manifestation of the *alastōr*, the avenging spirit itself (1497-504), 'undercutting herself as a fully autonomous agent', as Foley has claimed.[33] When the Chorus bring up the idea that under the rule of Zeus 'the doer must suffer' (1563-64), her realization that she might become the *daimōn*'s next victim demonstrates how far she has fallen from her lofty perch. She now seeks a pact with the *daimōn*: she will be content with all that has happened and give up her share of the royal wealth if only the *daimōn* will go elsewhere and persecute some other house (1566-76). Her initial confidence in bearing the sole responsibility for murdering Agamemnon dissipates completely. She even fears she might be the next victim of the evil spirit which for a brief moment she thought she was.

This is not her only misconception. With the appearance of Aegisthus and his bodyguards, she learns that the man whom she considered her protector (1435-37) has no plans to share power with her (1638-39, 1673-74). Furthermore, she learns that he has used her because of her gender as a tool to achieve this power: 'to snare him was the woman's work' (1636), he says when blamed by the Elders for not having the courage to execute the murder himself (1633–35). It is hard to overstate the blow it must have been to Clytemnestra, who boasted of her femininity before the Elders, to realize that the man she trusted has capitalized on her gender to accomplish his own aims and eventually remove her from power. Clytemnestra's misconception of the reality surrounding her is as staggering as is her confidence that she cannot err.

Cassandra, on the other hand, knows perfectly well not only what has been and what is happening as she speaks, but also what will happen in the future, knowledge to which only gods are privy. Metaphorically, Cassandra is the voice of the house. At the play's start, after seeing the beacon announcing the fall of Troy, the Watchman says that he is holding his tongue about what is happening in the house (36–38), but 'this house, this building, if it could but speak, would say it all most clearly' (38–39). It is in Cassandra's scene that the house has found this voice. While Cassandra's first utterances are inarticulate cries that weave themselves into a lament, and are incomprehensible to the Elders, eventually her prophecy is clear and explicit. She visualizes the past of the House of Atreus, its present, its future, but the most crucial knowledge for her is her fate when she enters the palace, the same knowledge Clytemnestra finally gains in *Libation Bearers*: that her son will kill her.

Conclusion

Cassandra is the most tragic (in the modern sense) character in the *Oresteia*. She is a prophetess who prophesied the truth but was never believed. She cannot convince the Chorus of Elders of her own and Agamemnon's impending deaths, which they could have prevented, as she could not convince her parents about the disaster Paris will bring on Troy. Most tragic of all, she knows that she is inconsequential. Cassandra is the paradigm of a war victim. Although innocent of agency in the case of Agamemnon, she adds additional fuel to Clytemnestra's hatred of Agamemnon. Clytemnestra had no real reason to kill her, but also no real reason to keep her alive after murdering Agamemnon. Cassandra's function in the household was terminated with the death of the man she was assigned to serve as a concubine. Clytemnestra cannot be exonerated from the murder of an innocent victim, but eliminating a sexual competitor is at least understandable. While it was societally permissible for a husband to have extra-marital liaisons, bringing a concubine to cohabit with a wife was not acceptable.[34] Cassandra blames Apollo for her upcoming death, and she is right to do so. It is not because she is somehow implicated in Troy's old transgression, as has been suggested, but because of her past deception of Apollo. That Aeschylus wants the audience to think so is evident by the way he scripts her last act on stage a few minutes before her entrance through the gates into the palace to be killed. She casts off her prophetic trappings, the staff, fillets, and her prophetic garb, which she claims Apollo himself strips from her. She tramples on them as Agamemnon has trampled on the expensive blood-red fabrics on his way to the palace. Unlike Agamemnon, however, she knows that Clytemnestra will die as well (1279–84, 1317–19).

The parallels between the tapestry scene and Cassandra's scene emphasize how integral the Cassandra scene is to the arc of the *Oresteia*. It reiterates the theme of cause and effect, with Cassandra mirroring Agamemnon's demonstration of his own culpability. The contexts of the trilogy, which superficially revolve around the events taking place in the ten years since Agamemnon left home, are expanded not only to include the curse on the House of Atreus, but also the complex involvement of the gods in the world of the mortals. By introducing the tragic prophetess into his plot, Aeschylus underscores the plight of being caught between the two worlds: a mortal woman, with the divine gift of prophecy, whom no one believes and who therefore cannot save herself. Cassandra and Clytemnestra are ultimately both caught up in a cycle of violence which neither of them can prevent.

Notes

1 Although Cassandra enters on a chariot in 781, she does not descend from the chariot and start singing and dancing until line 1072.
2 During lines 258–354, she speaks 77 lines; during lines 587–615, 28 lines; during lines 855–974, 82 lines; and during lines 1035–1068, 28 lines.
3 Clytemnestra speaks 215 lines out of her 276 lines on stage, which is 78 per cent of her presence. Cassandra whirls and talks to the Chorus for 180 lines out of the 258 lines of the 'Cassandra scene', that is, 70 per cent of the scene's lines.
4 In lines 1372–1673.
5 For Aeschylus' use of the third actor, see Knox (1979).
6 1035, 1039, 1049, 1053–54, 1059, 1070–71.
7 For Cassandra's meters, see Fraenkel (1950), vol. III on lines 1072–1177. On dancing, see Schein (1982); Ley (2007), 28–32, 70–80, 92, 150: 'The skene also awaits Cassandra, but the power of her vision is expressed fully in the playing space, in dance and song, and it contrasts strikingly with Clytemnestra's refusal to remain in the playing space . . .'. Cf. Easterling and Hall (2002), 3–38 *passim*.

8 For explanation of this claim, see Schein (1982), 11.
9 Roisman 2021: 23–36.
10 Sider (1978), 15–18 has brilliantly shown how Cassandra's stripping off her prophetic garb and possibly stepping on the *agrenon*, a net-like garment (1264–73), performatively parallels Agamemnon stepping on the tapestries.
11 Lebeck (1971), 76.
12 See Collard (2002), on 1082.
13 For this punishment of Cassandra and the complexity of understanding Cassandra's guilt and innocence, see Leahy (1969).
14 Sider (1978), 16.
15 Leahy (1969), 174–75.
16 A similar tactic of demonstrating culpability is found in Euripides *Hecuba* (986–90), when Hecuba lures Polymestor into lying that Polydorus is still alive, when Hecuba knows Polymestor has already killed the boy.
17 Raeburn and Thomas (2011), on 1260–63.
18 As presented in *Agamemnon*, Cassandra is most probably still a virgin, having had sexual relations with neither Apollo nor Agamemnon. Her rape by Oilean Ajax is not mentioned at all. Her refusal to honour the promise that she would have sex with Apollo is the reason the god rendered her true prophecies unbelievable. Cf. Debnar (2010), 132–33, 137–38.
19 For example, *pacheiē cheir* is used for Odysseus and Penelope solely (*Od.* 6.18, 19.448, 20.299, 21.6, 22.326). For the use of *kerd-* for Odysseus' family and his loyal slaves, see Roisman (1994).
20 For the various possibilities of sequencing the lines surrounding line 1228, see Raeburn and Thomas (2011), on lines 1228–30. For dog imagery, see Raeburn and Thomas (2011), lxvi–lxviii; female dogs were thought to be 'pre-eminently shameless'. For further discussion of dog imagery and attributes, see Franco (2014), 105, 125–26. For this self-comparison of Clytemnestra to a dog, see discussion in Roisman 2021: 23–36.
21 For the study of olfactory images in the *Oresteia*, see Lather (2018).
22 See Roisman (1986).
23 The epithet appears only six times in the *Iliad*, referring to four heroes: Patroclus (17.557, 18.235, 460), Stichius (15.331), Lycophron (*I*15.437), and Podes (17.589). For discussion, see Roisman (1984), *passim*.
24 For discussion, see Roisman (1984), 105–6.
25 In Sophocles, *Electra* 234, the Chorus as a group refer to themselves metaphorically as a 'loyal mother', implying that they, not Clytemnestra, had a mother's love and concern for her.
26 Ferguson (1972), 83 mentions this possibility but without any further elaboration. For a full discussion and grammatical ramifications of the use of *apistēn*, which is a compound adjective in an unusual female form in Greek, and of other *double entendre*s mentioned here, see Roisman (2018). For a similar intentional or unintentional manipulation of sound-play, see De Jong (2001), on *Od.* 18.306–43, where she discusses *erga gelasta* 'the laughable deeds' that can be understood also as *erg' agelasta* 'not laughable/grave deeds'.

27 Thomson (1966), lines 611–12 suggests that 'bronze' *(chalkos)* came over time to mean a metal in general.
28 For a brief summary of the various scholarly views on the phrase, see Hogan (1984) *Ag.* 612.
29 The story of the deceitful summoning of Iphigenia is as old as the *Cypria*, frg. 8 West. It is likely it has been also dramatized in Aeschylus' lost *Iphigenia*. The story has survived in Euripides' *Iphigenia at Aulis*.
30 Conacher (1987), 49.
31 For taunting by vaunting, see Parks (1990), *passim*; Keith (1924); Kyriakou (2001).
32 1468–69, 1481–88; 1505–20.
33 Foley (2001), 203–4, 211–34.
34 Foley (2001), 89–90.

5

Ritual in *Agamemnon*[1]

Richard Seaford

It is an astonishing thing to see and be moved by a drama written two and a half thousand years ago. And the more you know about the culture that produced it, the more astonishing it is. There is much to know about the culture that produced Aeschylus' *Agamemnon*. We cannot entirely put ourselves into the heads of the original audience, but we can go some way towards it. To be moved by and understand this play one should go as far as one can in that direction, and I am going to talk this evening about an aspect of Athenian culture that is important for understanding their tragedy, namely ritual.

I shall start by saying something general about ritual. Ritual is important to our lives. It was even more important for the Greeks. Ritual does not have to be religious. Shaking hands is a ritual, and we all perform rituals every day of our lives. So what is ritual? It is a stereotypical communicative action often designed to create cohesion between people, solidarity within the group. Another way of thinking about ritual is that it is an image of perfection, of perfect action that we carry with us through the chaos and vicissitudes of everyday life. Sometimes the feeling of perfection is so intense, so powerful, particularly if it is in a large group, that – certainly among the Greeks – there is a sense of deity being present as a result of the performance of ritual.

Ritual is a means of creating social cohesion which tends to be more important in pre-modern societies, such as ancient Greek society, than in our own society. Although we have numerous rituals, non-religious and religious, clearly ritual does not have the central role in the creation of social cohesion for us that it does in many pre-modern societies. We have other ways of doing that: our legal system, politics, money, various modern institutions and practices, some of which the ancient Greeks also had, although they had not had them for very long, and they were a more precarious means of creating society than they are for us. So, for the Greeks, as for many pre-modern societies, ritual is somehow at the centre of things, because it is the way that they can survive as a society, creating images of themselves for themselves and others as a group working perfectly together.

Ritual has a central role in Greek society, and it also has a central role in Greek literature and Greek art, sometimes even in Greek philosophy. An example is animal sacrifice. We have animals killed for us in abattoirs and eat them very often without thinking of the way in which they were killed, but for the Greeks the killing of the animal to be eaten is a public, open, dramatic act, which is at the centre of a number of other rituals. The animal in the sacrifice is given to the deity, but it also provides a feast for humans. So in an animal sacrifice, the animal – generally a cow or sheep or pig – is led in a procession to the altar, and all the participants in the procession, the human participants and the animal, wear crowns. There is music if it is a grand sacrifice, and it all has to go in a very peaceful and orderly way: when the animal arrives at the altar, the human participants form a ring around altar and animal, the music continues, water is sprinkled over the animal and over the participants (this will come up later when we discuss *Agamemnon*), somehow uniting them as all members of the ritual group. One text tells us that the animal had to consent to being sacrificed, otherwise people would feel guilty. So, you sprinkle the water over the head of the animal and it shakes the water off, and its nodding indicates that it is quite happy to be sacrificed, or so we are told some Greeks believed.

And then the animal has to be killed. This is a highly dramatic moment: the blood spurts out of the animal, there is a high-pitched screaming from the women, the blood is carefully collected in bowls. The animal is cut up and eaten in a very ordered, traditional, stereotypical way; some of it is given to the god, but most of it is eaten by the human participants. The essence of this is the solidarity and articulation of the human group, but it is also a movement through the intensely dramatic, even horrifying moment of killing the animal, to an eventual shared feast of meat and wine, when everybody relaxes. So, the ritual is not just an image of perfection, but it is often a very special kind of image of perfection that incorporates and overcomes pain and suffering to arrive at the joy of a collective feast at which the gods may in some sense be present.

My intention is to describe the ways in which Aeschylus' *Agamemnon* evokes certain kinds of ritual, not only the animal sacrifice but also *rites of passage*. Rites of passage are a special kind of ritual in which, comparably to the animal sacrifice, an individual or a group moves through suffering to a state of happiness, and often to incorporation into a group, so that their identity is changed. For example, in the wedding ritual the bride moves from being a girl into being a wife, which is (unlike a modern wedding) a process of movement through suffering to happiness – at least as imagined by the community. For the Greek girl the wedding is, initially at least, an undesirable transition: she does not want to leave the only home she has ever known, to enter into the control of a male who is much older than she is, whom she has probably never met, to a household where she will be isolated and exploited. She resists the transition, she weeps, but in the end – for society to continue – she has to accept her new status. The function of the ritual is to allow her to express her resistance and suffering, but also to incorporate her into her new household.

In other rites of passage there is a similar movement. There is a change of status that also involves a transition from suffering and resistance to incorporation into the new status or group. The two other rites of passage that I will use to access (so far as possible) the original emotional effect of *Agamemnon* are death ritual and mystic initiation.

First, death ritual. Death is obviously an event involving suffering and resistance, and at the same time is surrounded by a ritual which is designed to incorporate that person into the next world. Once again, there is even here an image of perfection. On the brute facts of suffering and death there is imposed a human construction, something cultural as opposed to natural, something that enables the Greeks and many other cultures to handle the fact of death. That is why death ritual is so fundamentally important, and leaving it unperformed is one of the worst things you can do (think of *Antigone* and the last book of the *Iliad*): it would signify the victory of chaos, death and suffering over our control of things, over our culture, over our imposition of form on chaos.

My other rite of passage is mystic initiation. The point of being initiated into the mysteries, which – unlike the funeral or the wedding – we moderns are not familiar with, is to equip yourself with a happy fate in the next world. You do that by going through a kind of rehearsal of death in which you are terrified: you move through suffering and resistance to eventually a happy state of joining the group with whom you will spend all eternity. So the ritual of mystic initiation involves a threefold transition from ignorance to knowledge, from being outside the group to being inside the group, and from suffering to joy.

How does knowledge of the importance of these four rituals to Greek culture elucidate *Agamemnon*? Remember that if you are in the original Greek audience, you are not just very familiar with these rituals, but they mean much to you, they carry a great emotional charge. There is almost nothing in our relatively very fragmented culture that is comparable. Ritual is much less important to us, and we do not have rituals shared by everyone. So we have nothing equivalent to the emotional intensity of those rituals that gave Aeschylus the tremendous advantage of being able to create emotional intensity simply by their evocation. It would be like in the last century or before that having the Book of Common Prayer as a shared cultural text meaning a great deal to most people and then evoking it in a drama. But even that is not really anything like the advantage the Greek tragedians had in having a shared, rich popular culture of spectacular rituals.

Let us start with passages that evoke wedding ritual. In the first choral song (the *parodos*) there is a description of Iphigeneia being sacrificed by her father Agamemnon. Everybody would know that she had been summoned to Aulis, where the Greek fleet was assembled to go to Troy, on the pretext that she was to be married. She was of marriageable age, and Euripides' *Iphigeneia at Aulis* was all about this particular deceit: she was summoned for her wedding, but really to be sacrificed to allow the Greek fleet to sail to Troy, and her father is the one who sacrifices her.

Greek tragedy is full of strange things that are for the first time since antiquity being understood. In the description of her sacrifice in *Agamemnon*, Iphigeneia does something strange. She lets her saffron cloth flow to the ground (there are many different ways of translating this). She then looks around at the company of men with a piteous expression, and is taken up and sacrificed. There was a stage in the Greek wedding where the girl was symbolically sacrificed. That is a fact that you must take into account in understanding this scene: the wedding was kind of death for the Greek girl. She was not really sacrificed, of course, but only symbolically. In the myth, in the tragedy, that fictional suffering becomes a reality. There is also a point in the wedding called the unveiling ceremony, or *anakalupteria*, which probably took place just before the bride left for the bridegroom's house in procession on a chariot. It consisted of the bride, who all through the meal had been veiled (and you can imagine everybody wondering what she looked like – was she beautiful, was she not?), and at the end of the meal the poor girl, probably only fourteen or fifteen years old, was unveiled and everybody sees her. You can imagine the fear of this moment for the bride, in which the company of men are all staring at her. It is this moment that is evoked by this passage of the first song, where she looks pityingly around her for a very different reason, that she is going to be killed. But it evokes the ritual, in which she is also looking pityingly round at the staring male company because she is about to go on a terrifying journey to her husband's house. This was ritual familiar to everybody, who would accordingly be moved by its evocation in the tragedy.

It is evoked at two further moments into the play, one of them in the later choral song about Helen, where she sailed away from the gauzy curtains (as David Stuttard's translation of the Greek *prokalummata* has it). *Prokalummata* could easily refer to the bridal veil (compare, for instance, Euripides' *Phoenican Women* 1485), and so our passage evokes bridal unveiling.

The bridal journey in a vehicle to her new home, immediately after the ritual of her unveiling, seems to have been sometimes imagined as a *sea-*

journey. The sea-journey of Helen to Troy with Paris is described in terms of a wedding in which, we soon hear, the brides weep. The brides here are the Trojan women who, because of the destruction that Helen will bring to Troy, will lose their husbands. This is all part of an elaborate wedding image, in which the weeping brides are the Trojan wives who are going to lose their husbands. Once again what has happened is that a ritual fact, the weeping of the bride, which in a real wedding is overcome when the bride is incorporated into a new home, becomes a fact that with the destruction of Troy cannot be reversed. Characteristic of tragedy is that the negative elements in the ritual, the suffering that the ritual is there to contain, triumphs. Nowadays people refer to death in a car accident as a 'tragedy'. But the Greeks would never call such accidents tragedies. Mere suffering – however horrible – was not material for tragedy. An example of truly tragic suffering is when the means for controlling and dealing with suffering, namely ritual, is subverted, so that the ritual is crushed by the suffering that it is designed to contain.

Agamemnon returns to his house with Cassandra, who refers somewhat cryptically to the ritual of unveiling of the bride: she stands outside the house, about to go into what she knows is her death, and she says, 'The oracle is no longer looking out of the veils like a bride'. Cassandra becomes like a bride who is going to go into a house not for incorporation and childbearing, but to be slaughtered. In the original production Agamemnon and Cassandra would have arrived on a chariot, perhaps with an accompaniment of soldiers, a procession, and would have taken up their position outside the house in this chariot, in front of which a woman stands (Clytemnestra). This scene would have been very familiar to the audience. We have many fifth-century Athenian vase paintings which depict precisely the moment of the ordinary wedding in which the bride and groom have travelled together and are now in a cart or chariot at the house of the groom, outside which a woman (the groom's mother) may be standing. In the Athenian wedding there was a configuration of figures, chariot and house identical to what was in *Agamemnon*.

Moreover, Agamemnon and Cassandra do, like bride and groom, have a sexual relationship. That is appropriate, but this quasi-wedding is going to end in disaster. In the normal wedding there occurred an animal sacrifice. Clytemnestra says to Cassandra, 'Come into the house, because the animals are standing already at the hearth to be sacrificed' and 'Come and participate in the lustral water'. Cassandra is here invited to be incorporated into the household, to join the solidarity of the group created by animal sacrifice. What Clytemnestra means is 'Come and participate in the animal sacrifice, be one of those people standing about the altar, receive the lustral water which is sprinkled on everybody'. But, as I pointed out earlier, the lustral water was also sprinkled on the victim. The victim, too, participates in the lustral water.

So Cassandra is, in this phrase, to be the victim. That is the deeper meaning of the phrase which the audience would understand. Once again, the negative element in the ritual, the suffering that it is designed to control, has broken out of it and is controlling the ritual. The ritual becomes, so far from being what ritual essentially is (the means of creating cohesion and good feeling), the means of inflicting unlimited and horrible conflict and suffering.

The second rite of passage that I promised to find in *Agamemnon* is death ritual. Here I refer simply to the way in which Clytemnestra kills Agamemnon. She kills him in his bath, and she wraps around him a cloth which traps him like a net. This is a rather surprising way, you may think, for somebody to be killed in Greek tragedy. It is certainly undignified; it is convenient perhaps – he is in the bath, he doesn't have his sword with him. But there is more to it than that. It is not a version which occurs in Homer or other earlier versions of the Greek myth. What is crucial here is that, when a man dies, his wife will wash him in a bath and then she will wrap him in a shroud, a cloth which she herself has probably woven. There is no doubt that this is what is being alluded to here. Once again, the audience would have understood the evocation of death ritual, even though modern scholars have not. Clytemnestra is handling Agamemnon as a wife handles the dead body of a husband, giving him his bath, wrapping him in a cloth, *but while he is still alive*, not as a means of expressing conjugal love for a dead husband in that intimate act but as a means of killing him, a means of expressing the most extreme hostility. Here again the ritual is transformed into its opposite – from being an image of perfection, a means of expressing extreme intimacy and love, into an image of disruption and horror, a means of expressing the most extreme hostility. The ritual is the means through which she kills him.

There is another passage of the play that is relevant here. When Agamemnon arrives and is just about to go into the house, Clytemnestra praises him in a series of arresting images which include, for example, 'the only pillar of the house'. I think that all the images that she uses were used in the funerary lament. This cannot be proved, but many of them are still used in Greek laments in rural areas of Greece today, and we know that there is much continuity between the ancient Greek lament and the modern Greek lament. So, when she praises him with all these images, perhaps the audience would know and think of the praise of the dead man at the funeral, even though Agamemnon is still alive. There is one very telling word that she uses in describing her praise: *apenthetos* ('without grief', translated by Stuttard as 'my grief is done') . Why would she say that, unless once again it is, with subtle duplicity, a means of evoking the grief of the funeral? That fits into the argument that Agamemnon is being treated as though he is already dead. The loving ritual turns into its opposite.

The third rite of passage that I described earlier, which was familiar to the audience – or at least to many of them – is the ritual of mystic initiation. In the very first line of the play, the Watchman says, 'I pray to the gods for release from sufferings'. A little later he sees a light in the darkness (a beacon-fire from a nearby mountain), and to him that means release from sufferings. It means that Troy has fallen, that Agamemnon is about to return and that his labours as a watchman are almost over. The phrase 'release from sufferings' will recur throughout the trilogy of which *Agamemnon* is the first play. Now, release from suffering is what the Mysteries ensure for you – not only within the ritual, in which you suffer a rehearsal for death that is a transition to happiness and knowledge, but also in the next world, where you will joyfully pass eternity initiated into your group. Release from suffering is at the heart of mystic initiation. In the Eleusinian Mysteries, the main mystery-cult of Athens, this release from suffering, this transition in the ritual from suffering to joy and from ignorance to understanding, was created by the introduction of a great light into the darkness. The light embodying release from suffering was at the heart of the extraordinarily intense experience of the Athenian initiates into the Eleusinian Mysteries, and it is also right there in the prologue. If you understand this, you feel the prologue quite differently.

I said earlier that the rites of passage in tragedy are characteristically reversed (or subverted) so that the negative element takes over, dominates and destroys the ritual. We have seen this happening with sacrifice, wedding and funeral. It is also the case with the mystical allusions: almost every release from suffering that you find in *Agamemnon* and the later plays of the trilogy – sometimes associated with light in the darkness – proves illusory and temporary. The point of the mysteries is that they give you eternal happiness. But the return of Agamemnon and the destruction of Troy, so far from being a permanent release from suffering which the mystic imagery would suggest, brings another disaster: the murder of Agamemnon and Cassandra. In the next play, *Libation Bearers*, the revenge taken by Orestes for the death of his father by killing his mother and her lover Aegisthus is presented as a mystic transition to happiness, but that too brings on more suffering, the suffering of Orestes pursued by the Furies. It is only at the very end of the third play, *Eumenides*, that, as the language makes clear, we have a true release from suffering ensured by the acquittal of Orestes in the first ever law-court in human history, and the reconciliation of the Furies, who will be installed in Athens and receive cult there. So there is no further possibility of reciprocal violence. This is the true release from suffering shared by the whole city of Athens as the trilogy ends. That permanent release from suffering, which seems to redeem all the suffering which has gone before, is celebrated once again by light, this time not the imagery of light, nor the light from a mountain as at the beginning of the trilogy, but torchlight actually on the stage as the Furies are conducted in a torch-lit procession to their new home in a cave under the Acropolis.

Finally, there are two other ways in which Greek tragedy was associated with ritual (besides evoking it). It was performed in a ritual context, in a festival of the god Dionysus. For instance, animal sacrifice took place during this festival both in and around the theatre. Secondly, tragedy emerged, I believe, from a complex of performance in which death ritual and particularly mystic ritual were prominent. It still shows, in for instance in *Agamemnon*, produced fifty years after the emergence the tragic genre from ritual, traces of its origin.

Note

1   This is the revised text of a lecture delivered by Richard Seaford prior to a performance of *Agamemnon* directed by David Stuttard for Actors of Dionysus.

6

Let the Good Prevail

Sophie Mills

In the *parodos* of *Agamemnon*, the chorus sings the memorable refrain, 'Chant the laments for sorrow, may all turn out well' (*ailinon, ailinon eipe, to d'eu nikato*, 121, 138, 159). Variations on this refrain echo throughout *Agamemnon* in the mouths not only of the chorus, but of individual characters. Similar sentiments appear in *Choephori*, while the end of *Eumenides* is notably full of compound adjectives containing the Greek prefix '*eu*' (good), indicating that the chorus's plea in *Agamemnon* will eventually be answered. But 'eventually' is the operative word: the good will prevail, but not in the lifetime of that chorus, because their prayer is to Zeus, and Zeus' time is not human time, and the suffering he imposes (never arbitrarily, however it may seem) on humans is intimately connected with the passage of time. Here, I will explore the implications of the chorus's refrain, consider its echoes through *Agamemnon*, along with a very brief glance at those echoes in the other plays in the trilogy, and consider how the plea of the chorus and its variants illuminate and exemplify the role of Zeus in the trilogy, as well as certain other themes of the whole *Oresteia*.

Wishes for the future in *Agamemnon* have certain themes or characteristics in common. To sing, 'Chant the laments for sorrow, may all turn out well' implies that the speaker is at a kind of middle point between evil and good, fearing the worst, but hoping for the better. Not only is this uncertainty repeated over and over in *Agamemnon*, but also, every such wish will remain unfulfilled, because they are emblematic of one of the central narrative arcs of *Agamemnon* and the whole trilogy, as character after character hopes for a good outcome to their particular part of the story but is disappointed. Such prayers indicate that evil is clearly in the ascendant when they are expressed, but that the speaker remains hopeful that some power exists in the universe, both strong enough to move circumstances from trouble to happiness and willing to be prevailed on to do so. This power is Zeus (cf. *Ag.* 160ff.). Zeus does, in fact, listen, and the chorus's wishes in the *parodos* of the first play will be brought to fulfilment in the third play, but on a divine, not a human timescale. Eventually, the good prevails: the house of Orestes will be restored, and the problem of Clytemnestra's valid but problematic claims to her own justice will come to some sort of resolution, but the times and the places that such a resolution will occur are not those imagined or desired by the characters when they wish for better things. The chorus of *Agamemnon* is not the chorus of *Eumenides*; the setting of *Agamemnon* and *Choephori* is not that of *Eumenides*; and time is not controlled by ephemeral, vulnerable human beings, but by Zeus, who is eternal. The limitations of human time and space make it impossible that anyone in *Agamemnon*, whether the old men of the chorus, Agamemnon, Clytemnestra, Aegisthus, or the Greeks and Trojans killed in the Trojan War, will live to see a happy ending for the royal House of Argos. Only Orestes comes to adulthood at the right time both to perpetrate a deed which demands a long exile and suffering and then to return to enjoy his native land and throne – in a sense, he is the eventual single lucky recipient of all the previous prayers from multiple quarters that all may turn out well.

Human time is difficult and limited: Zeus' time is neither. For human beings, time is also paradoxical. It both heals suffering in its course, and yet for those living through suffering, the passage of time can seem endlessly elongated, so that sufferers feel that they will never see the good prevail in their lifetimes. Time is thus aligned with Zeus, whose immortality enables the god to put into place another of the central, repeated themes of the trilogy, that through suffering comes learning (*Ag.* 177–78) and that the doer shall suffer (1563–64).[1] These principles are true both for individuals but also for society more broadly – both that within the trilogy and its spectators, as they are given the opportunity to watch, evaluate, and reflect on the sufferings of Agamemnon, his house and the Greek army and their multiple, complex, even conflicting causes.[2] Time and suffering are inextricably linked because momentary suffering is not real suffering and is unlikely to bring true learning. Instead, if suffering is to be endured so as to bring learning, the process must take time, so that what the human characters wish to happen quickly will not do so.[3] These facts of time and space also confirm a truth about Zeus: from a human perspective, he may often seem enigmatic and potentially cruel, but this is not the real truth, since he imposes suffering not through sadism, but to bring about a beneficial learning over time.[4] The end of *Eumenides* is notably optimistic and the dramatic structure of the trilogy that moves gradually from the gloom of Argos to the eventual light of Athens gives audiences a kind of 'Zeus' eye view', because in a few hours it creates the illusion of a very long passage of time[5] over many years, enabling the audience to see and begin to understand Aeschylus' vision of the working of Zeus' justice. That the change from woe to good will happen at Athens in the shadow of the Acropolis would have been uniquely meaningful to the original audience of 458 BCE.

Throughout *Agamemnon*, characters express the desire for the situation in Argos to be other than it is, inhabiting a midpoint between fear for what is and hope for what could be, sometimes expressing their thoughts through a third person imperative ('Let it be the case!'), sometimes through a wish for the future expressed in the optative ('If only!'). Even long before the chorus expresses its famous wish 'May all turn out well', repeated three times for emphasis (121, 138, 159), the Watchman laments that the previous greatness of the house is gone (19) and prays for a happy (*eutychēs*) ending to his suffering (*Ag.* 20; cf. 1). His whole speech, like that of the prayer of the chorus is full of foreboding, an expression that Agamemnon's house is badly amiss and all he can do from his limited human efficacy is to express a plea to whoever is listening that a change for the better may be possible. His prayer is answered by the sight of the beacon blazing (22–24), and at first he is excited that this new development will bring beneficial change to the household, and makes a wish for the return of his master to set his house to rights (34–35). But at 36, he returns to the present with foreboding as before: present circumstances weigh too heavily on him and he is unable to believe that the sign of fire truly signifies respite from suffering.

In their *parodos*,[6] the longest uninterrupted sequence of choral song in all of Greek tragedy, the chorus express foreboding similar to that of the Watchman and for similar reasons (97–103), but as is typical of the chorus in Greek tragedy generally, they also sometimes transcend their specific status in the here and now. Though they are characterized as old men of Argos, loyal to Agamemnon and chafing under the rule of Clytemnestra, they also have the power to frame the story of the Trojan War in a grander historical and theological context that briefly exalts them by granting them knowledge beyond their individual human status through the power to connect with, and explore, the workings of Zeus and his universe.[7] Thus they take us back ten years to the beginning of Agamemnon's expedition to Troy, a long time in which many things have happened on the human plane, although ten years is nothing in Zeus' sight.[8] Just as the Watchman and everyone in *Agamemnon* must wait for Zeus' justice to be done, wishing for it to be done sooner than it will be (and many will never see it in their lifetimes) so the *parodos* also explores the necessity of waiting, through various signs and symbols whose deliberate obscurity and complexity for readers and viewers reflect something of the complexity and difficulty of understanding the connection between individual human existence and divine immanence. The birds of prey who are in agony for their stolen children will eventually be granted a revenge from one of the gods (55–56, the uncertainty is telling) but it will only be 'in time', not immediately (58), nor can this revenge bring the chicks back. The Greeks will punish Troy, but it will take many years and lives and will not bring any end to the suffering of Agamemnon and his family.

The *Oresteia* is famous for the string of images that are repeated with variation throughout the trilogy.[9] One such image is that of the liquid poured on the ground – sometimes libations to the gods, sometimes human blood – seen first at *Ag.* 69–70.[10] The image of the libation itself can express visually the ambivalent midpoint of fear and hope that the chorus's refrain encapsulates. A libation is poured on the ground and can never be retrieved: those who pour it do so out of need for divine help and hope that they will receive it, but it must remain uncertain, at least in the moment, how effective their offering will be. Only later may its efficacy be proved. In an analogous way, the chorus hope that the good will prevail, and frequently express the hope but in the absence of clear proof, can never be completely sure. Human vulnerability and impotence are highlighted in the early part of the trilogy, as the characters can only express wishes for what they would like to happen, because they are unable to act effectively to make it happen, even though Zeus remains in the background, and, after a time of necessary suffering, will eventually enable the good to prevail. Human impotence, however, must paradoxically co-exist with trust in the power of words to influence events by bringing human plights to Zeus' ears.[11] Thus, though the chorus are old and feeble (72–82), they also express the importance of their remaining power to sing (104ff.) in a passage which especially exemplifies their ability to inhabit a role that transcends their status as old Argives, by invoking past time, things seen and unseen (cf. *Ag.* 167–72, 248), prophecies, signs and omens, in an attempt to imagine and connect with the bigger processes of Zeus' universe. Thus, at 108ff. they recall the omen, as significant as its meaning is unclear,[12] of the two eagles devouring the hare, during which comes the first instance of the refrain on which this essay meditates (121), and the explanation of it offered by Calchas the seer, a primary conduit between gods and humans, who has a special ability to divine the future and the gods' plans. His words as recounted by the chorus (126–137) also combine fear and hope: in time, Agamemnon and Menelaus will prevail, but Artemis is angry at the eagles for their violence to her own dear creature – clarity is hard to find here, as many commentators have noted,[13] but this deep ambiguity is a deliberate expression of Zeus' complex relationship with humanity at any given moment. Again at 138 the cry comes, 'Chant the laments for sorrow, may all turn out well', which reflects clearly Calchas' own assessment of the portent, as simultaneously auspicious and the opposite (145) 'with visions promising success grim with disaster', and he too asks for divine help, here from Apollo to prevent Artemis blocking the voyage from Aulis (150). The final repetition of the refrain joins Calchas' words with those of the chorus (158–59)[14] and this harmony creates a marvellous effect of unity in the mingled despair and hope that is a hallmark of so much of the trilogy.

Only Zeus has the power to negotiate between the conflicting claims which bring about suffering, learning, and the eventual victory of what is good. Thus, having recalled events on the human plane, the chorus can finally turn to Zeus and meditate on his power to transcend whatever is done on the human plane (160). No wonder, then, that they are unable to be sure even how Zeus should be addressed, expressing their sense of Zeus' uniqueness and their own inability to comprehend the god's power. Even Zeus, though, was subject to the power of time and had to wait for his time to rule until the third generation (167–72), eventually surpassing divinities whose rule was temporary and less satisfactory.[15] Part of Zeus' greatness, according to the chorus, is that he has set human beings on the path to wisdom by decreeing (176–81) the fixed law that by suffering we will learn.[16] Here the chorus directly express the inextricable connection between suffering, time and learning. The ambiguous promise of this process is encapsulated in the chorus's description of it as 'a kindness in the cruelty of gods', and with this echoing in our ears they resume the human narrative immediately afterwards at 184.

Agamemnon must face a hideous choice at Aulis: as the son of Atreus, he is subject to the gods working out his father's crime through his own suffering,[17] and though he himself does not understand this, others in the tragedy do, as do spectators who are given a broader view of causation, more akin to that of Zeus. Will Agamemnon abandon his role as leader of the army by refusing the divine command to sacrifice his daughter, or will he lay aside paternal love in order to lead his army of allies to Troy to punish the Trojans for their crime against hospitality? As he says (211), 'Each way lies horror', and the chorus quote his desperate wish (217), 'May all be well (*eu*)', that recalls their own earlier plea (121, 138, 159). This particular echo of the chorus juxtaposes particularly starkly the contrast between fearful knowledge of dire circumstances and a desperate hope that the situation will be made better by some external force. The next lines (218–47) narrate what happens when he dons the 'leash of certainty' (218) and becomes his daughter's killer. The narrative is so horrific that even the chorus only describe the moments leading up to the murder and not the actual deed itself (248), and perhaps because of its horror, they have to turn immediately to Calchas, Zeus' mouthpiece, endorsing the truth of his prophetic power: since this had included some reassurance of success in time (126, 145), it is then easier for them to affirm the reality of Justice (250) and the hopefully reassuring connection of suffering and learning (250–51). At 255 they echo once more their earlier refrain through a wish for a better future – 'May all be well (*eu*)'. But in the bigger context of cause and effect in the theology of this play, this better future is not going to arrive soon, given what they have just described.

Moreover, their wish is soon echoed by Clytemnestra, on stage for the first time: 'May daybreak bring good news born from the blackest night' (264–65), ostensibly words of good omen,[18] but because of previous hints that her feelings towards Agamemnon are hostile and that the chorus do not trust her, a more sinister tone may underlie her wish. As she describes in detail the path that the victory beacon took from Troy all the way to Argos, more ambiguity between hope and fear is generated. The approach of the fire is a sign that Troy has finally been justly punished, and that Zeus cares for justice and is in control of the world, as the following choral ode emphasizes,[19] but it also signifies that Agamemnon will soon come home and may not have an easy reintegration: at 310, the fire is described as swooping on the House of the Atreidae as the offspring of the Trojan fire – not a reassuring idea.[20] Nor is it reassuring, at least to those of the audience who recall Priam's bloody death at Zeus' altar and the rape of Cassandra by Ajax, to have Clytemnestra (338–48) invoke the possibility that the Greeks may treat their defeated opponents unjustly and suffer for it. There is a distinct menace in her further warning that even if the Greeks resist the temptation to unjust plunder so as to get home safely, some unseen trouble might yet lie in wait for them at home (347). For Clytemnestra, it would not be a disaster if Agamemnon never returned, so her wishes for the future are especially ironic, almost reversing the standard formula of everyone else's prayer: whereas the chorus and others state 'Chant the laments for sorrow, may all turn out well', Clytemnestra's desires are better represented by 'Chant the good, may all turn out sorrowfully', so while her wish at 349 – 'May all turn out well. May it be seen most clearly' – outwardly resembles the standard wish that runs throughout *Agamemnon*, the rest of the speech, along with the broader context of the play, colours it with irony and uncertainty. The good for Clytemnestra may be very different from the good for others.

At 498–500, the chorus, seeing the Herald approach, acknowledge again their position between hope and fear, speculating on the news he will bring: 'He will either spit out his report that we might celebrate . . . I cannot face the other, the alternative. No. No. No, let his news be good (*eu*) that we might add it to the good news (*eu*) we already have.' Although the Herald is at first overjoyed to have returned to his homeland and that Troy has been justly conquered, he quickly begins to fall into more familiar patterns. At 551, he acknowledges that 'it has turned out well (*eu*)', but immediately qualifies this: in this long period of time some things have gone well, but others are troublesome (*epimompha*; cf. *katamompha*, 145). 'Only the gods live all their lives completely free from sorrow.' And while his following speech dwells on the miseries of campaigning which now are thankfully over (567–68), the way he mentions the dead, who are free of misery for quite different reasons, and his insistence on referring to pain, even in victory (574), give his joy a muted tone. When the chorus ask him about Menelaus' return, even his veneer of joy and release after a hard campaign cracks (620–21). The Herald's account of Menelaus' disappearance recalls Clytemnestra's earlier warning that any deviation from proper conduct will bring disaster on the returning Greeks[21] – at 635 (cf. 649), the chorus even ascribes the disappearance to divine wrath – and the Herald himself comes to inhabit the midpoint between fear and joy (636–49) that is so typical of this play and that the chorus has voiced so memorably in the *parodos*, as news of victory proves ultimately impossible to disentangle from other news of the storm that destroyed the Argive fleet which left the sea 'blossoming with shipwrecks and the corpses of the dead' (648–60). After all this, his wish at 674, 'May all turn out for best' seems highly ironic: it is hard to imagine much good arising any time soon from what has happened already.

At 854, Agamemnon himself expresses another variant of the wishes for a happy future that recur throughout this play in contexts that undermine them in some way: 'And now that victory is ours, may it stay so forever.' Given the chequered history of Agamemnon's so-called victory – filicide, a miserable and bloody ten-year campaign that caused multiple deaths, followed by a difficult, storm-tossed homecoming – such a victory will not be as easy as his words would imply. His perspective as a human is necessarily limited: much time is still to pass, and Zeus is not yet finished with the suffering that brings learning. In this scene, Agamemnon's words are often sombre and he recognizes his own human vulnerability in attempting to reject Clytemnestra's excesses.[22] One might perhaps imagine that his suffering in the Trojan War has indeed brought him some learning, but not enough learning to understand the larger workings of Zeus' justice which requires that his past misdeeds, and those of his father, must exact a fatal price from him, since his problematic past has yet to be accounted for. The doer must suffer – a 'thrice-old word' says so (*Cho.* 313–14).[23]

In response to this scene, at 975ff., the chorus expresses a mixture of unease and hope that this unease is unfounded. In particular, at 998–1000, they express anxiety for the future but pray that their 'forebodings never come to pass, but fall like barren seed, unblossoming', following their wish with another statement, which, though its text is corrupt and the thought highly convoluted, clearly expresses hope and trust in Zeus' abundance at 1013–16. But though their belief in the saving power of Zeus will be vindicated at another place and time, again that time and place are not yet, and in their subsequent interactions with Cassandra it is notable that they understand her references to the past horrors in the House of Atreus (1105–6, 1242–44) but either genuinely do not understand what she is saying of the next instalment of suffering for the house

(1112–13, 1119–20, 1130–31, 1152, 1245, 1251, 1253, 1255) or are resistant to it.[24] Indeed, at 1249, they actively reject it: 'I say, let it not be so!'[25] Like Calchas, Cassandra has a closer connection to divinity than the ordinary human characters do. Also like Calchas, she points the way to some future hope for the house, promising (1280–90) the advent of an avenger who himself must go through the process of doing wrong and suffering for it, but who will eventually survive his troubles, according to what the gods have promised.

The chaotic aftermath of the murder of Agamemnon and Cassandra continues to resound with themes from the *parodos*. Though they are appalled by what Clytemnestra has done and by how she justifies it, at 1485–88, they can only ascribe what has happened to Zeus: 'This comes from Zeus, the architect of everything, the source of all that is. For nothing mortal reaches its fulfilment without Zeus and nothing here has not been sent by God.' This divine ordinance, it is implied, must be for the good, however completely mysterious Zeus' will is at this point, and they put their trust in a coming Justice (1535–36). At 1562–64 they reaffirm once more the law that the doer will suffer as long as Zeus is on his throne. Who is the doer? Who the sufferer? At this point, the dead and the living are simultaneously doers and sufferers, although Clytemnestra and Aegisthus both claim that what they have done is entirely just. Clytemnestra wrongly suggests that her actions have put an end to the internecine slaughter in the royal house (1574–76); Aegisthus, that the good (1578)[26] has now indeed prevailed because Agamemnon has finally been made to pay for his father's crimes against Thyestes (1577–82) and justice has been done (1604, 1607, 1611). From the bigger context of the theodicy of the play, as represented by the chorus in the *parodos*, it is clear that they are deluded. The chorus now follow Cassandra in looking to Orestes to help good prevail (1646, 1667).

But, because of Zeus' long timeframe and the necessity that any doer must also be a sufferer, Orestes' arrival at Argos will not bring the instant restoration and good that is so longed for. Continued hope in justice and in Zeus are still expressed (61–65, 244–46, 409, 639–52, 775, 784–835). Indeed, twice in the play, the hope of the chorus in the *parodos* is echoed: at 782, the nurse utters the familiar plea, 'May all turn out for the very best, with the gods' blessing', while just before Aegisthus' cries are heard, at 868, the chorus utters the hope, 'May it end in victory.' But while Orestes undertakes his mother's murder with the direct endorsement of Apollo on the divine plane and human endorsement from Pylades (900–3), and expresses a new awareness of the moral difficulties of such a murder,[27] its justice is still incomplete. It cannot be the true justice of Zeus, because Zeus' justice is predicated on time. Orestes must still undergo the passage of time that will provide proper learning through suffering.[28]

But in the final play of the trilogy, in a different time and space from what has gone before, the good prevails. In *Agamemnon*, the chorus and many others were at a midpoint between hope and fear, crying woe but hoping for better: Athena and the Erinyes treat that midpoint somewhat differently. A middle way, steering a compromise between conflicting claims, is said to bring victory: the chorus at 517 state that there is a place where what is terrible is in fact good (*eu*), affirming the connection between suffering and wisdom (520-21) that the chorus of *Agamemnon* claimed,[29] as crucial in establishing justice, and they praise a middle way (526-29).[30] Athena herself (690-91, 696-99) reaffirms these connections (cf. 927-37). By 902 the good has indeed prevailed, as indicated in the remarkable number of uses of the prefix *eu*, three alone in Athena's first welcome to the Erinyes (906, 908, 910), and then again at 944, 992, 1019, 1026, 1030, 1031, 1032, 1035, 1038. Zeus has answered the prayers of the chorus of *Agamemnon* in his own time.

Notes

1. Cf. *Ag.* 250, 532-33, 1527, *Cho.* 313-14, 1009, *Eum.* 520. See especially the discussions of Dodds (1960), 255-64 and Lebeck (1971), 59-73. The power of Zeus is central to the play and his name permeates it. Apart from the specific passages discussed in this paper, cf. *Ag.* 285, 355, 62, 470, 509, 526, 677, 703-4, 748, 973, 1042, 1036, 1387, 1391, 1485: Dodds (1960), 257-58.
2. Some commentators (e.g. Lloyd-Jones 1956, 62; Denniston and Page 1957, 85-86) reasonably object that characters such as Agamemnon learn nothing. If so, then the claim must be intended to have a broader application beyond the play: Conacher (1987), 12; Lebeck (1971), 26-29. But the moral sense of certain characters later in the trilogy does seem more developed than those of Agamemnon or Clytemnestra, even if one cannot quite call it learning. *Cho.* 973-1043, in which Orestes stands over the bodies of his dead mother and her lover, visually mirrors the equivalent scene in *Agamemnon* (*Ag.* 1372-1447) in which Clytemnestra stands over the dead Agamemnon and Cassandra, and the mirroring effect between the two scenes helps to underline some significant differences between them. In his scene, Orestes is arguably more aware of the moral complexities of what he has done than his mother was, understanding that from one perspective what he is doing is wrong (cf. *Cho.* 930): Dodds (1960), 261-65. Additionally, I suggest that the Erinyes themselves are ultimately persuaded to learn through the humiliation of defeat to accept a degree of limitation placed on their powers by Athena as Zeus' daughter and representative.
3. The chorus' essential optimism and faith in Zeus' justice is especially evident in *Ag.* 750-62, where they dissent from what they claim is the ancient belief

that great prosperity brings evil, claiming instead that only evil begets evil, while a just father will beget happy children. But the process takes much longer than the chorus suggest.
4   This Zeus resembles that of Achilles in *Iliad* 24.527-33, whose two jars sometimes offer all evil and sometimes a mixture of good and evil, but never offer humanity unmixed good.
5   Agamemnon does not even appear in his own play until l.810. On time in Aeschylus, see de Romilly (1968), 59-85, esp. 77-82.
6   Useful discussions of the *parodos* include Fraenkel (1950), vol. 2, 26-146, esp. 96-99, 112-13; Lebeck (1971), 7-24; Herington (1986), 121-22; and Conacher (1987), 76-96.
7   Significantly, the last reiteration of their refrain (159) is woven with the words of the seer Calchas, who himself has the power to connect with the divine world: Lebeck (1971), 30.
8   De Romilly (1968), 77-78 notes that though the play is nearly 1700 lines long, a mere 300 lines of these deal with the present time, and much material dealing with the past is in the mouths of the chorus, who, by definition, cannot themselves have experienced these events, so are channelling a special knowledge akin to that of Calchas or Cassandra.
9   Lebeck (1971), esp. 1-5.
10 Cf. *Ag.* 1019, 1121-22; *Cho.* 48, 66, 149, 400; *Eum.* 107, 149, 261-62, etc. with Lebeck (1971), 80-91.
11 See Goldhill (1986), 16-23.
12 This obscurity and difficulty in themselves underline the essential ambiguity between hope and fear and uncertainty that the chorus' refrain economically expresses.
13 See, for example, Fraenkel (1950), vol. 2, 96-99; Lloyd-Jones (1962), 187-91; Peradotto (1969).
14 'And in response with one voice we chant the laments for sorrow, may all turn out well'.
15 At least for anyone familiar with Hesiod *Theogony* 160-89, 455-506.
16 On this passage, see Lloyd-Jones (1956), 61-65.
17 Because the son's life is a prolongation of the father's, guilt is inherited: Dodds (1960), 256; cf. de Romilly (1968), 80.
18 Fraenkel (1950), vol. 2, 148-49.
19 See especially *Ag.* 355-62, 369-78, 461-70. Zeus' name is repeatedly invoked in this ode, 355, 362, 367, 470.
20 Lloyd-Jones (1962), 193.
21 Cf. Goldhill (1986), 6-7 and in general, 5-9.
22 *Ag.* 821-23, 838-40, 846-50, 922-30, 946-49. For varying assessments of Agamemnon's character in this scene, see Fraenkel (1950), vol. 2, 441-42 (extremely favourable), Denniston and Page (1957), xxxiii-xxxiv, 151-52 and Lloyd-Jones (1962), 194-95 (both less enthusiastic).
23 All translations of *Choephori* and *Eumenides* are from Sommerstein (2008)

24 Cf. Lebeck (1971), 31-3-2 who (31) connects the chorus with Cassandra through 'intuition hovering on the threshold of consciousness but repeatedly denied admittance'.
25 By 1331–42, the chorus is beginning to see that the process of learning is much lengthier than they had hoped.
26 'See how the sunlight blazes so benignly (*pheggos euphron*) on this day now Justice is restored'.
27 Peradotto (1969), 239–43; Dodds (1960), 261–65.
28 Hence the repeated statements in *Eumenides* that Orestes has been wandering for a long time and undergone many purifications: *Eum.* 237–39, 280–85, 445–52.
29 The sentiment of *Eum.* 521 'to learn good sense under the pressure of distress' (*sophronein hupo stenei*) echoes *Ag.* 180–81: 'although unwillingly, mankind learns how to live within the bounds' (*kai par'akontas elthe sophronein.*)
30 Dodds (1960), 260–61: 'This is the final liberating moment, not, like the others a choice between evils, but a choice of Good'.

7

Agency in *Agamemnon*

Robert Garland

'It's absurd how mortals blame the gods, alleging that we cause all the bad things that afflict them when actually they're the ones who bring sufferings upon themselves beyond what fate decreed, all because of their own utter stupidity.'

These words, spoken by Zeus at the beginning of the *Odyssey*, take us to the heart of the problem of agency.[1] Human stupidity is the root of human suffering. But there are other forces that shape the lives of mortals, notably fate, though fate, it seems, can be overridden by stupidity. That said, we, Homer's audience, know not to ignore the part played by the gods, even if we accept Zeus' proposition that they are often falsely blamed.

In *Agamemnon*, a complex and inextricable web of agents are in play, including the gods, foremost among whom is Zeus; *daimones* or divine beings, such as the Furies; the curse that has fallen on the House of Atreus; and finally, abstractions such as Justice, Ruin, Fate and Necessity.[2]

The chain of events is as follows: Zeus sends a Fury to seek revenge for the theft of Helen; Artemis induces Agamemnon to sacrifice Iphigenia in response to the killing of a pregnant hare; Agamemnon bows to Necessity in performing that sacrifice; Clytemnestra urges Agamemnon to tread on the purple coverings to excite the envy of the gods; the family's dystopic past stirs and muddies the pot; and through it all, in some vague way, the justice of Zeus is preparing to come out on top because, the Chorus tells us, it always does. Making sense of who or which agent does what defies rational analysis, not least because the chain of events is both overdetermined and differently evaluated by different speakers.[3] Even so, struggling to comprehend agency takes us to the core of the play's vision of human destiny, which in the words of Fraenkel represents 'a sublime effort to unriddle the ultimate cause of the fate and suffering of man'.[4]

A number of factors complicate the effort to unriddle this metaphysical Sphinx. One is that the text is hopelessly corrupt in places, rendering it impossible to comprehend to whom the speaker is attributing causality. Another is that it is impossible to determine what force should be attributed to the abstract nouns that are assigned agency. The two most prominent are

'Justice' and 'Ruin'.[5] Others include 'Anger', 'Envy', 'Malice', 'Persuasion', and 'Strife'.[6] Translators often assign these words an initial capital, signalling that they are to be treated as personifications, as I shall here. Capitals didn't exist in Greek, however, so there's no means of knowing whether Aeschylus intended his fifth-century audience to view them as agents as such. Next, Greek religious vocabulary is not easily translatable. 'Fate', for instance, can refer either to unalterable events in an individual's life or to destined events in general. Similarly, *daimōn* can mean either a divine entity, one's personal destiny, or, more loosely, luck, usually bad luck. Many events are explained both by human agency and by divine intervention. Agamemnon is both free and an instrument of Zeus' determination to punish Troy. Next, Aeschylus' poetry evokes a world where imagery and actuality play off each other, so that in Zeitlin's words 'the imagery is often the medium through which the action finds expression'.[7] Lastly, there is no overarching perspective that serves as a corrective to the fallible attempt on the part of mortals to understand the world they inhabit. We, the audience, are wholly dependent on the Chorus and the *dramatis personae* for our explanation of why things happen. In sum, there is perhaps no drama in the Western canon that leaves its audience so much at liberty to forge a link between cause and effect, and it would be fatuous to claim that I have arrived at a final resolution. Indeed, it is highly doubtful whether any final resolution is possible.[8] To quote Fraenkel again, 'it would be absurd to attempt an exact calculation as to the degree of efficacy in each of the different elements that work together towards Agamemnon's fatal end', and the same is equally true of every other event that happens in the play.[9]

I propose first to offer a synopsis of the play with specific reference to agency and then to analyse the explanations that are provided by the Chorus and the *dramatis personae*.

* * *

The play opens with the Watchman praying to the gods for 'release from toils'. He is rewarded moments later with a fire signal that indicates Troy has fallen – a fortuitous coincidence presumably. We are hardly entitled to suppose that his prayer has been answered.

The Chorus enter, unaware of the momentous news that we, the audience, have just learned. They narrate events that occurred ten years previously, beginning with the abduction of Helen and the departure of the Greek fleet to Troy. In response to this violation of hospitality, Agamemnon and Menelaus uttered a war cry, which some god – they don't at first know whether it was Apollo or Pan or Zeus – heard. The god duly dispatched (*pempei*) a Fury 'in belated revenge' (55–59). In the next breath they assert that it was Zeus Xenios, the protector of hosts and guests, who dispatched – *pempei* again – Agamemnon and Menelaus against Paris. They reveal that the outcome of the campaign will be determined by *to peprômenon* or Fate, whose course cannot be altered either by sacrifices or libations (68–71). 'It is what it is' aptly summarises their judgement.

The Chorus describe their pitiful condition. 'We are dishonoured because of our aged flesh ... and our strength is no more than that of a child', they declare (72–75). On and on they go, enumerating the indignities and disadvantages of old age. They are, of course, establishing character, as well as exonerating themselves from agency – a necessary dramaturgic device. When the moment comes for them to step in and prevent Clytemnestra from murdering Agamemnon, all they'll be able to do is express their foreboding, and when they hear Agamemnon's piercing death cry, all they'll be able to do is dither, express their anxiety and remain passive.

The Chorus are able to narrate events prior to the sailing of the fleet because they were eyewitnesses. Given the fact that they were too old to serve in the army, it is tempting to assume that the scene they describe took place not at Aulis but at Argos.[10] Why would they have been with the fleet at Aulis? Their role as narrator is facilitated by the fact that 'Persuasion sent by the gods' breathes upon them – the gods in question presumably being the Muses (104–06). A 'fierce bird of omen' sends – *pempei* yet again – the expedition to Troy (111–12). In the next sentence this bird turns out to be an eagle and suddenly there is a pair of them.

In full sight of the army, the eagles devour a pregnant hare. Agamemnon's reaction to the portent, which was sent by Zeus, becomes central to the audience's assessment of his character. '*Moira* or Fate will plunder by violence all the cattle that the people possess, so long as no *aga* or Malice sent from the gods casts darkness on the great curb of Troy to repulse it, once it has been drawn up as an army', the seer Calchas declares in lines of lyric intensity, not to say opacity (131). Artemis is 'venomous because of pity' – a haunting oxymoron – because 'she loathes the eagles' feast' (134, 137).

Calchas sings a paean in the hope that his patron Apollo will provide a favouring wind before Artemis demands 'a second sacrifice', i.e. one in addition to the 'sacrifice' of the pregnant hare (150). Such an event, he ominously predicts, would be 'the architect of strife bred in the race' (151), since a 'mindful child-avenging Wrath' is waiting in the wings (152–55). He doesn't spell out who the sacrificial victim would be, but the audience understand this to be a reference to Iphigenia and they identify the mindful child-avenging Wrath with Clytemnestra.

The Chorus sing the so-called Hymn to Zeus (160–83). Zeus alone is capable of relieving the burden of their anxiety (160–65). It is unclear whether they are re-imagining the anxiety they experienced ten years ago or whether they are describing their current state of mind, viz. their sense of foreboding at Agamemnon's return. It is Zeus, they tell us, who sets mortals on the road to understanding by establishing a causal relationship between suffering and learning, ominously characterized as 'a favour that comes by violence' (182). Though the principle of 'learning by suffering' is often seen as central to Aeschylus' religious viewpoint, how it relates to the central action of the play, viz. the murder of Agamemnon, is unclear (176–78). None of the characters learns anything, least of all Agamemnon.[11] Enlightenment, if it is available, is limited to the audience alone. The conclusion is irresistible that the Chorus is asserting this principle merely in its capacity as a *dramatis persona*, not as the author's mouthpiece.

Calchas' prayer for a favourable wind falls on deaf ears. As a result of the fleet being prevented from sailing, the army became 'harmfully idle, starving, ill-anchored, and purposeless' (193). The seer 'cried out for another remedy for the baleful storm' (198–99). Like Calchas, the Chorus refrain from explicitly stating that Artemis demanded the sacrifice of Iphigenia. They leave that to the audience's imagination.

The Chorus report the speech that Agamemnon delivered to his army. He claims that refusing to sacrifice his daughter would be as grievous as doing so, since he is under a moral obligation not to become 'a deserter of his fleet' (212).[12] He goes so far as to claim that the sacrifice will be *themis*, i.e. right and proper in the eyes of the gods (215–17). It is as if he is deliberating aloud. Any lingering misgivings he still had at this moment were brushed aside, the Chorus inform us, when he 'donned the halter of *anankê* or Necessity' (218).[13]

The graphic re-creation of the sacrifice that follows, with Iphigenia begging her father for mercy, removes any vestige of sympathy for Agamemnon on the part of the audience. The *parodos* ends with a re-statement of the Chorus' belief that Justice 'turns the balance scales in a way that teaches wisdom to those who suffer' (249–50).

Clytemnestra enters and, after announcing the fall of Troy, vividly describes the plight of the defeated as if she were seeing it in real time (320–37). Suddenly, however, her vision clouds and she utters a pious prayer for the army's welfare:

> If the army returns without having committed any offence against the gods, the sufferings of the dead may be appeased, if no unexpected calamity occurs.
>
> 345–47

The double conditional suggests her prayer has precious little chance of fulfilment. 'The dead' obviously include Iphigenia. In reality, Clytemnestra is hoping that the Greeks are indeed committing sacrilege, as the Herald will casually confirm a mere two hundred lines later (525–28).

Does it actually matter if the Greek army offends the gods? Clytemnestra is hardly going to spare Agamemnon either way. If anything is at stake here, it's merely what we might call a feel-good factor. Clytemnestra would prefer to have the gods and the dead on her side because this will help alleviate any reservations she might still have at the prospect of committing murder.

In their first *stasimon* the Chorus sing a victory hymn to Zeus and Night for having thrown 'an enveloping net over the towers of Troy' (357–58). This is perhaps a reference to the wooden horse, which they equate with 'the all-catching fishing net of Ruin' (361). 'Ruin', *atê*, is used of someone whose insufferable pride has brought about her or his downfall. They express their reverence (but not their thanks) to Zeus for having directed his arrow against Paris, whom they regard as the cause of the war (362–64). There are some people who erroneously deny that the gods punish wrongdoers but such individuals, they assert, are impious (369–72).

If an excessively wealthy person kicks away the altar of Justice, Persuasion will be the consequence, presumably in the form of bad advice, and this will drive that person to Ruin (381–86). Though the Chorus are applying this formula to Paris, it equally describes what happens to Agamemnon. In both cases, the wealthy person is the victim of events over which he had only limited control. Paris was induced to abduct Helen by Aphrodite; Agamemnon was induced to sacrifice Iphigenia by Artemis/Zeus.

The Trojan War has led to many casualties on the Greek side – a point the Chorus emphasize by referencing the 'easily stored cinerary urns that Ares the money-changer of bodies … sends back from Ilion to their dear ones' (438–41). Resentment against the war simmers beneath the surface, intensified by the fact that it occurred 'because of someone else's wife' (448–49). Are we to understand from this that the Chorus are suggesting that the war was caused by a woman's agency? Or that it was caused by agents who used a woman to further their own ends? If the latter, are the Chorus pointing the finger at Aphrodite or at Paris?

Unidentified citizens have uttered the equivalent of a curse, most likely against Agamemnon, though the Chorus refrain from naming him (456–57). The gods have taken note of the heavy cost of war and are in the process of destroying the man who has become 'prosperous against justice', which is applicable both to Paris and to Agamemnon (461–68).

The Herald enters, confirming, as we noted, that the Greeks have destroyed temples and altars in Troy (527).[14] He suggests that this was carried out with the permission, even the assistance, of Zeus as the 'upholder of Justice' (524–28).

The Herald reveals that Menelaus was caught up in a storm. Assuming that this event was due to 'the wrath of the *daimones*', the Chorus inquire about the outcome, whereupon the Herald declares that it is wrong to pollute an auspicious day by speaking of something evil (636-37). Though the text is uncertain, the Herald seems to violate his own injunction a few lines later, by revealing that the gods were responsible for the storm (649).

At the beginning of their second *stasimon* the Chorus blame Helen for bringing misery to ships, men and cities. The fact that her name is similar to the Greek for 'hell' indicates that the gods had foreknowledge of the havoc she would cause (681-98).[15] *Eris*, Strife, and *mênis*, Wrath, are evoked as (partially) responsible for Troy's ruin in what seems to be a reference to the judgement of Paris (699, 702).

The Chorus give voice to an allegedly traditional belief, namely that good fortune causes insatiable woe. Their own belief is that great prosperity leads to hubris, and hubris to ruin (750-62). This is hardly original. The Athenian lawgiver Solon had advanced this idea a century and a half earlier.[16] They end with the declaration that Justice not only honours the man who is righteous but also guides all things to their end (773-81).

Agamemnon enters in a carriage accompanied by Cassandra. He claims equal credit with the gods both for his homecoming and for 'what I did' – as he obliquely puts it – at Priam's city' (811-12). The gods, he says, are *metaitious*, i.e. either 'jointly responsible' or 'jointly guilty'. Though we might regard his choice of vocabulary as a sign of his arrogance, he is only stating what we have already heard from the Chorus, viz. that he was sent by Zeus to destroy Troy. He concludes his poetic description of Troy's downfall with the words, 'It is necessary to give much-remembered thanks to the gods for this, since we have exacted punishment for the presumptuous abduction', viz. of Helen (821-23). The destruction of Troy was, in other words, the product of both divine and human agency. He then greets the gods, 'who, having sent me forth, brought me back home' (853-54).

After describing at length her state of mind during Agamemnon's long absence, Clytemnestra says, 'Let envy stay away' (904). Divine envy towards Agamemnon is, of course, precisely what she wants to arouse. 'Justice has led you back to a home you didn't expect to see again', she declares (911). What she means is that retribution has led Agamemnon back to a very different homecoming from the one he was expecting.

We have reached the theatrical climax of the play. At the bidding of Clytemnestra, Agamemnon reluctantly treads on the purple *heimata* – a word which is often translated as 'carpets' but which literally signifies 'coverings' (921). Though he recognizes that 'it is necessary to honour the gods with things such as these' (922) and though he urges his wife to respect him 'as a man, not as a god' (925), it only takes ten lines of stichomythia to break down his resistance. 'May no envious eye strike me down' is the feeble hope he utters as he steps upon them, repeating what Clytemnestra said earlier (947).

Before entering the palace, Agamemnon orders Clytemnestra to welcome Cassandra into the house as his personal slave. The Greek audience would have understood that Cassandra was expected to gratify her master's sexual needs. It might seem illogical to assume that the girl's presence at her husband's side would have further fuelled Clytemnestra's desire for vengeance, not least because she herself was in an adulterous relationship with Aegisthus. However, cause and effect hardly defer to logic when it comes to the emotions, especially those that are aroused by marital infidelity, quite aside from the fact that logic is conspicuously absent throughout the drama. It thus makes good sense that Clytemnestra feels betrayed, and therefore yet more vengeful, by her husband's very public act of shaming her.[17]

Once Agamemnon has departed, Clytemnestra prays to Zeus the Fulfiller to fulfil her prayers 'and to take care to fulfil what *you* intend to fulfil as well' (973-74).

The Chorus are gripped with fear. Like the Watchman in the Prologue, however, they are reluctant to speak openly:

> If one *moira* or Fate ordered by the gods had not prevented another *moira* from obtaining more [viz. than what was due?], then my heart, anticipating my tongue, would have revealed these things.
> 1026-29

The image of two fates contending with each other is puzzling. Which two fates are the Chorus referring to? Are they associated with events or with individuals? How can one fate subdue another?[18]

In the scene that follows, Cassandra describes how 'ancient evils' in the royal house have passed from one generation to the next, beginning with the murder of Thyestes' sons by Atreus and followed by the murder of Atreus by Thyestes' son Aegisthus (1072-1330). These atrocities resulted from Thyestes' seduction of his brother's wife, which Cassandra describes as the 'first cause of *atê* or Ruin' (1192).

Before prophesying the fate that awaits both Agamemnon and herself, Cassandra explains how she incurred the wrath of Apollo, who, because she reneged on her promise to sleep with him, punished her by declaring that his gift of prophecy would become a curse, since no-one would believe her (1208-12). This accounts for her relationship with the Chorus.

Moments after Cassandra's departure, the Chorus hear Agamemnon's first death cry. They call for silence, uncertain who the victim is, despite the fact that they have already worked out that Agamemnon faces the possibility of imminent death. When they hear the second cry, they determine to take counsel together (1346–47). Though we don't expect them to intervene, they go to extreme lengths to remain bystanders by fragmenting into three distinct lobbies (1348–53):

In my opinion, we should issue a proclamation, requesting that the citizens bring assistance to the house.
For my part I think we should rush in as quickly as possible and catch them in the act, swords in hands.
And I for my part am in favour of this proposal and vote that this is what we should do. There's no time for delay.

No time for delay? Never was a truer word spoken. However, the verb the Chorus member uses for 'vote' – *psêphizomai* – transports us to the legislative world of the Athenian Assembly, where dilatoriness is the order of the day.

Clytemnestra reappears, exulting in her deed, for which she takes full responsibility.[19] I stand where I struck him and by the deed I accomplished. It's what I did. I don't deny it.

1379–80

Her third strike was 'in thanksgiving to Zeus of the Underworld' – a blasphemous suggestion since there is no evidence that Zeus actively sought the murder of Agamemnon. She commits further outrage by comparing the blood that spurts from Agamemnon's death blows with 'the spring rain bestowed by Zeus' (1389–92).

Immediately after her confession, she and the Chorus hold a mock trial. Proclaiming her innocence, Clytemnestra swears by Justice, *atê* and the Fury, 'by whom [or to whom] I sacrificed this man' that she is now freed from anxiety so long as Aegisthus – 'no small shield regarding my boldness' – remains faithful to her. It is noteworthy that she does not directly implicate him in the murder (1431–36).

The Chorus deplore the destructive role that Helen played in causing the slaughter of thousands at Troy, which in turn led to the murder of Agamemnon – one woman's crime leading to that of another (1453–57). Clytemnestra responds by defending Helen, perhaps in solidarity with another woman or perhaps in order to keep the Chorus focused on the guilt attaching to Agamemnon. In the next stanza the Chorus take us back further into the past by evoking the *daimōn*, 'which afflicts both this house and the twins descended from Tantalus' (1468-69) – a reminder of Tantalus' guilt in serving the flesh of his son Pelops to the gods. Clytemnestra concludes by ascribing responsibility to 'the ancient, ruthless avenging curse of Atreus ... [which] has rendered in payment this adult [Agamemnon] for the children [of Thyestes] as a full sacrifice' (1501-4).

The dispute between Clytemnestra and the Chorus is complicated by the fact that Greek does not differentiate between 'guilt' and 'responsibility'. This is not merely a semantic nicety. It goes to the heart of the moral complexity at the play's core. Clytemnestra is certainly acknowledging responsibility but in no way (presumably) is she admitting guilt.

The Chorus threaten Clytemnestra first with banishment and then with death (1410-11, 1429-30). After Clytemnestra has defiantly defended her crime, they evoke the *daimōn* 'who wields power proceeding from women of similar inclination or temperament' (1468-71). This seems to suggest that the *daimōn* is not an external force but rather one that is lodged inside an individual. Even so, the wording is sufficiently obscure to enable Clytemnestra to shift the blame away from herself. She commends the Chorus for having acknowledged that the *daimōn* is responsible for all that has happened and characterizes it as 'that which belongs to the race', i.e. the House of Atreus (1477).

The Chorus now have a revelation. If the *daimōn* is the proximate cause, Zeus must be the ultimate cause, since Zeus is the cause and explanation of everything. What is accomplished for mortals without Zeus? What is not ordained without the god? (1487-88).

Clytemnestra declares that 'the ancient, bitter *alastōr* or spirit of vengeance appearing in the likeness of the dead man's wife' is responsible for Agamemnon's murder (1500-4). She is perhaps casting herself in the role of a minister of justice rather than passing on responsibility to a divine being. The Chorus concede that an *alastōr* might indeed have been her accomplice (1507-8).

'Justice', they prophesy, 'is being sharpened for other deeds involving injury on the whetstones of *moira*' (1535-36). Are the Chorus suggesting that a higher power is preparing retribution for the crimes committed? Or are they merely giving voice to the hope that everything will turn out right in the end? They again state axiomatically that 'the one who acts' – or perhaps 'the one who does evil' – 'suffers' (1563) and further that 'the race' (i.e. the House of Atreus again) 'is attached to Ruin' (1566). A truce of sorts is arrived at and Clytemnestra expresses her satisfaction at having formed a pact with the *daimōn* of the house, which she hopes will now finally depart (1568-73).

When Aegisthus enters, he introduces an additional pretext for Agamemnon's murder, namely revenge for the gruesome feast that his uncle

Atreus served to his father Thyestes. Though he gives credit to the Furies (1580), he characterizes himself as the 'just weaver of this crime' (1604), by which he presumably means that he at least planned, though he did not cause or execute, Agamemnon's death. 'Justice', he says, 'brought me back' (1607). He has observed Agamemnon, he goes on to say, 'in the nets of Justice' (1611). It is noteworthy that he does not give Clytemnestra any credit for righting a wrong nor indeed does he address her directly.

* * *

In the course of the play Aeschylus raises a number of questions regarding agency, to which he provides no simple solution:

1. Why did the Greeks send an expedition to Troy?

Aeschylus never mentions the Judgement of Paris, which in popular thinking was regarded as the ultimate cause of the Trojan War, and he only alludes briefly to the goddess *Eris* or Wrath, who incited the dispute for the golden apple which prompted the judgement. The Chorus hold Helen and Paris both accountable for the war, though Helen, because of her name, seems to have been fated to be a cause of human misery, for which reason she lacks full agency (399–402, 681–98). In their view, Zeus Xenios, the god of hospitality, 'sends' Agamemnon to Troy. He does so in response to the outrage to which the Atreidae gave vent. It's unclear how much responsibility they are apportioning to the Atreidae on the one hand, and to Zeus on the other. Are they suggesting that Zeus put the thought of the campaign into their heads? What is clear is that Agamemnon undertook the expedition, in their mind, with Zeus' full support. Human agency is primarily characterized by Menelaus' *pothos* or 'yearning' for Helen. He loves his wife desperately. The Chorus do not suggest that either family honour or injured pride was a factor in the decision to recover Helen.

2. What is the explanation for Artemis' anger?

Calchas surmised that Artemis was outraged by the portent which Zeus sent to indicate that the impending war will be successful. He did not explain why she held the Atreidae in some way responsible for the portent. However, Agamemnon accepted unquestioningly that the goddess could be appeased only by the sacrifice of his daughter.

It is true that Artemis is the protectress of young creatures but why does she have such a strong reaction to an everyday occurrence? If she were to take exception to every act of prey, her venom would have no respite. If, on the other hand, she interprets the event as a symbol of some dire event, what precisely is that dire event? Suggestions by commentators include the murder of Thyestes' children by Atreus, the sacrifice of Iphigenia, and the sufferings that the impending war will inflict on innocent victims.[20] The last is the most cogent explanation, though I know of no other occasion when Artemis pities war victims. However, we should not exclude the possibility that she does so on this occasion, particularly since, as Lloyd-Jones points out, she is depicted 'as a loyal partisan of Troy against the invaders'.[21]

It is equally unclear why Artemis holds Agamemnon accountable for a portent sent by Zeus. Irrespective of the explanation for her anger, it is morally objectionable that she should direct her wrath towards the Atreidae simply because they fit the portent through analogy.[22] It is also morally objectionable that Zeus, who requires the destruction of Troy, should place Agamemnon in such a dilemma.

In conclusion, the most likely explanation for Artemis' anger is that she was incensed by the slaughter that the war was going to occasion, but this leaves us wondering why this should have mattered to her in the first place. Nothing in the text suggests she was motivated by compassion for the victims of war – only by the killing of the hare and her leverets.

3. Did Agamemnon have any choice in his decision to sacrifice his daughter?

The Chorus evidently believe that Agamemnon was a free agent up to the point that he donned the halter of Necessity, since he wavered before taking the fateful decision. His indecisiveness was therefore a consequence of his free will. At the moment he cast doubt aside, he surrendered his agency. And at this point, Troy's doom – and his death – become equally inevitable.[23] It is true that he saw himself under pressure not to desert the fleet, but that fact did not rob him of free will. It is unclear whether his fear of deserting the fleet was prompted by public-spiritedness or by fear of compromising his authority. Whichever was the case, he took the decision to sacrifice his daughter only after soul-searching. He thus engineered his own downfall, since, having taken this decision, he became set on a course of destruction – his own and that of others – which he could not alter. At the same time, by an act of double determination, it was this act which ensured that the will of Zeus was enacted, since it was Zeus who determined that Troy had to be punished for Paris's violation of the sacred law of hospitality.

It's true that Artemis caused adverse winds and that Agamemnon performed the sacrifice to appease her, but, as Peradotto points out, '[she] merely creates a situation in which he may either cancel the war, or else pursue it by inflicting on his own household the kind of slaughter he will perpetrate at Troy'.[24] The fact that Agamemnon chose the path he did is indicative of the kind of person he is. In other words, he is the victim as much of his own flawed character as he is of Artemis' wrath.

4. Why did Troy fall?

The Chorus indicate that Troy fell because of the dispensation of Zeus. Agamemnon, however, on his return home, apportions credit for its destruction equally to himself as human agent and to the gods. The Chorus maintain that Justice, too, played its part in the outcome because the abduction of Helen was a crime, though it is unclear whether they regard Justice to be acting as a free agent or merely functioning as a consequence of that crime.

5. Why was Agamemnon murdered?

Clytemnestra was motivated to murder Agamemnon in revenge for the sacrifice of Iphigenia, whereas Aegisthus, who had no hand in the deed, saw it justified by the outrage committed by his uncle Atreus towards his father Thyestes. It is noteworthy that Clytemnestra did not justify her crime by instancing her affection for her daughter. She claimed that her act was assisted by a variety of supernatural agents – by the gods, by an unnamed *daimōn*, by Fate and by Justice. Further grounds for Agamemnon's murder in the eyes of the audience include the fact that he instigated a war that led to the deaths of many Greeks, offended the gods by permitting his army to commit sacrilege at Troy, and had the temerity to flaunt his war bride in his wife's face.

Though Agamemnon is compliant in yielding to Clytemnestra's invitation to step on the purple coverings, it is hardly the case that the gods would have intervened to save his life if he had resisted.[25] Doing something that he knows to be highly ill-advised is certainly foolish but there is no evidence that he does it out of hubris, even though Clytemnestra obviously hopes that the gods interpret it that way. Admittedly the act is reminiscent of his shedding of the blood of Iphigenia, but we are hardly entitled to assume that this association is contributory to his demise, unless we infer that it rouses Clytemnestra to greater fury.[26] Clytemnestra also asserts that the *daimōn* of the House of Atreus has agency, a view that is endorsed by Cassandra. In other words, the house's violent past is also contributory to Agamemnon's demise by generating another round of intrafamilial killing.

6. Why in general do terrible things happen?

The answer on one level is simple: one bad deed leads to another. The causal link in the chain of events described by the Chorus and enacted by the characters is, on the surface, entirely straightforward. The abduction of Helen leads to the dispatch of the Greek army to Troy, which leads to the sacrifice of Iphigenia, which leads to the destruction of Troy, which leads to the murder of Agamemnon. A parallel chain of events is familial. The seduction of Atreus' wife leads to the banquet of Thyestes' children, which leads to the curse upon the House of Atreus, which leads to the sacrifice of Iphigenia, which leads to the murder of Agamemnon. However, Aeschylus invariably suggests that what may appear to be an obvious link between cause and effect only at best offers a partial explanation. No division is ever achieved or even proposed between the parts played by human and divine agency. Likewise, image and metaphor are linked indissolubly.

In sum, the action of *Agamemnon* suggests a terrifying world of moral and metaphysical confusion, in which Zeus, by seeking vengeance for the violation of hospitality, becomes directly responsible for the sacrifice of an innocent virgin, the destruction of an entire city, and the assassination of a king who, whatever his faults and shortcomings, is hardly a monster of depravity. Though Agamemnon's assassination will be avenged in *Libation Bearers*, this will require a son to become the murderer of his mother.[27]

If Justice exacts so heavy a price, why in gods' names should we, Aeschylus' audience, hope that it will prevail?

Notes

1 Hom. *Od.* 1.32–34.
2 In addition, chance, or perhaps more accurately circumstance, makes a fleeting appearance (187, 664).
3 Sommerstein (2010 [1996]), 368 writes: '[A]lmost every important event in Aeschylean tragedy is the fruit of parallel human and divine action, usually from different motives'. Bednarowski (2015), 193–94, 196 points out that in the parodos Agamemnon is initially presented as 'an instrument of the gods brought low through divine wrangling', whereas the later account of Iphigenia's sacrifice emphasizes his personal responsibility. As a further complication, the second stasimon 'raises the possibility that Agamemnon is in fact a victim of his father's crimes according to the doctrine of inherited guilt'.
4 Fraenkel (1950), vol. 2, 113.
5 Lines 131, 361, 383, 386, 772–81, 1192, 1566, 1607, 1611.
6 Lines 106, 155, 382, 385, 664, 698, 763.
7 Zeitlin (1965), 463.
8 As Edwards (1977), 18 points out, 'Like most of us, Aeschylus may not have been completely clear-headed and logical about the roots of human action'.

9   Fraenkel (1950), vol. 3, 625.
10 The view that the portent was received at the palace in Argos rather than on the beach at Aulis has been suggested by a number of scholars (e.g. Sommerstein 2010, 177).
11 Dodds (2007 [1960]), 263 argues that, whereas Agamemnon's last words convey 'no final flash of insight', Clytemnestra learns 'too late and incompletely', whereas Herington (1986), 122 and Langwitz Smith (1973), 9 are of the opinion that the point of view is merely that of the Chorus.
12 Sommerstein (2010 [1996]), 363–65 argues that Agamemnon was free to abandon the expedition but chose not to do so because it would have been a blow to his prestige.
13 Dover (1973), 65 describes *anankê* as 'applicable to any physical, legal or moral force to which resistance is shameful, painful, perilous or for any other reason difficult'. Many instances of it, he further acknowledges, 'are resistible in principle'.
14 Sommerstein (2008), 61 believes that the reference to the destruction of altars and buildings of the gods at line 527 was 'added by a producer or actor for a revival in the late fifth century', though as he further points out the Greeks have in any case offended the gods by killing Priam at an altar and abducting Cassandra from a temple.
15 For discussion of Helen's name, see Rutherford (2012), 226–29.
16 Solon frr. 4.7–9, 6.3–4, 13.7–16 West. For discussion, see Denniston and Page (1957), 136; Conacher (1987), 28–29.
17 I am most grateful to David Stuttard for pointing out to me that Clytemnestra's appetite for revenge would have been further roused by the sight of Cassandra, both on grounds of betrayal and humiliation.
18 Scott (1969), 341 suggests that one fate applies to everyone and the other is specific to selected individuals 'as a special dispensation' and that this latter fate refers to Agamemnon, who was permitted by Zeus to sacrifice Iphigenia in order to advance his campaign against Troy and is therefore spared the inevitable consequences of this action. Lloyd-Jones (1978), 56 interprets *moira* as referring merely to social status, which was thought of as 'god-given' in archaic thought.
19 Conacher (1987), 49 notes: 'No other speech in Greek tragedy contains so many (ten in all) and such insistent references to the speaker's responsibility for a deed'.
20 Conacher (1987), 10 writes: 'The poet is concerned ... to provide a portent in which we can see, in a flash of the mind's eye, without rational analysis, the sack of Troy, the sacrifice of Iphigenia, and the awful feasting on Thyestes' young'.
21 Lloyd-Jones (1983 [1962]), 61.
22 See Elata-Alster (1985), 28.
23 The halter of necessity has been the subject of endless discussion. Denniston and Page (1957), 88 are of the opinion that Agamemnon had no choice in the matter. They assert that the reference to necessity 'is not to the action which

he now undertakes but to *the inevitable consequences* of that action' (original emphasis). Lesky (1966), 84 argues that Agamemnon is *both* forced to put on the halter of necessity *and* wants to do it. Edwards (1977), 31 sees Agamemnon as a 'man of inherited guilt who, because of it, in a situation of terrible choice had the mad folly to incur terrible pollution and make his ruin inevitable'. Conacher (1987), 13 argues that Agamemnon 'has *chosen* to stain his hands with his daughter's blood rather than betray his position as leader of the expedition and of this ... no rationalization by the critics can clear him' (original emphasis).

24 Peradotto (2007 [1969]), 227–28. Conacher (1987), 85–92 offers a useful summary of the debate concerning Agamemnon's guilt.
25 Fraenkel (1950), vol. 2, 441 believes Agamemnon yields both because he is 'a great gentleman, possessed of moderation and self-control' and because of weariness. Denniston and Page (1957), 151 claim that he does so out of hubris. Simpson (1971), 96 is closer to the text in suggesting that Clytemnestra 'masters him and imposes an act of *hubris* upon him', though I cannot see how *hubris* can be imposed.
26 The 'path of purple cloth', as Taplin (2018), xxiv–xxv phrases it, 'is a fascinating, inexhaustible *coup de théâtre*, one of the greatest of all time'. He notes that Agamemnon never makes direct contact with Argos 'and is instead caught up in the beguilement of wealth, tangled in Clytemnestra's wrappings of words'.
27 This is essentially the same conclusion as that of Sommerstein (2010), 169, who writes, 'what we are shown in *Agamemnon* is a rotten, stupid world, and one almost finds oneself wondering, at the end of the play, if the "good sense" to which Zeus has "made a road" is nothing but the recognition that it *is* a rotten, stupid world'.

8

Wealth and Injustice in *Agamemnon*

Michael Carroll

The extended general reflections in the choral odes of *Agamemnon* constitute one of the play's most distinctive features, and a topic explored with particular insistence by the Argive Elders is that of wealth and its relation to wrongful behaviour. To Aeschylus' audience the theme would have seemed a traditional one. In his *Works and Days*, the early archaic poet Hesiod stressed that divine punishment awaits those who, rather than contenting themselves with 'god-given' possessions, acquire wealth by unjust or fraudulent means (320–26), and this tenet was memorably echoed, several generations before Aeschylus' time, by the Athenian poet Solon.[1] In later archaic poets like Solon we also find a marked preoccupation with the dangerous consequences of excessive wealth, often articulated in the form of the idea that an overabundance of prosperity (*koros*) leads to thoughts and actions marked by excessive self-assertion (*hybris*), and to the disastrous reversal of fortune such arrogance inevitably incurs (*atē*).[2]

The solemn, authoritative tone adopted by the Elders in their general reflections reinforces the impression that they are tapping into the accumulated wisdom of the Greek poetic tradition at such moments. This tone is in stark contrast to the agitation and hesitancy they display at other points in the play. A particularly abrupt shift of register occurs towards the end of the first *stasimon* (*Ag.* 355–487). The Elders have finally been persuaded by Clytemnestra that Troy has fallen, and the ode begins with a meditation on the reasons for Troy's fate. Attention gradually turns to the discontent at Argos concerning the death toll in the war, and the final stanza before the epode raises the possibility that trouble lies in store for the returning Greeks. The Elders end this stanza – in one of the passages directly relevant to the topic of this chapter – by indicating their preference for 'prosperity that inspires no resentment' (*Ag.* 471), and expressing the wish to be neither a sacker of cities nor at someone else's mercy (as the surviving Trojans now are). Then in the epode (475–87), a section in a different metre that concludes the ode, their tone changes. Suddenly the Elders – or some of them, if (as many scholars think) the Chorus divides into two or more groups at this point – start to doubt whether the war has really come to an end, and tetchily suggest that it would be typical of a female ruler not to wait until the facts have become clear.

It might be tempting to dismiss this as an example of inconsistent characterization, even if the Elders' *volte-face* raises the dramatic stakes ahead of the appearance some lines later of the Herald who is to confirm the news of Troy's fall.[3] In recent decades, however, scholars have become more attuned to the flexibility of the choral voice in tragedy. At times the fictional identity of the chorus comes to the fore as it interacts with other characters and responds to developments in the action; in *Agamemnon*, the Elders' edginess, ambivalence towards Clytemnestra, and tendency to fluctuate between despair and wishful thinking are all consistent with their status as venerable but relatively powerless representatives of the community whose loyalties lie with the king and the established order. At other times, however, the chorus in tragedy speaks with greater authority and critical detachment than its fictional identity might seem to warrant. The reason for this, scholars have argued, is that the men playing the part of the fictional collective are at the same time performing as members of an Athenian civic chorus in a dramatic festival dedicated to Dionysus. This immediately situates their performance in a long-standing tradition of choral cult celebration and grants them access to the stories and wisdom associated with that tradition. The chorus never explicitly casts off its fictional identity, but the less that identity is foregrounded in a particular passage, the more authoritative its utterances tend to be.[4]

If this helps to explain why the Elders are able to channel the voice of poetic wisdom at certain moments, a further question is how much their general reflections actually illuminate the events of the drama. The topic of wealth in particular has (at least until recently) attracted less scholarly attention than its prominence in the choral odes of *Agamemnon* might seem to deserve, and some scholars have openly doubted its relevance to the action; Dodds, for example, argues that 'money questions have no real place in the tragedy of the House of Atreus'.[5] As an initial response to Dodds we can point out that the theme is not restricted to the Elders' choral meditations. In the scene before the first *stasimon*, Clytemnestra suggests that the victorious Greek soldiers will not suffer disaster as long as they do not yield to the desire for material gain and 'pillage what they ought not to' (342). The acts of sacrilege committed by the Greeks during the sack of Troy were an established part of the mythical tradition, and the acuteness of Clytemnestra's words (however feigned her concern) is borne out by the Herald's account in the following scene of the storm that destroyed much of the Greek fleet on its way home (636–80).

The theme of excessive wealth is integral to the stagecraft, moreover, in the powerful scene in which Clytemnestra persuades Agamemnon to enter the palace by stepping on the precious textiles she has ordered to be spread before him. Agamemnon is well aware that the fabrics will be destroyed in the process (948–49), and his decision to tread on them nevertheless is a blatant manifestation of the excessive self-regard associated with *hybris*.[6] The link between Agamemnon's attitude and the wealth of the royal house is underlined at the start of the speech delivered by Clytemnestra as the King walks into the palace. Clytemnestra declares that, since the resources of the sea can never be exhausted, including the shellfish from which the purple dye for the textiles was extracted, the royal house – which 'does not know how to be poor' – has the means to replace the fabrics ruined by Agamemnon's feet (958–62).

It does not seem unreasonable, on the other hand, to suggest that wealth is not as significant a factor in the events of the *Oresteia* as, say, the urge for revenge on the part of the human agents or the influence of the divine sphere. We can acknowledge that the great prosperity of the House of Atreus is consistent with the link between excess and *hybris* posited by poets such as Solon, and still wonder if the Elders are missing the point somewhat by returning to this theme again and again in their reflections. Could it be, perhaps, that these passages serve to underline the *limits* of traditional wisdom when applied to the cycle of vengeance in the Argive royal family? Or are the Elders' meditations on wealth in fact more central to the meaning of *Agamemnon* (and of the trilogy as a whole) than scholars have generally recognized?

One passage in which the Elders themselves might seem to downplay the explanatory value of wealth comes towards the end of the second *stasimon* (681–781), the choral ode that begins immediately after the Herald's account of the storm that struck the Greek fleet. In the final three stanzas of this ode, the Elders move from the specific case of Troy's fall to general principles, and they begin by drawing a contrast between an old explanation for human suffering, 'spoken long ago' (751), and their own view, a view that supposedly sets them apart from others. According to the belief that they oppose, great prosperity gives birth to – that is to say, has as an inherent consequence – 'insatiable misery' for the rich man's family. The Elders are here alluding to the traditional idea that particularly successful individuals incur the resentment (*phthonos*) of the gods by virtue of this success and sooner or later suffer the consequences.[7]

The Elders then proceed to summarize their own position: it is the impious deed, they explain, that gives birth to other deeds of the same breed (that is to say, to other impious deeds), while 'houses that keep to straight justice' have as their offspring a fortune that remains fair forever (758–62). In the following stanza (763–72), they expand on the first of these possibilities, this time using the language of *hybris* rather than impiety: an old act of *hybris*, they declare, tends to give birth to a new act of *hybris*, which has as its breeding ground the sufferings of mortals.⁸ The level of textual corruption in the following lines makes them very difficult to interpret, but the Elders are perhaps saying that the birth of the new *hybris* appears to be arbitrary (it happens 'at this or that time') but is in fact determined in advance, and that at the same time a divinity – who seems to be identified as the goddess Ruin (*Atē*) herself – is born from the old *hybris*. We shall come back to these details later, but worth noting for the moment is the way in which the metaphorical language of procreation in both stanzas helps to bring out the differences between the two positions outlined by the Elders. The Elders' opponents hold that prosperity gives birth to misery, but that leaves open the question of *how* one leads to the other: in contrast to the usual relationship of resemblance between parent and child, the two states seem fundamentally opposed. The Elders' position, on the other hand, is consistent with the principle that like begets like.

These two explanations for misfortune are often characterized in the scholarship as 'amoral' and 'moral' respectively, since to be extremely prosperous does not, on the face of it, seem a transgression deserving of punishment in the way that an act of impiety or *hybris* is. Whether this is the exact contrast that the Elders have in mind is a question we shall come back to, but scholars who interpret their words along these lines often feel drawn to cast doubt on their assertion that they are alone in holding the second view. Had poets like Solon not long ago suggested that it is not simply excess, but excess accompanied by *hybris*, that leads to ruin? And do we not find versions of the broader belief that the gods punish wrongdoers as far back as the Homeric poems and Hesiod's *Works and Days*?⁹

The Elders are of course speaking from the perspective of individuals living long ago in the mythical past, so it is perhaps unfair to query their claim to novelty in this way. But something else that tends not to be acknowledged is the awkwardness of making the Elders' words fit the Solonian ideas they are supposedly restating.¹⁰ Let us assume for the moment that when the Elders speak of one impious act begetting others, they are referring to the process whereby impious behaviour becomes engrained in a person, family, or community: the more such acts are committed, the easier it becomes to commit others.¹¹ According to the traditional wisdom, such a process ends in disaster, but one problem with this way of interpreting the Elders is that they fail to mention the disastrous final stage before moving on to the fair fortune of just houses. Instead, it has to be supplied by the audience: one impious deed leads to others of the same nature, *and eventually to the ruin of the person, family or community in question*. On the other hand, the Elders do seem to allude directly to this final stage in the following stanza when they refer to the birth of the goddess Ruin. One option, then, is simply to accept that it is left unmentioned in the previous stanza and attribute this abruptness to the compression of thought characteristic of Aeschylus' style.

On this interpretation, the implication seems to be that *hybris* need not be accompanied by excessive prosperity, since the Elders make no reference to wealth when outlining their own position on the causes of disaster.[12] That the two are frequently found in tandem, however, is suggested by what they go on to say in the final stanza of the ode (773–81): the presence of Justice is easy to make out in cottages filled with smoke, and the goddess favours those who – like the inhabitants of such hovels – live a life of moderation, but she distances herself from the impure inhabitants of gold-spangled dwellings. This return to the theme of wealth prepares for the dramatic moment in the following scene when Agamemnon walks across the precious tapestries. If we accept the interpretation of the previous two stanzas outlined above, however, it represents a somewhat surprising way to end the ode: after presenting prosperity and *hybris* as distinct explanations for misfortune and indicating their support for the latter, the Elders now suddenly lay stress on the close association between the two.[13]

How do the Elders' pronouncements in these final three stanzas of the second *stasimon* compare with what they say elsewhere concerning wealth? The other most important passage on the topic comes towards the beginning of the first *stasimon*. After some introductory lines hailing the Greek victory, in the first stanza the Elders take as their starting point this 'blow' from Zeus that has struck the Trojans (367–84):

> Of a blow from Zeus they are able to speak;
> that at least can be tracked down.
> He acted as he decreed. Some deny
> that the gods deign to concern themselves
> with mortals who trample on the grace
> of untouchable things – but those people are not pious.
> Revealed as the offspring[14]
> of deeds not to be dared is the ruin
> of men swelling with pride more than is right,
> when houses flourish to excess,
> beyond what is best. Let it be
> painless, sufficient for someone
> well endowed with sense.
> There is no defence for a man
> who, through excess of wealth,
> has kicked the great altar
> of Justice into oblivion.

The scale of the destruction suffered by Troy, the Elders suggest, is a sure sign of Zeus' involvement, as even the Trojans (the 'they' of the first line) can now see. Indeed, Troy's fate directly contradicts the belief – held only by the impious – that the gods pay no attention when a person defiles the principles of proper behaviour. The Elders then move further back along the causal sequence. Those who commit wrongful acts that lead to ruin are consumed by a pride that exceeds that which any person ought to feel, and such an attitude is found in circumstances of inordinate prosperity. The Elders next describe an alternative scenario: a person who is sufficiently wise will settle for an amount of wealth that has no painful consequences. The phrasing of the last four lines allows for more than one interpretation, but it is best to understand them as a summary of the sequence already outlined by the Elders: when excessive wealth induces a person to act unjustly, ruin is the inevitable consequence.[15] This allows the kicking of the altar of Justice to correspond directly to the trampling of the grace of untouchable things mentioned earlier in the stanza, as well as to Agamemnon's destruction of the precious tapestries later in the play.

As already mentioned, Solon and other poets from the later archaic period frequently describe excess and *hybris* as successive stages in a process that ends in disaster. In a fragment of direct relevance to the present passage, for example, Solon declares that 'excess (*koros*) gives birth to *hybris*, whenever great prosperity comes to people whose mind is not sound' (6.3–4 West). Sometimes we hear instead that *hybris* leads to *koros*, or the two stages are presented as coinciding, and such variations reflect the fact that what is being described here is really a cyclical phenomenon.[16] Excessive wealth may lead to greater arrogance and misbehaviour, but a self-centred person without scruples will also be more inclined to keep accumulating wealth.

The Elders follow the more common sequence in this stanza, though in reverse order: starting with the disastrous end-point, they move backwards to the doing of unjust deeds, the attitude of self-assertion that lies behind this behaviour – *hybris* can apply to both the actions and the mindset – and finally to the conditions of excessive prosperity that underpin such an attitude. But how does wealth become excessive in the first place? What sets the destructive cycle in motion? In the fragment from Solon quoted above, the poet suggests that the problem arises when great wealth comes to a person whose mind is not 'sound'. In a similar vein, the Elders suggest that someone 'well endowed with sense' will be satisfied with wealth that is in no danger of becoming excessive. One way of interpreting these statements is to see those who lack the sense to avoid excess and the behaviour as morally deficient, possessed of some objectionable weakness that leaves them prone to the lure of wealth; there is an unmistakable tone of reproach in many of the passages in archaic poetry that deal with those who cannot rein in their own desires. Another possibility, however, is that – at least some of the time – individuals possessed of excessive wealth have fallen prey to impulses and intellectual failings that few humans are wholly immune to. In suggesting that wealth with no painful consequences is what will satisfy a person of intelligence, the Elders highlight the key issue: how is one to know what amount of wealth fits that description except with the benefit of hindsight? It is this same problem that Solon wrestles with towards the end of his *Elegy to the Muses* when he laments that 'no limit of wealth lies revealed to men' (13.71 West). Because the line dividing mere prosperity from excess is obscure to mortals, a seemingly unobjectionable desire for wealth can over time merge into the pursuit of a goal which becomes progressively more difficult both to fulfil and to renounce; as Solon observes, 'those of us who now have the greatest riches are doubly eager for more' (72–73).

Whatever exactly leads a person to accumulate too much wealth, at the beginning of the next stanza the Elders give a vivid insight into why the line between safe and dangerous wealth matters so much in the world of the *Oresteia*. Their concern is now with the pressure exerted on the unjust man at the moment when he is faced with the choice of committing a wrongful act: 'Audacious Persuasion deploys force, the irresistible daughter of Ruin who plots in advance' (*Ag.* 385–86).[17] Here the Elders represent the unjust man's demise as the result of a combined effort on the part of two goddesses. Ruin has already decided on his downfall, and the Elders describe Persuasion as Ruin's daughter because she plays the subservient role of advancing Ruin's plan.[18] Paradoxically, it is force – a form of agency that would seem directly at odds with persuasion – that the goddess uses as the means to that end. What should we make of this oxymoron? Since to be persuaded to act in a certain way implies some level of consent, we can assume that the unjust man actively wishes to commit the act of *hybris* that will lead to his downfall. That Persuasion uses force, however, seems to mean that her agency has a reliability that persuasion generally lacks. The goddess is 'irresistible', and no other outcome is really possible.

In the following lines the Elders turn to the punishment that inevitably ensues when such an act is committed. No cure is effective, pleas to the gods are in vain, and the community as a whole suffers as a result of the unjust man's actions. Then towards the end of the stanza they explicitly relate these general reflections to what happened at Troy: Paris was exactly such a man, as he showed when he 'defiled the table of hospitality' (*Ag.* 401–2) offered to him by Menelaus and Agamemnon. This violation of the bond of guest-friendship (*xenia*) is the equivalent of the trampling and kicking mentioned in the previous stanza, but the example of Paris also fits the earlier part of the explanatory sequence. The great wealth of Troy, and of the Trojan royal family in particular, is an important part of the story from the *Iliad* onwards, and is taken for granted in the second *stasimon* when the Elders declare that Helen initially seemed to the Trojans to be a 'gentle embellishment of wealth' (741), that is to say, the crowning glory of the city's riches.

The first two steps in the sequence are also directly applicable to Agamemnon, and it is no coincidence that in the rest of the ode the Elders' attention gradually turns to the resentment of the Argive community towards their leaders. As we have seen, the great wealth of the Argive royal house comes to the fore in the 'tapestry scene' later in the play, and it is striking that Clytemnestra has an effect on Agamemnon similar to that of the goddess Persuasion on the unjust man. The final line spoken by Clytemnestra before Agamemnon yields begins with the command, 'Be persuaded!' (943), and the fact that Agamemnon steps on the tapestries despite being fully aware that such behaviour incurs the wrath of the gods (918–30) makes Clytemnestra's persuasive powers all the more mysterious and unsettling; at that moment, the Queen seems a human embodiment of the divine forces bent on Agamemnon's destruction. Furthermore, in the account in the *parodos* (the first choral ode of the play) of the events that led to the sacrifice of Iphigenia, there is a hint that the divine sphere played a role in those events similar to that ascribed to Persuasion in the first *stasimon*. However exactly we interpret the famous yoke-strap metaphor of *Ag.* 218, later in the same stanza we are told that Agamemnon was able to bring himself to commit such an act because 'mortals are made bold by audacious derangement (*parakopa*), which counsels shameful deeds and is the first source of misery' (222–23). In archaic Greek thought, it is precisely such derangement, inflicted by the gods, that leads a person to ruin, and in *Eumenides* the chorus of Furies use the same word *parakopa* to describe their effect on their victims (329).

What the opening two stanzas of the first *stasimon* suggest, then, is that in circumstances of excessive prosperity a person becomes unable to resist prioritizing self-interest over righteous behaviour, and that both the act of *hybris* and the punishment that inevitably follows are planned in advance by the divine sphere. There is no need to take from this that *hybris* can never be found in other circumstances, but the Elders' focus is firmly on its relationship with excess. It is because Persuasion becomes irresistible once the line between appropriate and inordinate wealth has been crossed that it is so vital to stay on the right side of the limit, and it is in this light that we should understand the Elders' assertion towards the end of the ode that they approve 'prosperity that inspires no resentment' (471). There may be rare individuals who cross over into excess, realize their mistake, and reduce their wealth accordingly; in the third *stasimon* the Elders speak in metaphorical fashion of a man whose ship is caught in a storm and, in an effort to stay afloat, uses a 'sling of due proportion' to cast part of his cargo overboard (1008–13). The Elders are evidently thinking of Agamemnon here, but the mood of hopefulness is quickly dispelled: once blood has been shed, they observe mournfully, there is no way that the deed can be undone (1019–21). In order to remain in command of the Greek expedition the King found it within himself to kill his own daughter, and for this outrageous desecration of the principles of justice he will shortly pay the price.

It is time now to turn back to the three final stanzas of the second *stasimon*. In light of their reflections in the first *stasimon*, we might expect the Elders to have expressed themselves somewhat differently when outlining the position that sets them apart from others: it is not simply great wealth, they could have said, but great wealth followed by acts of impiety or *hybris* that leads to ruin. Why, then, do the Elders speak of the impious act begetting other impious acts and of old *hybris* giving birth to new *hybris*? Is it possible that they are in fact making a rather different point in these stanzas? The key to grasping the nature of the contrast being drawn by the Elders is to turn back to the earlier stanzas of the ode. From the very start, the second *stasimon* is dominated by the pattern of a positive state of affairs turning into a negative one, and for the most part there is some unifying element underlying the transformation. The beguilingly beautiful Helen was revealed to be a destroyer of ships, men and cities; the wedding bond between Helen and Paris turned out to be a source of mourning; the adorable cub in the fable narrated by the Elders became a bloodthirsty lion; and a mindset of indulgent complacency at Troy was swept aside to reveal that a Fury – a divinity of vengeance – had been living in their midst all the while. Finally, according to the view opposed by the Elders, great prosperity leads to insatiable woe, though in this case it is less obvious what underlies the transition from positive to negative, and indeed that is precisely the Elders' objection.

In view of the consistency with which the pattern has been repeated up to this point, we would expect the sequence which the Elders go on to describe to correspond again to the shift from prosperity to disaster. For this to be the case, though, the second generation of impious deeds would need to represent those committed by other people *in response* to the initial wrong done to them.[19] And there is much to be said in favour of this interpretation. First of all, the Elders can then be understood to offer two complete thoughts in their initial summary of the position they favour: one impious deed provokes a further set of impious deeds in retaliation, while just behaviour results in a prosperity that lasts. This also fits with what the Elders say – as far as that can be made out – in the following stanza. The new *hybris* represents the act of revenge provoked by the initial act of *hybris*, and this flourishes among the sufferings of mortals because the crime committed against the victim is what motivates them, or whoever acts on their behalf, to retaliate. That the birth of the new *hybris* seems arbitrary but is determined in advance reflects the fact that, unbeknownst to the perpetrator, punishment is inevitable from the moment the deed is committed. And the birth of Ruin alongside the new *hybris* also makes more sense on this interpretation, since it is through the new act of *hybris* carried out in requital that the original act of *hybris* is punished: disaster comes upon the malefactor by means of further *hybris*.

The clear implication of the Elders' words, though they do not say it outright, is that the Greek army's response to Paris' crime is the equivalent of the new *hybris* born from the old. This helps to explain why the Elders initially speak of multiple impious deeds born from a single one: as mentioned earlier, in other versions of the myth various acts of sacrilege are committed by the Greeks during the sack of Troy, and the Elders have just heard from the Herald about the destruction suffered by the Greek fleet.[20] Far from being a bland restatement of traditional wisdom, then, the position defended by the Elders is one for which it is difficult to find close parallels in earlier poetry. We can understand why it was *possible* that the Greek army would lose all restraint when the moment of victory came, but the idea that, in general, *hybris* is requited by further *hybris* is much more startling. The only explanation, it seems, is that it is the gods who ensure that the cycle of self-generating violence continues.

On this interpretation, there is no suggestion that excessive wealth and *hybris* should be thought of as competing explanations for human suffering. The Elders' point, instead, is that the conditions of excess which give rise to *hybris* are unable to provide the unifying principle they have been seeking from the start of the ode: there is no direct link between the fortunes possessed by the royal house of Troy and by the Greek commanders, and even when a sequence of wrongful acts unfolds within a single family – as in the case of the House of Atreus – the excessive prosperity of the family does not explain why the crimes of its members are committed against one another. Thus there is no need to understand the Elders' remarks in the second *stasimon* as inconsistent with what they say in the first *stasimon*, or see anything strange in the return to the theme of wealth in the final stanza of the ode (when they declare that Justice honours the poor man and departs from gold-spangled abodes).

The lines chanted by the Elders immediately before they hear Agamemnon's death cries (1331–42) rarely receive more than a passing mention in discussions of the play, but the interpretation developed so far allows us to see this passage as a climactic encapsulation of many of the themes and problems discussed in the Elders' earlier choral reflections. Success, they observe, is something that mortals are by nature never sated with, and those who live in 'houses at which people point their fingers' (i.e. the houses of the very wealthy) never refuse to let further wealth enter when it arrives at their door. Here the Elders echo the lines from towards the end of Solon's *Elegy to the Muses* quoted earlier, where the poet observes that wealth has no limit for mortals and that the best off are the most eager to acquire further riches. The Elders then move to the specific case of Agamemnon: despite the god-given success he has enjoyed he is soon to be killed, and they now know that in the process he will pay for the kindred blood shed in the previous generation (1338–40). In the previous scene Cassandra had painted a horrifyingly vivid picture of the group of Furies within the royal house who have become drunk on human blood and refuse to leave (1186–93), and the Elders now see that in Agamemnon's case the sequence of impious actions can be traced as far back as Atreus' murder of his brother Thyestes' children, and the adultery of Thyestes with Atreus' wife which provoked that astonishingly cruel act of vengeance.

From such a perspective the 'moral' and 'amoral' explanations of human suffering seem rather to blur into one another. The Elders never suggest that those who 'kick the altar of Justice into oblivion' are anything other than fully responsible for their crimes and deserving of punishment, even in cases when those crimes are themselves acts of retaliation for the injustice of others. All the same, their reflections in the first *stasimon* suggest that the only way for a person to remain invulnerable to the temptation of *hybris* is to avoid crossing the line separating due prosperity from excess. What hope is there then for individuals, like Agamemnon, who have been born into great wealth? And how many of the rest of us would really be willing to part with a great fortune that suddenly came into our possession? Leaving aside those individuals mentioned by the Elders in the first *stasimon* who have the wisdom to remain satisfied with modest means, for the majority of mortals the importance of luck as a factor in staying clear of *hybris* and the inevitable punishment cannot be underestimated. When the Elders ask at the end of the passage preceding Agamemnon's death cries whether anyone who has heard of the King's impending fate can 'boast of having been born to a destiny free from harm' (1341–42), they are not simply resorting to a commonplace.[21]

To conclude, let us turn back to our earlier question: how much do the choral reflections on the topic of wealth in *Agamemnon* actually illuminate the events of the drama? The first thing to stress is that the Elders do not simply repeat ideas familiar from archaic poetry. The sequence outlined in the first *stasimon*, with excess leading first to *hybris* and then to ruin, may recall ideas expressed by poets such as Solon, but the paradoxical description of Persuasion wielding force is a characteristically Aeschylean touch. Again, the unhelpful labelling of the positions articulated in the second *stasimon* as 'amoral' and 'moral' respectively is perhaps one reason many scholars have overlooked the novelty of the position defended by the Elders: the gods oversee a system of punishment that is both efficient – when they have decided on a person's downfall, they first use that individual to bring about the demise of another individual they wish to destroy – and self-perpetuating.

If we take seriously what the Elders say about the importance of the line between appropriate and inappropriate prosperity, moreover, their pronouncements on wealth provide crucial context for the events dramatized in the play. The weakness of character that allows Paris and Agamemnon to yield to temptation and commit the acts that lead to their downfall is not simply a sign of moral depravity but a consequence of the conditions that have surrounded them since birth, and it is much less obvious that living in circumstances of great prosperity should be thought of as a moral transgression than the acts they go on to commit. From the divine perspective, however, what matters is that in their prosperity and arrogance such individuals have strayed too close to the boundary separating gods from humans. Agamemnon is aware that by walking across the tapestries he risks incurring divine resentment (*phthonos*), but the destruction of the textiles is really just a symbol of the affront to the gods represented by mortal excess and haughtiness more generally. The Elders' reflections may not capture the whole meaning of what transpires in *Agamemnon* – for the relevance of the events in the previous generation we are reliant on Cassandra's intuitions and Aegisthus' one-sided retelling, for example – but they are nevertheless central to the vision of the world communicated by the play. How much the pessimism of that vision is softened by what unfolds in *Eumenides* is a question for another time.

Notes

1 Solon fr. 13.7–13 West.
2 On *hybris* the classic work is Fisher (1992); see also Cairns (1996) for some important qualifications of Fisher's position. On *atē* in Aeschylus, see Sommerstein (2013).
3 Cf. Denniston and Page (1957), 114: 'A momentary dramatic advantage, for those who look forward, is allowed to outweigh a serious flaw in the structure for those who look back; we may well judge that the advantage was too dearly bought'.
4 For an overview of these developments in the scholarship on the tragic chorus, see Gagné and Hopman (2013), 18–28.
5 Dodds (1960), 25 (Dodds is endorsing a similar view expressed by Solmsen). Recent studies that explore the theme of wealth include Seaford (2012),

ch. 11; Bakola (2013); and Gruber (2013). For a list of earlier works that pay due attention to the topic, see Bakola (2013), 227 n3.
6 Cf. Cairns (1996), 19.
7 For a recent discussion of divine *phthonos*, see Eidinow (2016).
8 The phrase translated here as 'the sufferings of mortals' could also be taken to mean 'evil men', but that fits less well with the interpretation defended later in this chapter.
9 Cf., for example, Denniston and Page (1957), 136 ('The opinion which the Chorus here advances as an exceptional and personal one was not in fact at all novel ...'); Sommerstein (2008), II, 89 ('There is nothing new about the belief about to be stated ...'); Raeburn and Thomas (2011), 145 ('... in fact similar ideas – though with more focus on greed than piety – had long since been articulated at Athens by Solon').
10 An exception is Thiel (1993), 188, who nevertheless defends the standard interpretation.
11 Scholars are not always sufficiently clear about how they understand this statement, but the interpretation sketched out here is explicitly held by, for example, Thiel (1993), 188–93 and Raeburn and Thomas (2011), 145–46.
12 This is how they are understood by Conacher (1976), 29: '[There is] a far greater insistence here on the impious deed (*apart* from wealth) as the cause of catastrophe than is always present in the extant Solonian fragments'.
13 Cf. Conacher (1976), 29: 'So despite the initial emphasis on ... the impious deed, rather than great wealth, as the cause of a family's recurrent woes, the "dangerous wealth" theme is still present ... Perhaps the Aeschylean Chorus has not advanced so far beyond Solon after all'.
14 I here tentatively adopt Bamberger's emendation ἔκγονος; for arguments in favour, see Bollack and Judet de La Combe (1981-2), vol. Iii, 393–98.
15 For the three grammatically possible renderings of these lines, see Sommerstein (2008), II, 46, n83.
16 Cf. Denniston and Page (1957), 136. On the cycle of greed and *hybris*, see Balot (2001), 92–93.
17 In translating τάλαινα (*talaina*) as 'audacious' here, I follow Wilson (1971), 297 (who has 'daring').
18 Cf. Sommerstein (2013), 7–8.
19 The position defended in what follows is substantially the same as that put forward by Bollack and Judet de La Combe (1981–82), vol. II, 95, 106–8, 139–41, 148–56.
20 In the case of the storm, the retaliation suffered by the Greeks has a purely divine source, so the pattern described by the Elders presumably only applies when human agents are involved.
21 For Conacher (1987), 48, by contrast, this question is a 'perfunctory moral platitude'.

9

'There is the sea – who can drain it dry?' Natural and Unnatural Cycles in *Agamemnon*

Rush Rehm

Confronting the garments that Clytemnestra has laid out for his arrival, Agamemnon fears that he commits an act of egregious waste by walking on them: 'May no god strike me with envy.[1] / I feel great shame to ruin under my feet the wealth of the house, / spoiling the woven work purchased with silver' (*Ag.* 948–49).[2] Agamemnon tries to limit the damage by removing his sandals, prompting his wife's bold response: 'There is the sea – who can drain it dry? / It breeds ever-renewing supplies of purple dye / for precious fabrics, as endless as silver coinage. / With the gods willing, we can find a remedy for this waste. / . . . our house does not know how to be poor' (A. *Ag.* 958–62).

Clytemnestra refers to the dyes made from the secretion of various Mediterranean molluscs,[3] producing a rare and costly colorant often applied to silk, appropriate to the royalty of Argos. She claims that their presence in the Aegean – and their dye-producing capacity for the palace – is inexhaustible. Any consumption can be restocked; waste is not an issue, for each and every loss can be replaced. Her comparison of the endless supply of dye and silk to silver coinage does not simply mean that they are expensive, as Agamemnon suggests ('purchased with silver', *Ag.* 949). She conflates the replenishment of material from the natural world with the 'endless' circulation of money, as Richard Seaford points out. The idea that real-world resources resemble currency mistakes the symbol of wealth for the actual 'stuff' that money can buy, physical material that can be ruined or consumed by use.[4]

In *Agamemnon*, Aeschylus exposes the danger of assuming – as Clytemnestra does – that the endlessly regenerative powers of nature can restore whatever humans inflict on it: insatiable wealth, wasteful consumption, revengeful bloodletting, foreign wars. As we shall see, nature turns on those who do violence against it and against those who share in nature's bounty.

When her husband takes his final steps on the fabrics, Clytemnestra returns to the natural world as guarantor of renewal, in this case the agricultural cycle:

> With the root back in its home soil
> leaves will grow again to shade us
> from the scorching heat of summer.
> And in winter, your return brings warmth
> to our hearth and home.
> When the seasons change once more
> and Zeus turns the unripe grape to wine
> a cool wind will rise in the house.
> The master walks his home.
>   Zeus, Zeus, harvester, answer my prayers.
> Turn your mind to the harvest at hand.[5]
>
> Ag. 966–74

Agamemnon's homecoming guarantees that nature's restorative powers will return to Argos, season by season, year after year. The ambiguity of Clytemnestra's closing prayer, however, leads us to wonder how this cycle may be affected once she reaps her 'harvest'.

After Agamemnon's murder, Clytemnestra ecstatically re-lives the event, returning to the image of growth from the soil. She compares her joy at spilling her husband's blood to that of 'seed corn rejoicing in the spring rain / that gives it birth, and it bursts into life!' (1391–92) The stream of his blood provides her with a vitalizing source, like rainfall that germinates the seeds. Following her previous speech (quoted above), we may assume this new growth will yield another harvest, as the cycle begins anew. Nonetheless, Clytemnestra hopes that this process has reached its end, pointing to her husband's corpse as proof of finality: 'This is the mixing bowl [for adding water to wine] that he filled with horror / and, coming home, drained to the dregs' (1397–98). The unripe grapes of her earlier speech (970) have matured, have been turned into wine, and Agamemnon has drunk it all down. In Clytemnestra's mind, Agamemnon consumed the evil he himself created, generating no further losses for the house.

Under pressure from the Chorus, however, Clytemnestra admits that Agamemnon's death may not have drained the bowl; by murdering him, she has tapped a source that could refill it with new horror. To ward off this prospect, she offers a truce with the *daimōn*, the 'spirit' that threatens the family with a new round of violence:

> I would make a pact with the spirit [*daimones*]
> in the race – to accept what stands,
> hard though it is to bear.
>   But for the future,

let it leave this house
and wear out another family with murder.
I will rest content with a small share
of what we have – only let the madness
of mutual slaughter depart.

Ag. 1569–76

Acknowledging the cyclical nature of vengeance, Clytemnestra utters the vain wish that she can turn the destructive spirit away from her own family and onto someone else's.

The goddess Athena makes a similar appeal in *Eumenides*, the final play of the trilogy. Like Clytemnestra, the goddess hopes that the destructive force (represented by the Furies, who now threaten Athens) will go elsewhere for its victims:

Do not plant . . . in the young men of my city
that maddening spirit – not aroused by wine[6] – for battle,
like that of the fighting cock ready to make war
in its own nest. Let there be foreign wars, and plenty,
for those with a passion for glory, but spare us civil war
here at home.

Eum. 860–65

Clytemnestra would sidetrack the fury in the race onto another family; Athena would direct the violent quest for glory to external wars with outside enemies. If the destructive drive (whether for vengeance or combat) remains endemic, then the best one can do is deflect the inevitable destruction onto a foreign target – another house, another family, another city – so long as it stays far from home.

We know from the second play in the trilogy that the violence within the House of Atreus does not come to an end. Clytemnestra's peace proposal gains no more traction than her actual offerings at Agamemnon's grave (*Cho.* 138–51). As Orestes puts it, invoking an old saying, 'Even if someone pours out everything he owns / to pay for one life taken, it's wasted labor' (A. *Cho.* 520–21). Only the interference of Athena and the trial in Athens in *Eumenides* preserves the House of Atreus from future bloodshed, freeing Orestes from a death sentence for matricide. As for Athena's hope that foreign wars might provide an alternative to civil strife, Orestes vows that Argos will honour Athens 'with the spear of allies' (*Eum.* 774). If his city ever attacks Athens, his spirit will rise from the grave to stop them. Orestes' final words surely resonated with patriotic Athenians in the audience in 458 BC, proclaiming that Athens has 'a grip no enemy can escape, / one that preserves you and brings you victory in war' (*Eum.* 776-77).[7]

It appears that the cycle of violence has stopped within the House of Atreus, and – more importantly, as Athena hopes and Orestes vows – that Athens will find allies that will lead it to triumph over foreign enemies. However, *Agamemnon* raises serious doubts about such a conclusion, for the Greek conquest of Troy doubles back on the conquerors. Epitomized by Clytemnestra's boast that 'the house does not know how to be poor', Aeschylus portrays human agents bound up in a network of insatiable desire – for revenge, for glory in war, for 'justice', and for ever more 'prosperity'. This desire insures a cyclical process of destruction.

Just before Agamemnon's death cries are heard coming from the palace, the Chorus address the human craving for more:

> For mortals, prosperity has no bounds.
> No one can turn it away from the halls
> that men most greatly admire,
> by saying 'Stay out! No entrance!'
> So for this man [Agamemnon], whom the blessed ones
> granted to seize the city of Priam –
> he comes home honoured by the gods.
> But if he will pay for previous bloodshed
> by giving to the dead payment in full
> with his own death and others to come,
> then who among mortals can boast they are born
> with fortune [*daimones*] and are out of harm's way?
>
> *Ag.* 1331–42

In her plea that the *daimōn* leave her house and afflict another (quoted above, *Ag.* 1569–76), Clytemnestra fails to recognize what the Chorus knows: insatiability cannot be kept away by cutting a deal or saying 'off limits'. As Seaford points out, 'the passage seems to assimilate the insatiability of reciprocal violence [Agamemnon's payback for past bloodshed, with more to come] to the insatiability of prosperity'.[8] The Chorus make just this connection, juxtaposing Agamemnon's impending death with the success and honour he has accrued for his triumph at Troy.

As we shall see in the next section, Aeschylus compares the destruction that results from interlocking 'spheres of insatiability' – wealth, revenge, military conquest – to an assault on the natural world. Once elemental forces come into play, categories like 'friend' and 'foe' prove permeable and are incapable of controlling the consequences.

The fire speech: Bridging the gap

Agamemnon begins with the Watchman describing his nightly task, looking for 'a single beam of light that says Troy has fallen' (*Ag.* 9). Over the course of a year, he has learned 'all about the stars, / which bring us summer, which winter, / the whole story'. His waiting ends when he catches sight of the beacon 'shining like the dawn' (22). Aeschylus sets the action of his play within the diurnal, seasonal, and cosmic cycles of the heavens, which operate beyond the control of humans. To be sure, Clytemnestra has arranged the beacon-relays, but the fire that brings the news operates elementally, doing more than she imagines.

Following the *parodos*, in which the Chorus relate events prior to the war, Clytemnestra delivers her extraordinary 'fire speech'. Combining geographical detail with charged poetic imagery, she describes the path of the beacon-fires that bring news of the Greek victory at Troy. The message travels (with intermittent stops) at the speed of light, drawing together the four basic elements – earth, air, fire, and water – of early Greek cosmogony. The beam of light races through the sky and over the ocean, then reaches a peak or promontory, where watchmen ignite the next fire, the flames rising again into the air, the light racing across the water, reaching the next bit of land. So the pattern repeats, a relay of fire-borne news heading to its final destination in Argos.[9]

Scholars have reconstructed the details of the path of the beacons, and the locations of the outposts work remarkably well in real-world terms.[10] The relay stations also carry important mythical and political meanings. For example, the first fire is lit on mile-high Mt. Ida southeast of Troy, where the judgement of Paris (that led to the Trojan War) traditionally took place.[11] The blaze ignited there mirrors the fires that reduced the city of Troy to ash, merging the means of bringing the news with the actual conflagration of the conquered city.

The next stage in the relay, the Aegean island of Lemnos, was famous as the haunt of Hephaestus, the blacksmith god associated with fire. Clytemnestra invokes his name to explain how the news reached Argos so quickly (*Ag.* 281), fire conceived as a divine force that can span distances faster than normal human means. The watchmen on Mt. Athos kindle the next fire that sends the news to the Makistos range in Euboea, across the narrow straits from the port of Aulis. There, ten years before, storm winds trapped the Greek ships, preventing them from embarking for Troy, and forcing Agamemnon to sacrifice his daughter Iphigenia (*Ag.* 184–245).

After Mt. Messapium in eastern Boeotia, the next outpost is Mt. Kithairon, on the border between Boeotia and Attica. Kithairon plays an important role in other Greek tragedies (notably Sophocles' *Oedipus Tyrannus* and Euripides'

Bacchae), and it dominates the view to the west from Eleutherae, the village associated with Dionysus Eleutherios. This cult of the god gave its name to the Athenian festival (also called the City Dionysia) where Aeschylus presented *Agamemnon* in 458 BC. The next station, described as 'the mountain where goats roam' (*aigiplagkton*, *Ag.* 303), probably refers to Mt. Aegalio ('goat-wandering') that rises between Eleusis and Athens. The adjective 'goat-wandering' carries a hint of the name of Clytemnestra's lover, Aegisthus, also derived from the word 'goat' (*aikz*).[12]

Clytemnestra names the final beacon-station as the 'steep heights of Arachnaion', the 'Spider Mountain' range that extends towards the Mycenaean citadel.[13] Ancient Mycenae lies between two smaller mountains in the Arachnaion group, Mt. Zara to the south and Profitis Ilias (or Agiolias) to the north. Near the top of the latter peak, excavators have found remains of a Mycenaean beacon-station (*phryktoria*),[14] lending archaeological reality to this mythic speech. By the end, the light falls 'on the house of Atreus, / descended directly from the blaze kindled on Mt. Ida' (*Ag.* 310–11), linking Troy and Argos by a chain of fire.[15] Bringing together sea and sky, sun and moon, plain and mountains, Clytemnestra also unites two distant cities whose fates appear as polar opposites.

War in *Agamemnon* has a way of breaking down distinct categories, to the point that 'winner' and 'loser' begin to resemble one another. The power of fire as a natural element subsumes the apparent controlled message of the beacons, and also the flames that destroy Troy. Let us look at how Aeschylus presents the Trojan War, and the way in which the Greek triumph turns back on itself, bringing suffering and disaster on the victors.

The war at Troy: Triumphant illusions

Following her fire speech, Clytemnestra describes the Greek triumph at Troy, beginning with the radically different responses to the outcome:

> Shouts ring loud in the city, but there are two songs I hear.
> Pour oil and vinegar in the same jar –
> they draw apart like enemies.
> So the end of Troy cuts two ways,
> for the victor and for the fallen.
>
> *Ag.* 321–25

The Greeks relish their victory, doing as they please in the conquered city, hungry for 'whatever breakfast the city holds' (331). After fulfilling their rapacious desires, the Greek soldiers sleep 'like happy men, freed from the frost / and dew of the open air, a night / when no guard stands watch' (335–37). At the other extreme, the defeated Trojans clutch the bodies of their dead, knowing that a life of slavery awaits them (326–29). Prophet-like, Clytemnestra warns her countrymen to 'honour the gods of the city / and of the land they have conquered, and their temples, / or those who plunder will be plundered in turn' (338–40). If the Greeks fail to respect these divine forces, 'the anger of the slaughtered may wake, / and evil break out again' (346–47).

Although Clytemnestra begins her account with the drawing apart of incompatible liquids, oil and water, she ends by suggesting that a Trojan-like disaster may await the Greeks. They face a long homecoming across the sea, 'turning the bend and coming back for the second leg of the double run' (*Ag.* 344). The racing metaphor recalls the relay of the beacon-fires that brought the news of victory, linking Troy's fall to the return of the Greek fleet. Clytemnestra's literal 'double-talk' undermines her initial insistence on the totally separate fates of the Trojans and the Greeks, and her admonitions suggest that disaster may find the victorious Greeks as they sail for home.

Long before Clytemnestra's appearance, the Chorus indicate that a similar fate awaits Greeks and Trojans alike on the battlefield: 'broken to their knees, / ground in the dust ... / ... the same / for Greeks and Trojans' (*Ag.* 64–67). Following Clytemnestra's exit, the Chorus seem to forget the reality of death in combat, celebrating the Greek victory as absolute triumph. No Trojan escapes 'the all-covering fish net that neither adult / nor young could leap through, / the great net / of slavery, which is total ruin' (358–62). The image of a trawling net that sweeps up big fish and small contradicts Clytemnestra's later claim of the inexhaustibility of the sea. No renewal offers itself to Trojans trapped in the net of ruin.

But what of the impact on the Greeks who cast this net on Troy? The Chorus return to the recognition that their countrymen died during the war and came home as cremated ash:

War[16] is moneychanger of bodies –
his balance rests on the point of a spear.
From the fires of Troy
he sends dust weighted with tears. / ... /
Packed in the hold, urns swollen with powder
to take the place of a man.

Ag. 438–44

As for the Greeks buried at Troy, 'even there, around the walls / of Troy, lovely bodies / have won their resting place, / the conquerors covered by enemy soil'

(*Ag.* 452–55). The Chorus that began with jubilant celebration of a foreign triumph gradually turn to rage and dismay at the Greek losses, which bring wrenching grief to those who wait at home: 'Anger creeps / against the sons of Atreus . . . / The people's voice is heavy / with a curse; the debt will be paid' (450–51, 456–57).[17] The earlier image of the god of war weighing out cremated 'powder' as if it were gold dust, then balancing it with once-living bodies, confirms that the destruction of war extends in untoward directions.

The Chorus welcome the arrival of the Herald, the first living Greek soldier to come back from the war. Initially, they greet him as someone who can deliver the real story, not like Clytemnestra with her beacon relay that 'signals voicelessly / . . . with fire smoke' (496–97). They hope for face-to-face confirmation of good news, and pray that anyone who wishes for the opposite 'reap the fruit of his mind's perversity (502). As the scene progresses, however, we watch their joy at the Greek triumph mutate into grief.

After a prayer of thanksgiving for his return, the Herald announces in ringing tones the destruction that Agamemnon and the army wreaked on the enemy: 'He dug up Troy with the pick-axe of Zeus / the Avenger, working over the ground: / altars smashed, temples rubble, / the seed of the whole land destroyed' (*Ag.* 525–28).[18] The Herald insists on the utter ruin of the city, for the Greeks made Paris pay for his crime 'with total devastation, / mowing down to the ground his ancestral home' (535–36). His description of the final harvest of Troy mirrors Clytemnestra's claim that Agamemnon has put paid for his crimes, draining them to the dregs. Both perpetrators of violence – Clytemnestra in Argos, the Greek army at Troy – believe they have utterly vanquished their foe, with nothing left in the balance.

However, the image of Agamemnon ruining the seed of the land (*Ag.* 528, 535–36) anticipates Clytemnestra's comparison of her husband's blood to life-giving rain that germinates the seeds in spring (1391–92). The latter carries the possibility that the cycle of bloodshed will continue. Although the defeated Trojans have no power to avenge their city's destruction, the forces of nature – presumably guided by some divine hand – step in to make the victors suffer. With this in mind, we can better appreciate the Herald's account – unprecedented in Greek tragedy – of the nightmare that faced the common Greek soldier at Troy:

> I could tell you of pain –
> crowded nights on the gangways,
> each day groaning with the sea.
> Then, at last, dry land, the greater horror.
> We slept near the walls of an enemy city.
> From the sky a steady drizzle and when it broke,

the meadow dew slowly rotting our clothes,
and everywhere, everywhere, lice.
I could tell you of winter that slaughtered birds,
the unbearable snow from Ida.
And the heat in summer, when waves melted
and calm seized the exhausted sea.

Ag. 555–66

This passage powerfully communicates the actual experience of soldiers at war – first on the sea, and then as they lay siege to the enemy's city. Heat, damp, cold, vermin plague the Greek army, independent of any actual combat.

The Herald then tries to repress these unpleasant memories: 'Our suffering is past. / ... It is right to boast in the light of the sun, / my words soaring over land and sea: / "Remember the time that the Greek army seized Troy!"' (*Ag.* 567, 575–77). As with Clytemnestra gloating over the corpse of Agamemnon, the Herald insists that victory has put an end to suffering. His exultation is cut short by the Chorus, who ask the whereabouts of Agamemnon's brother Menelaus. Echoing their prayer that any who wish the city ill should 'reap the fruit [*karpoito*] of their own perversity' (502), the Herald admits that he cannot 'make bad news sound good, / so that it might bear fruit [*karpousthai*] for any length of time' (620–21). He describes the storm that destroyed the Greek fleet sailing home from Troy.

Fire and water, long the most hateful of enemies,
swore an oath and conspired together,
pledging the destruction the Greek ships.
In the night, a wave of troubles surged up:
winds from Thrace, lightning, and pelting rain,
dashed the ships together and out of sight,
as if driven by a shepherd turned betrayer ...
When the bright sun rose up from the sea,
we saw the Aegean flower [*anthoun*] with corpses
and the churning timber of broken ships ... / ... /
either swamped by the waves,
or smashed into pieces on the rocky shore

Ag. 651–60, 665–66

Recall the image that Clytemnestra uses to contrast Greek joy with Trojan grief – 'Pour oil and vinegar in the same jar – / they draw apart like enemies. / So the end of Troy cuts two ways' (*Ag.* 322–24). The Herald shifts the image from the domestic sphere into a realm of primal elements – high winds, rocky shore, fire, and water *forget* their enmity and join forces in the storm that destroys the Greek armada. The earlier language of harvests and fruit-bearing, of germinating seeds and ruined fertility, come together in the striking image of the salt sea bursting into flower, with corpses as petals, along with the broken timbers of the wreckage. Only luck (664) saved Agamemnon's ship, but we know that his luck will change.

The Herald's experiences sailing to Troy, the long years of war, and the disastrous voyage home have much in common with Clytemnestra's account (320–30) of the fall of the city and the potential dangers awaiting the Greeks on their return She imagines the soldiers sleeping in the city's dwellings, 'sheltered from the soaking dew / and frost of the open sky' (*Ag.* 335–36); the Herald complains bitterly of the rain and dew-soaked encampment near the enemy walls (559–62).[19] Clytemnestra warns the Greeks not to plunder what they should not, for they face a long journey home (341–43); the Herald boasts that the Greeks razed the city to the ground, smashing the altars and temples, destroying the seed of the land (524–28). Clytemnestra emphasizes the two-fold nature of the homecoming – 'the second leg of a double run' (344). The Herald proclaims that 'The house of Priam has paid double for their "mistake"' (537).[20] Like the beacon-fires that link the destruction of Troy to the impending death of Agamemnon, the double-payment paid by Troy ironically suggests the repercussive suffering that awaits the Greeks.

Storm winds had disastrous consequences for Agamemnon even before the expedition sailed for Troy. In the *parodos*, the Chorus describe how northern winds from Thrace (*Ag.* 192) confined the army in the port at Aulis, where the interminable wait 'shredded the flower [*anthos*] of the Greeks' (197) and led Agamemnon to sacrifice his daughter Iphigenia. Ten years later, similar winds from Thrace (654) stir up the storm that destroys the fleet on its homeward journey, causing the sea to 'flower' [*anthoun*] with Greek corpses. The image of storm winds appears again when Clytemnestra welcomes Agamemnon home, comparing him to 'the mainstay and mast of a warship, / . . . / land to a sailor lost at sea, / daylight after a night of storm' (897, 899–900). After Agamemnon's murder, the Chorus dread 'the beating of a rainstorm that will smash the house / with a shower of blood' (*Ag.* 1533–34), anticipating the vengeance that Orestes will take in the next play. Following the matricide, the Chorus lament 'this third storm / that has strewn its wreckage / through the royal palace' (*Cho.* 1065–67). As these passages indicate, storms (both real and metaphorical) join other elemental forces in responding to human acts of waste and destruction.[21]

We learn directly from the Herald, and indirectly from Clytemnestra, that the sack of Troy took the form of a total obliteration. On his arrival home, Agamemnon confirms the annihilation of the city:

Now smoke holds the conquered city.
Only the winds of ruin live, stirring up
in the dying embers the trace of former wealth. /.../
[So] the beast of Argos ground the city to dust.
Shield-bearing young of a wooden horse
timed their birth to the setting stars.
A lion leapt the walls and gorged itself
on raw flesh, lapping up the blood of kings.

Ag. 818–20, 824–28

Casting our mind back to Clytemnestra's fire speech, we can imagine the beacon-flames arising Phoenix-like from the holocaust that reduced Troy to ashes, eventually reaching Argos with the light 'descended directly from the blaze kindled on Mt. Ida' (*Ag.* 311).

Agamemnon's account of the end of Troy also includes an image of generation – the wooden horse 'delivers' the armed Greek soldiers, 'young of the wooden horse' who lay waste to the city and devour the population. The horse as a container stuffed with death-dealing young recalls the cremated remains of the Greek dead, shipped home from the front: 'From the fires of Troy / he [War] sends dust / weighted with tears; / urns stowed in the hold, / filled with ashes instead of living men' (*Ag.* 440-44). The cargo in the Greek ships and the warriors in the 'pregnant' Trojan horse connect those who suffer death with those who deal it out. The Trojan horse as a mother giving birth to killers reverses the Chorus's account of the pregnant hare, on which the twin eagles (representing Agamemnon and Menelaus) fed, turning an omen good for the war into a horrible spectacle of bloodshed. This incident so outrages the goddess Artemis that she demands the Greek general Agamemnon 'pay' by sacrificing his daughter Iphigenia.

We can trace the impulse that sets off these perversions to Clytemnestra's claim that the natural world cannot be violated, because it always renews itself. In this view, nature goes on forever, never suffering depletion or death, much like the Greek gods. As James Redfield points out, given their immortality, the Greek divinities are 'spheres of power rather than significance'.[22] By never diminishing or coming to an end, they lack significant meaning, for time will correct any aberration or make up for anything that happens. Individual actions remain insignificant because their consequences can be undone, forever. In similar fashion, nature understood as inexhaustible can always restore whatever damage it might suffer; therefore any specific harm carries little weight, because it doesn't matter in the long run. The sea will never dry up; the molluscs will always reproduce; the supply of precious dyes will never fail; the palace will never know poverty. Clytemnestra can sacrifice all the wealth of the house to celebrate Agamemnon's return, and never feel the loss.

Unnatural waste and destruction features prominently in *Agamemnon*: the feast of Thyestes, in which Thyestes unwittingly ate the cooked flesh of his own sons (1095–97, 1217–22, 1590–1602);[23] the sacrifice of Iphigenia; the annihilation of Troy; the murder of Agamemnon; Clytemnestra's heartless slaying of Cassandra, the last Trojan. *Choephori* focuses on the matricide, understood as a god-driven call to vengeance and as a primal act of polluting bloodshed. Orestes' potential death at the hands of the Chorus of Furies threatens to perpetuate the carnage, until the Athenian jury acquits him and Athena converts the Furies into Eumenides ('Kindly Ones'). Let us look briefly at the end of *Eumenides*, and relate it to the destructive violence that precedes it.

Blessings, curses, and open borders

Angered at Athena's vote to free Orestes, the Chorus threaten her city, drawing on the agricultural imagery so important a part in *Agamemnon*. Reflecting their autochthonous origin ('We take our place under the earth, / in the sunless dark', *Eum.* 395–96), the Furies curse the very ground of Attica: 'On the earth / we will let loose poison, / unbearable poison that drips into the soil. / … / Spreading leaflessness and childlessness …, / a plague deadly / to humans will race over the land' (*Eum.* 781–87, again at 811–17). Once they accept Athena's offer of a home and sacred rites in Athens, the Chorus of 'Kindly Ones' pray for the city they previously cursed: 'May the bright rays of the sun / speed the prosperous gift of life, / bursting forth from the earth' (924–26).

The Chorus continue their blessings in a manner that 'corrects' most of the perversions of the natural cycle we find in *Agamemnon*:

> Let no wind damage the trees, / … /
> crossing the borders of this land,
> with searing heat that blasts the budding plants.
> Let no crop-destroying
> plague creep over the land.
> May flocks flourish, raised by a good
> shepherd [Pan], and bear twin lambs,
> at just the right time; and may the rich earth
> always bear fruit,
> blessed with the god's gift of rain.[24]
>
> *Eum.* 938–48

Winds are kept in check; so is the scorching heat; harvests are bountiful; animals breed in abundance; the rain brings bounty from the earth; violence is repressed or non-existent.

In each occurrence of violence in the trilogy, however, the natural world reacts, and these elemental powers – often linked to a divine power, and beyond the control of humans – have the final say. With that in mind, one detail in these benisons for Athens should give us pause, and make us wonder how 'localized' such blessings or curses can be. The Eumenides would keep any scalding winds from 'crossing the borders' into Attica (*Eum*. 941). If such winds were to rise up, they surely would not respect territorial boundaries. So too, a plague that poisons the land will not stop at a political border, but infect wherever it spreads.[25]

Of course, the prayers and maledictions of the Chorus are only that, a wish for the future. The same applies to the desires of Clytemnestra that her murder of Agamemnon will have no afterlife; that the house will suffer no repercussions; that the rain of Agamemnon's blood in which she revels will not water the impulse for revenge in others. So, too, for the Herald and Agamemnon, the Greek conquest of Troy must represent a complete action, sealed-off so that no fall-out affects the victors. In each case, events prove them wrong.

Welcoming her husband, Clytemnestra boasts that the resources of nature are infinite, so that any ruin caused by humans will ultimately vanish in the fecundity of replenishment. The blessings at the end of *Eumenides* offer an inspiring vision of that prospect, in which fertility and wellbeing burgeon throughout the land of Attica. However, the prior curses of the Chorus suggest that potential disaster can break out at any time, in response to violent disruption. The human-generated cycle of vengeance and violence relies on a mistaken notion that nature can and will absorb any and all depredations. It cannot, and its cycle of regeneration is not endless, nor does it ultimately respond to human wishes or divine blessings.

Aeschylus had no idea how far the human assault on the natural world would go – that scorching winds, blasted earth, and dying oceans would threaten life on the planet. We may never 'drain the sea dry', but we know that global warming can make it rise until it overwhelms the land, breeds wilder and wilder storms, and kills the very life that it once fostered. Our desires for more may be insatiable, but Aeschylus demonstrates the fatal limits that will trap us if we think we can cut a deal with forces far more powerful than we are.

Notes

1 Literally, 'May no eye of envy strike me from afar'; the implication seems to be that of an envious god, not some jealous Argive. The translations are my own (Rehm 1978, with some modifications).

2 The word usually translated 'tapestries' or 'carpets' means 'things spread out', and later Clytemnestra refers to the fabrics as 'raiments' or 'garments'. Perhaps we are meant to think of rich, but thin, dyed silk, a textile that has no business being lain on the ground, much less walked on.
3 The species include *Haustellum brandaris* and *Hexaplex trunculus*; see Sommerstein (2008), n201 on *Ag.* 959.
4 Seaford (2012), 200–5 and (2004), 148–49, 163, 166–68. Clytemnestra implies that real-world resources like expensive dyes and fabrics operate like silver coinage, circulating more or less indistinguishably (as in the popular phrase 'it's only money'), and never run out.
5 Sommerstein (2008), n204 on *Ag.* 967, thinks that the survival of the root (Agamemnon) means that whatever happens above ground, the tree will grow back to its old glory. However, when Clytemnestra topples the symbol of the house, she cannot be hoping for Orestes' return so that the 'tree' flourishes again. A less vivid translation renders her last two lines, 'Zeus, Zeus, fulfiller, fulfil my prayers; / whatever you intend, fulfil it for me' (*Ag.* 973–74). Lebeck (1971), 73 concludes: 'As leaves are the *telos* ['end', 'fulfilment', 'goal'] of the root, as wine is the *telos* of the grape , Agamemnon's death is the *telos* for which Clytemnestra prays'. If so, then Zeus as ultimate 'harvester' makes imagistic and poetic sense.
6 Commentators say little about this odd qualification, *aoinos*, 'without wine'. It appears that Athena does not mean drunken quarrels but something threatening to political order. One might take a backward glance to *Agamemnon* and the image of winemaking that Clytemnestra uses immediately before and after murdering her husband. For similarities between Athena and Clytemnestra, see Winnington-Ingram (1948), 143–47.
7 Sommerstein (2008), n159 on *Eum.* 773, points out that not long after the *Oresteia*'s premiere in 458, a thousand Argives joined the Athenian army in battling the Spartans at Tanagra (Thucydides 1.107.5); those who fell received a public funeral in Athens (Pausanias 1.29.8–10).
8 Seaford (2012), 202. Compare the Chorus's warnings against extravagant wealth, for ruin comes 'to a house rich with excess, / exceeding what is best. Let enough / prove sufficient, causing no pain / for those endowed with good sense' (*Ag.* 377–80).
9 The cities are separated by some 330 miles as the crow flies, but the beacons cover a far greater distance, given the need for the firelight to cross the Aegean from sufficiently high peaks.
10 Exact realism does not apply in every case. To fill in one of the gaps, Sommerstein (2008), n62 on *Ag.* 287, follows West (1990), 181–83 in positing lost lines that would add the crag on Peparethos (on the island of Skopelos) as the natural intermediary between Mt. Athos and Mt. Makistos (Mt. Kandili) on the north of the island of Euboea.
11 Hedreen (2001), 182–83, 190–200.
12 The Watchman slyly suggests the interloper's presence in the palace after catching sight of the beacon, calling for Clytemnestra to 'get out of bed'

(*Ag.* 27). Aegisthus later enters in person to dominate the close of the play (*Ag.* 1577–1673).
13 Here again, the name of a beacon station suggests a character or image that occurs later in the play, as if the environment itself carried aspects of the story. The Chorus describe the murdered Agamemnon caught 'in this web of the spider [*arachnês*]' (*Ag.* 1492), and the imagery of webs and nets runs through the trilogy; see, for example, Lebeck (1971), 14, 63–68, 132.
14 See http://www.mycenae-excavations.org/about.html, accessed 23 December 2019.
15 The beacon-fire resembles a living being, 'descended directly from' [or 'true offspring of'] its parent flame on Mt. Ida' (*Ag.* 311).
16 The Chorus say '*Ares*', the god of war; a divine personification that echoes Clytemnestra's '*Hephaistos*' (*Ag.* 281) for 'fire', in both cases combining the force with its associated god.
17 As Rose (1992), 212 reminds us, 'Aeschylus presents this phenomenon as an outrage, one that inspires the active resentment of the people'.
18 Sommerstein (2008), n112 on *Ag.* 526, deletes line 527 as a late-fifth-century interpolation; however, Denniston and Page (1957) on *Ag.* 527, and Lloyd-Jones (1979) note on 527, do not. Greeks familiar with the myth knew that the Greek violation at Troy involved great sacrilege, including the murder of a suppliant Priam at the altar of Zeus, and the rape of Cassandra, who took refuge at the temple of Athena; see Hedreen (2001).
19 The Watchman also complains about his 'dew-soaked bed' (*Ag.* 12), linking the physical hardships facing those at Troy who serve the king (Agamemnon) and those at home who must obey the queen (Clytemnestra).
20 Sommerstein (2008), n115 on *Ag.* 537, observes that – given the total destruction of Troy – '"double" seems very much an understatement'.
21 Peradotto (1964) presents a masterful discussion of natural elements in the *Oresteia*, on which I have drawn extensively. He concludes that 'the benevolence or hostility of nature [in the trilogy] depends upon the moral decisions of men, especially of rulers' (378).
22 Redfield (1994), 132.
23 Aeschylus includes several instances of slaughter, feasting, and blood drinking, in which the natural act of feeding turns into a monstrous perversion of itself: the twin eagles devouring the pregnant hare (*Ag.* 114–20), *not* a natural occurrence (see Fraenkel, 1950, vol. II on *Ag.* 156f, p. 96, and Jones, 1962, 125–26); the image of the conquering Greeks like a lion gorging on Trojan flesh and lapping up the blood (827–28); the lion cub raised in the palace that ravages livestock, 'an uncalled-for feast / that steeps the house in blood' (731–32); Clytemnestra's nightmare in which she gives birth to a snake that drinks her blood along with her breast milk (*Ch.* 527–33); the Furies' threat to drink Orestes' blood in payment for the shedding of his mother's blood (*Eum.* 264–67).
24 Here I follow West (1990), 291–92, who emends lines *Eum.* 946–48, followed by Collard (2002) note on *Eum.* 964–68, and Taplin (2018), note on 947–48.

25 The miasma from Polyneices' unburied corpse in Sophocles' *Antigone* provides the clearest example in extant Greek tragedy. Creon thinks he can 'control' the corpse, but the pollution spreads throughout Thebes, spread by birds and other carrion eating animals, fouling the altars of the city; see Rehm (2018).

10

Similes and Other Likenesses in Aeschylus' *Agamemnon*

Anna Uhlig

It has long been recognized that dense and intricate poetic imagery is a distinctive feature of Aeschylean drama. Detailed examination of figurative language proves to be amongst the most rewarding and illuminating ways to delve into his plays. By 'poetic imagery' and 'figurative language', I mean the use of words in a manner that is not, strictly speaking, 'literal' or that goes beyond the boundaries of what we might call 'normal speech'. I put all of these terms between quotation marks because there are many theorists and philosophers of language who justifiably argue that all linguistic expression is a form of 'figurative language'. Granting that this may well be the case, it is nonetheless evident that there is a certain difference between saying 'I got caught in the rain on my way home' and expressing a similar sentiment in the form 'I had to swim home'. The latter employs the verb 'to swim' in a figurative sense, drawing on the familiar association between swimming and water to suggest that the trip home was extremely wet. The language thus creates an 'image' (though not necessarily a visual one) of what the rainy trip was like.

The basic type of metaphorical expression exemplified by the sentence 'I had to swim home' is a staple of fifth-century Athenian tragic drama, whether by Sophocles, Euripides, or Aeschylus. But there is something distinct about the way that Aeschylus makes use of imagery within his plays. He deploys figurative language with such frequency and weaves its thematic strands together so artfully that it can almost function like another character in the dramatic action. It is for this reason that Aeschylean 'imagery' is so often the subject of academic articles and books, and also why it is important to have some understanding of the constituent members of this rather amorphous category.

That said, there is no single, universally agreed upon rubric for the classification of verbal imagery. Naming categories of figurative language, and charting their relationships to each other, has been a contentious undertaking for almost as long as critical terms have been applied to poetry. But, as with so many objects of long-standing intellectual debate, one is always free to forgo essentialism and instead adopt a contingent model that suits the endeavour – in this case, the text – at hand. When it comes to *Agamemnon*, the model suggested by the text places an unusual emphasis on figures of similitude. In particular, the play represents a sustained engagement with the formal structure known as the 'simile', which draws an explicit link between two things through a linguistic claim of likeness (in English, usually the word 'like' or 'as'): She is happy as a clam; I am hungry like the wolf.

In discussions of figurative language, simile is often treated as a simpler, less inspiring correlate to metaphor, the use of 'non-standard' language without any explicit marker, as in my 'swim home' sentence above. Aristotle, for example, claimed that simile is simply a metaphor 'that needs a clarifying word' (*Rhet.* 1407a15). Modern theorists, animated by the idea that metaphor exposes fundamental principles of all language, have also tended to relegate simile, and its overt structures of likeness, to little more than a footnote. But one need look no further than Homer, whose figurative language is almost entirely comprised of extended (so-called 'epic') similes, to wonder if similes are really so simple or unimportant when it comes to understanding Ancient Greek poetry.

Leaving such generalizing reflections aside, let us examine the particular case that Aeschylus' *Agamemnon* presents for taking seriously the figure of simile as a complex tool of poetic imagery in its own right. My aim, as I hope will be clear, is not to elevate simile above other forms of figurative expression, such as metaphor or parable. There is much to be gained from an appreciation of how *Agamemnon* draws on each of these tools to create a composite network of imagery. Nonetheless, a specific focus on similes, as a distinct form of poetic expression, permits an appreciation of how likeness plays an outsized role in characterization and the construction of meaning in the play. As we will see, Aeschylus' fascination with structures of similitude is not limited to the figurative realm. It also reflects one of the critical premises of the playwright's approach to telling the murder of Agamemnon.

* * *

The most striking argument for the importance of simile in *Agamemnon* emerges not from any specific passage of the text, but from comparing the frequency of simile usage across Aeschylus' surviving plays. While this picture is necessarily partial (it excludes the vast majority of Aeschylus' works, which do not survive), it nevertheless reveals that Aeschylus employed simile to different degrees from play to play. On the low end, *Persians* contains only three similes and *Prometheus Bound* (which may not be by Aeschylus) five. The majority of surviving plays hover somewhere around ten similes:

Eumenides has eight, *Choephoroi* and *Seven Against Thebes* each have nine, and *Suppliants* has ten. *Agamemnon*, by contrast, has nearly three times that average, with a remarkable thirty-three.[1] Even taking account of the fact that *Agamemnon* is slightly longer than Aeschylus' other surviving plays, the extreme numerical variation invites scrutiny.

When one looks at the thirty-three similes of *Agamemnon* as a group, one is immediately struck by how, in addition to their frequency, the play's similes are unusually varied in form. Although there are certain speakers, such as Cassandra, around whom a disproportionate number of likenesses cluster, similes are spoken by and about nearly every character who appears on stage. The range of imagery (the similes' 'vehicles', in the technical terminology favoured by scholars) is even broader, extending from animal comparisons to human vocations to natural phenomena and abstract forces. As if in parallel to the broad compass of imagery they employ, the similes also make use of a wide variety of formal structures, employing no fewer than eight different terms to mark the relationship of likeness that is at the core of the figure.

The variation within similes in *Agamemnon* hints at the versatility that Aeschylus discerned in this particular mode of figurative expression. At the same time, it is noteworthy that the terminology that Aeschylus most frequently employs to establish similitude in *Agamemnon* is not one that is commonly found throughout surviving archaic or Classical Greek poetry. Of the thirty-three unquestionable similes in *Agamemnon*, fourteen – nearly half – are structured around the 'improper', and otherwise quite rare, adverbial usage of *dikēn*: the noun 'justice' in its accusative form.

Although found elsewhere in Aeschylus' work, *dikēn* similes are far more frequent in *Agamemnon* and the other *Oresteia* plays than in his other surviving works. As Peter Wilson has argued, it is unlikely that this is simply a coincidence, given that the very idea of justice is a central thematic concern of *Agamemnon*, and the *Oresteia* as a whole.[2] Viewed in this way, one might say that 'justice' introduces the very first simile of *Agamemnon*, when the solitary Watchman laments that he has been 'been crouching *like a watch-dog* here on the Atreidae palace roof' (2–3, my italics). It is 'justice' that allows Clytemnestra to wonder if Cassandra's language is 'unstructured *as a swallow's* rasping scream' (1050, my italics). And it is 'justice', as the play draws to an end, that casts the Chorus's sense of doom as '*like a black crow* rasping its hoarse tuneless hymn of exaltation' (1472–73, my italics).

The conflation of 'justice' and 'likeness' through the adverbial use of *dikēn* introduces a degree of uncertainty and instability into the similes of *Agamemnon*. Sometimes it can take a moment to recognize that Aeschylus is composing a simile, as when Cassandra describes Clytemnestra's murderous plans at lines 1229–30. The passage is normally translated along the lines that

Stuttard follows here, 'like a black malignant demon she will work her will'. But the same Greek could be plausibly rendered 'accomplishing the justice of a malignant black demon'. In moments such as this, the ostensibly simple operation of comparison (the function 'this is like that') on which similes are founded is shown to be far from straightforward.

The profusion of *dikēn* similes in *Agamemnon* harmonizes with another complicated model of comparison that 'justice' introduces into the trilogy, namely the trial through which the trilogy is resolved in *Eumenides*. Orestes, having avenged his father's murder by killing his mother, is made to stand trial for the deed in Athens. Although Orestes' defence is partially premised on the divine sanction for his actions (it was Apollo who demanded the killing), the trial is primarily an exercise in comparison. The murder of Agamemnon is set next to the murder of Clytemnestra, and the jury is asked to decide which is more deserving of vengeance. The fundamental resemblance between the two deaths, the similarities of which are repeatedly and explicitly thematized throughout *Choephoroi*, is matched by the filial responsibilities that both victims claim from Orestes. It is only through Athena's adjudication in favour of the male parent that the seemingly comprehensive equivalency of the two deaths is interrupted. Gender intrudes on the trial's otherwise balanced equation, tipping the scales in favour of what Froma Zeitlin has called the trilogy's 'dynamics of misogyny'.[3]

But before Athena steps in with her deciding vote, *Eumenides* presents a vision of civic justice that functions, to an almost exaggerated degree, as a kind of legal simile: this murder is like that one. The figurative language of likeness that threads through the trilogy is expanded to comprehend the essential questions of life and death that its plays explore and seek to understand. Nor are Agamemnon and Clytemnestra the only ones whose deaths are assimilated to the *Oresteia's* grim calculus of similitude. Alongside their murders, we are asked to apply a frame of likeness to the deaths of Cassandra and Aegisthus, as well as to those of Iphigenia, the children of Thyestes, and the countless Argive dead at Troy, these last poignantly marked by the mournful equivalence by which Ares trades 'corpses in exchange for living men' (438).

* * *

Death is not the only fulcrum for extravagant comparison in *Agamemnon*. The living, too, find form through an almost indecipherable network of mirrored likenesses. The most extreme example of this tendency is found in the so-called 'lion in the house' passage, recounted in the third *stasimon*. The Chorus break off recounting Helen's ill-fated arrival in Troy to tell the story of how 'a man once reared a lion-cub in the palace' (717). The lion was beloved by the man and his family. 'But gradually it grew and it revealed its innate character to those who'd nurtured it' turning on the royal family and slaughtering them all. The 'lion in the house' is not a simile (though it does contain one, to which we will turn in a moment). Unlike a simile, the short narrative, which is best labelled a parable or an allegory, does not explicitly identify likeness. It gestures towards equivalences without stating them outright.

Given the context in which the lion parable is situated, the first likeness adduced by most readers is to Helen herself. Just as the lion was adored before turning on its foster family, so too did Helen arrive at Priam's palace to a warm welcome, only to prove herself a fatal intruder. The parable thus replays the *stasimon*'s first two stanzas. The lion-cub's growth mirrors the transformation of Helen's bridal song to lament as recounted in the earlier part of the *stasimon*. But, as Bernard Knox demonstrated in a now famous article, the similarities suggested by the lion-cub do not end with Helen.[4] In fact, Knox makes clear, Aeschylus endows the lion-cub with particulars that allow him to stand as analogue to nearly every human character in *Agamemnon*, as well as many in the trilogy's subsequent plays. I won't rehearse Knox's masterful analysis here, but encourage readers to seek out his interpretive insights for themselves.

For Knox, the parable is a quintessential example of how Aeschylus uses networks of imagery to weave complex structures of meaning across his dramas. But even as the lion-cub serves as a broad paradigm for Aeschylean imagery in all of its complexity, it also calls attention to the fact that, in *Agamemnon*, this imagery frequently finds shape in 'simple' relationships of likeness. It is in this light that we should be sure not to overlook the simile embedded in the lion-cub tale. Describing how the royal family doted on the docile young cub, the Chorus claim that 'the children loved it and the old men pampered it, *just like a new-born child*' (724, my italics). The simile is not ground-breaking, given the context. It appears to do little more than emphasize the integration of the animal into the human household. But in so far as the simile explicitly reminds us that likeness is also a way of playing a role, of inhabiting a place or adopting a behaviour not quite one's own, it helps to recast the operation of similitude as one of transformation. By being *like a new-born child* the lion-cub is able to fulfil the role of new-born child, at least temporarily.

Multiple characters and events can be linked through their resemblances, as the 'lion in the house' parable so aptly illustrates. But it is equally significant that a single character can have multiple aspects, exhibiting similarities to different things at different times. So the lion-cub is 'like a new-born child' in the first phase of its rearing, and only after time (the Greek *chronistheis* literally means 'he passed time') does the animal turn murderous, no longer performing the similitude that once defined his position in the palace.

* * *

Before looking at the importance of overabundant similitude in *Agamemnon*, it will be helpful to note one moment in which likeness is conspicuously limited. Midway through the *parados*, the Chorus interrupt their account of Agamemnon's sacrifice of Iphigenia at Aulis in order to offer their reflections on the power of Zeus (the so-called 'Hymn to Zeus', 160ff.). The digression begins with a reflection on the proper name for Zeus, followed by an expression of *aporia* (bewilderment) at the prospect of finding something to which Zeus may be compared (*ouk echo proseikasai* at line 163 translates literally to 'I am unable to compare').

It has often been asserted that, by questioning how Zeus should be addressed, the first sentence of the Hymn to Zeus calls attention to the (uncertain and relativized) nature of language itself, a subject that scholars have seen thematized in particularly sophisticated ways in *Agamemnon*.[5] But when one takes account of the close integration of thought across this stanza, the Chorus's reflections on nomenclature appear more limited in scope, resulting directly from their inability to find adequate similitudes with which to speak. A single name must suffice when likenesses do not provide avenues for exploring multiplicity.

The failure of comparison that inaugurates the Hymn to Zeus is, however, the exception in *Agamemnon*. The stark singularity which the Chorus attach to Zeus' name stands in contrast to the exuberant variety of *comparanda* that are invoked elsewhere, as when Clytemnestra celebrates her husband's return with a catalogue of 'names' (*prosphthegmata* 903) that she might use of him:

> I should speak of him, my husband, as the watchdog of our house, our saviour, mainstay of his ship, the deep-set pillar shouldering the vaulting roof, the only son, the dry land seen by sailors, when all their hope is gone, the sun's rays breaking out in stormy weather, the cool spring splashing on the stones for thirsty travellers.
>
> 896–901

Although Clytemnestra's Greek does not couch her likenesses in the formal structure of simile, she seems to be engaging in an exaggerated version of what Richard Hunter has called the 'likeness' game, in which companions adduced comparisons for each other's attributes and behaviours.[6] Although it is most often associated with sympotic revelry and ribald humour, the likeness game could also be played in earnest, and it is in this more sober guise that the game appears in *Agamemnon*. Clytemnestra here plays on a range of similitudes to paint a picture of Agamemnon as strong, dependable and beloved (never mind that she actually thinks none of these things). The density of the imagery emphasizes its variability, as each likeness adds something new to the verbal portrait.

Clytemnestra is often found as both the speaker and object of similes, but no character in *Agamemnon* is more closely linked to the figurative structures of likeness than the Trojan princess Cassandra. Not only does she give voice to the greatest number of similes after the Chorus, she is also the character most frequently described by similes. After attention shifts to her silent presence onstage at line 1035, no fewer than ten similes are deployed to describe her various attributes.

Clytemnestra imagines that her speech will be 'primitive, barbarian, unstructured as a swallow's rasping scream' (1050). And that, in death, she sang her last laments like a swan (*kuknou dikên*) (1444). The Chorus view Cassandra's arrival at Argos as 'like an animal just taken from the wild' (1063). She is 'like a hunting-dog, keen-scented' as she noses out the murderous past of the House of Atreus (1093), 'just like a nightingale' lamenting her own death (1140) and yet is able to face her fate 'bravely like a beast to sacrifice' (1298). Cassandra gets in on the game as well. Her speech, she assures the Chorus, 'won't blush coyly out from gauzy veils *like some new bride*, but *like a fresh breeze* it will fan and race to meet the sun-rise' and surge up like a wave (*kumatos dikēn*) (1178–83). Picking up the scent of past murders, she likens herself to 'a marksman' who has hit his target (1194). Sensing her impending death, Cassandra refuses to 'tremble like a bird caught in the woods' (1316).

Within the scene as a whole, the numerous similes paint a complex picture of Cassandra. Bestial and birdlike, but also, in her own estimation, a force of nature and a human agent: a marksman, but not a bride. The likenesses produce an interconnected, yet not entirely consistent series of images. Even as they help us to understand Cassandra, they preclude any conclusions as to her character or role in the drama. Such an inconsistency squares with Cassandra's earlier experiences at Troy where, clad in her prophetic robes, she was

> mocked by my family, my enemies, all their conviction empty, and they called me names, talaina, like a gypsy sham, a refugee, I bore their taunts of beggar, pauper, tramp.
>
> 1271–74

Like Agamemnon on his return to Argos, Cassandra in Troy inspired a fulsome likeness game, but with an aim to disparage rather than to praise. Cassandra's unhappy experience of the likeness game differs in another important respect: the insults were occasioned by her priestly attire, the outward symbols of Apollo's unfortunate gift of a prophetic vision destined never to be credited by others.

Cassandra's recollection of past likenesses in Troy brings out two critical facets of her experience in Argos. On the one hand, Cassandra's memory of insults at Troy is immediately occasioned by her decision finally to reject her priestly robes. Addressing herself directly to Apollo, a presence unseen by all but herself, Cassandra removes the physical markers of her divine gift.

> So why keep these symbols still of my disgrace, this sceptre and this garland? No! Damnation take them! There's my response to you, there on the ground! Go, give some other girl your wealth of ruin – not me. Look! Look! Apollo himself's stripping me of my prophetic costume.
>
> 1264–70

Undressing on stage, Cassandra seeks to extract herself from the role of prophet. Through this act of defiance she hopes perhaps to escape the likenesses that the costume invites, even as she recognizes that the same fate may yet await 'some other girl', much as the lion-cub's attributes could be seen in many.

Cassandra's action gives material form to the likeness game in which her prophetic gift has enmeshed her. Her sceptre and garland are physical correlates to the verbal similitudes that transform her by turns into a bird and a dog, a bride and a beggar. Likeness, the scene suggests, is not limited to the names we use. It is not simply a performance in and of language. It is a practice undertaken by bodies as they adapt to different roles. The insight is doubly pertinent, inviting us not only to contemplate the role that the Trojan princess has been forced to play, but also the tools by which actors in the theatre transform themselves to fit the many roles that they are asked to play.

Through the range of similes applied to her and her conspicuous performance of embodied similitude, Cassandra represents a powerful locus for contemplating likeness in *Agamemnon*. At the same time, her own prophetic language translates the dramatic action into an extended similitude. Her vision of the House of Atreus and the events past and future that take place there are often presented through formal similes. Clytemnestra is plotting murder 'like a witch, who works her poison' (1260), the putrid smell of the house is 'like the stench that issues from the grave' (1311). She even undertakes her own likeness game in her search for a proper way of describing Clytemnestra:

> She is – how should I name her for her butchery insatiate, this beast, this amphisbaena, this, this Skylla crouching in her cave, this gorgon drowning sailors, this, this mother spawning death, her hot breath fetid

for her family, the breath of Ares, god of battle, stirring fighting into death. Oh, how she raised the cry of victory, all boasts, bravado like a general who's turned a battle into rout.

1232–37

Not all of Cassandra's visions are so clear in spelling out relationships of likeness.

But the Chorus nevertheless grasp they are meant to be thinking in similitudes. When Cassandra warns the Chorus to 'keep the bull from the heifer' (1125–26), they are unable to understand her precise meaning but are able to achieve a generalized comparison: 'I compare these things to evil' the chorus respond (1131), employing the same verb of comparison (*proseikazô*) that they used to describe their failed comparison of Zeus in the *parodos*. Later they are overcome by fear when they recognize Cassandra's description of the feast of Thyestes, claiming to hear her speak 'not in likenesses' (*ouden exêkasmena*) (1244).

This last comment reflects one of the core facets of the similes and similitudes of *Agamemnon*: no matter how simple they may appear, they are never straightforward. Even when we (think we) 'know' how the relationship of comparison is being drawn, the imperfectly aligned structures of similitude ('like' as opposed to 'is') introduce just enough difference to produce a space for reflection and contemplation. The Chorus (believe that they) 'truly' know the story of Thyestes and his children, so they deny similitude and see only absolute identity. But when it comes to things that are less familiar, such as the imminent murder of Agamemnon, they can grasp meaning only through the frame of likeness.

* * *

We now have a general sense of how Aeschylus deploys likeness as a critical figurative mode within *Agamemnon*. But no real understanding of the importance, and distinctive character, of similes within this play can be achieved without examination of the most famous, and certainly the longest, simile in the play: the vulture simile that the Chorus use at the outset of the *parodos* to illustrate the wounded rage of the Atreidae as they embark upon their war against Troy.

> calling in their fury for a strong retaliation – *like vultures screaming in their lonely grief, which soar and circle high above the empty nest, their young all dead, their great wings dipping, rising in the sun like oars, now all their vigilance, their long hours caring for their growing chicks is gone; but*

> *there is one high on the mountain-crag – Apollo, Pan or Zeus – who hears the birds' lament, their piercing screaming tearing at the skies they share, and so in time against the one who did this thing, he sends the stalking demon of revenge, the wraith of retribution.*
>
> 48–59

Whereas the play's other similes are mostly one or two words in length, the vulture simile of the *parodos* provides a full narrative and emotional portrait of the birds, grieving for their lost young. The structure is, unmistakably, that of the 'epic' simile, the extended form of similitude most closely associated with the *Iliad* and *Odyssey*. Epic similes can run over multiple hexameter lines and, given their length, often take on a narrative power of their own, employing relationships of likeness to subtly shift the focus of the events that they are meant to be illustrating, as when, in a particularly extreme example in Book 23 of the *Odyssey*, a simile that begins as a likeness of Odysseus' tears of joy shifts seamlessly into an emotional portrait of his wife Penelope (*Od.* 23.231–39).

The shifting focus of epic similes, like the multiplicities embedded in the seemingly simple 'lion in the house' parable, can suggest connections between characters as well as revealing different facets of or perspectives on a single character. Thus the vulture simile, in so far as it compares the Atreidae to grieving (avian) parents, suggests darkly ironic connections to the grief that their war will cause, both in the specific case of Clytemnestra grieving the loss of her daughter Iphigenia and to the general experience of the people of Argos who will mourn their many sons lost at war. At the same time, the simile achieves a marked shift in focus over the course of its narrative development. At the outset, the Chorus emphasize the agency of the Atreidae in prosecuting the war. But by the end of the simile, divinely sanctioned vengeance has become the dominant motif. No longer is the marital might of the Atreidae at the centre of the Chorus's thought. Rather, they now assert that the simile illustrates Zeus' agency; how 'in power, greater than the power *they* wield, Zeus of the family, Xenios, the god of guests and friends, sends out the two Atreidae against Paris Alexandros' (60–62).

The vulture simile employs a distinctly Homeric voice to exploit the flexibility of thinking with likenesses. As the first developed imagery at the start of the *parodos*, it also inaugurates an extended reflection on, and radical reimagining of, the extended epic simile that will continue throughout the programmatic opening choral song. To understand how this more protracted engagement with the simile form works, it is necessary to consider the specific Homeric similes on which Aeschylus drew in developing his vulture imagery.

Traditionally, scholars have identified two specific similes as models for Aeschylus' vultures: *Iliad* 16.428–31, a martial simile in which Patroclus and his Trojan opponents are said to shriek like vultures as they make their way into battle and *Odyssey* 16.213–21, a more emotional portrait that likens the weeping Odysseus and Telemachus to sea-eagles or vultures lamenting for their lost young. But scholars have overlooked another Homeric simile that seems to have had a role in shaping Aeschylus' vultures. Although it has no vultures, the famous simile of the cranes and the Pygmies, which marks the beginning of what is now called Book 3 of the *Iliad*, also represents a critical influence on Aeschylus' vulture simile. In recognizing the importance of this third Homeric model, we not only enrich our appreciation of the vulture imagery itself but gain a better understanding of the role of this striking likeness within the larger frame of the *parodos*.

The simile comes as the Trojans and Achaeans are marching into battle. The shriek (*klangē*) of the Trojan forces is compared to that of cranes, who are described as involved in a somewhat obscure conflict with the 'men of the Pygmies'.

> And then when each side was arrayed with their commanders, the Trojans marched forward with a shriek (*klangē*) and cry just like birds, like the shriek (*klangē*) of cranes in the sky, who have fled the winter and unimaginable storms and fly with a shriek (*klangē*) from the flows of Ocean bringing death and doom to the men of the Pygmies and from high in the air bring forward the evil strife. And so the Achaeans marched forward in silence breathing might, eager in their breasts to come to each other's defense.
>
> *Iliad* 3.1–9[7]

Like Aeschylus' vulture simile, Homer's cranes and Pygmies simile recounts an extended narrative of animals in conflict. The fact that the cranes are not only rousing to battle, but must undertake a lengthy voyage to find their enemies, is a further point of resemblance with Aeschylus' Atreidae as they prepare to sail for Troy. No less significantly, Homer's cranes and Pygmies simile engages in an overt shift across its length: the opening similitude is drawn between the noise of the Trojans and the cranes, but the conclusion highlights a relationship of inversion, contrasting the Achaeans' silence with the clamour of the birds (and thus the Trojans).

But the most important reason for considering this simile as a model for Aeschylus is the threefold repetition of the noun shriek (*klangē*), which results in an especially vivid link between Trojans and cranes. In Aeschylus' vulture simile, the war-cry of the Atreidae is signalled by the verbal form of this same 'shriek' root (*klazontes*, 48). Within Aeschylus' simile, the term is only used once and not repeated. The description of the vultures' 'piercing screaming' employs other terminology. But after the vulture simile's conclusion the same verb for shrieking (*klazō*) is used three additional times over the course of the *parodos*, and in ways that suggest Aeschylus meant to link the various voices of his choral ode in a complex relationship of sonic similitude not unlike that achieved by Homer in his cranes and Pygmies simile.

A little later in the *parodos*, when the prophet Calchas interprets the portentous eagles whose appearance at Aulis conveys Artemis' anger at the Atreidae, he is said to 'shriek out' (*apeklanxen*, 156) his prophecy. The eagles are themselves an internal correlate to the vultures of the opening simile, a reprise of the figurative narrative marked both by close similarities and striking differences. The grieving vultures of the simile are now transformed into ruthless hunters, and the parental grief is now felt by their prey, the hapless hare. Both birds are explicitly designated as likenesses for the Atreidae, a fact which draws attention to the range of roles that the leaders inhabit. The Chorus recount how Calchas 'looked on the Atreidae, battle-ready both and proud, and recognised in them the eagles glutting on the hare' but by using the same verb of shrieking that introduced the vulture simile to describe his interpretation, they bind these two avian images into a kind of unconventional extended simile of its own. These birds are like these birds are like the Atreidae.

A further layer of likeness is added in the Hymn to Zeus. As we saw above, the digression is already introduced by the contemplation of Zeus' incomparability. But comparison nonetheless makes its way into the Hymn when the Chorus praise whoever shrieks (*klazōn*) 'the cry of victory for Zeus' (174). The shrieking here is both similar and different to that which came before, just as Zeus himself is said to be unlike previous gods (Uranus and Cronus) who were overthrown (168–72). The pattern of likenesses extends.

The verb occurs one further time once the Aulis narrative is reprised, and is again used to describe the speech of Calchas. The seer is said to have shrieked (*eklanxen*) for 'a second salve to soothe the storm-winds, baleful and more bitter for the generals' (201). This final usage clearly echoes the previous application of the verb to Calchas' prophecies at 156, while at the same time incorporating some of the vengeful spirit that motivated the initial shrieks of the Atreidae (48). But it also inaugurates a new phase of this oddly dislocated play of similitudes, in so far as Calchas' second speech will ultimately result in the sacrifice of Iphigenia, a brutal act which is described as a silencing of the young woman's voice.

Iphigenia's inability to speak is the primary focus of the Chorus' account of her death. They tell of how Agamemnon instructed his henchmen 'to gag her mouth, her lovely mouth, to muffle any words that might bring down a curse upon the house' (235-37). And they describe how Iphigenia, bound and gagged, cast 'darting looks to melt the heart, lovely as a girl looks in a picture, wanting so to speak, as often in her father's halls she'd sung at banquet, her voice pure, lovely as a virgin's voice is pure' (240-45). The description contains its own internal likenesses, both in the form of a simile comparing Iphigenia to a painted image and as a temporal contrast between a past full of song and a present of silence. But the thematization of Iphigenia's silence also fits her murder into the pattern of similitude marked out by the cranes and Pygmies simile: Iphigenia's fatal silence inverts the shrieks that have filled the *parodos* up to this point, mirroring Homer's concluding contrastive focus on the silence of Achaeans. Even in this likeness, there is an important difference, since the silence in the Homeric model is a positive attribute, highlighting the courage and discipline of the Achaean forces. In Aeschylus' hands, silence stands for death, and extends from Iphigenia to the Chorus, who refuse to speak 'what happened next' (248).

Through the lens of the cranes and Pygmies simile, we can see how the parodos reimagines Homeric simile in a sophisticated new form. This particular form of the likeness game not only lets us see new facets of the different parts of the ode, but understand its various components in relationship to each other. At the same time, by setting this radical experiment in similitude at the outset of his play, Aeschylus forestalls any assumption that his approach to simile will be in any way simple.

* * *

Even so, a more nuanced understanding of *how* similes and similitudes work in *Agamemnon* is not the same as an explanation as to *why* the play is so fascinated by this particular type of relationship. If similes in *Agamemnon* are a lens through which to view multiplicities and transformations, it would be foolish indeed to try to divine any single or definitive explanation for their prominence in the play. Nevertheless, the extreme Homeric tenor of the *parodos* does invite some speculation of a more generalized character.

In particular, we should not forget the unique role that the narrative of Agamemnon's fateful homecoming plays in Homer's *Odyssey*. The events that comprise Aeschylus' *Oresteia* are recounted on numerous different occasions over the course of Homer's epic poem, almost always as an explicit analogue to the situation faced by Odysseus and his family. From within the narrative logic of the *Odyssey*, the characters of the *Oresteia* exist only as likenesses; as models, positive and negative, from which the agents of the epic can better understand themselves and their choices. The choices of Agamemnon and his household are examined as if through a prism, with each new instance of similitude inviting a new perspective on the tale. Homer asks by turns that we consider now the fate of Aegisthus, now the choices of Orestes, now the emotions of Agamemnon, now the guile of Clytemnestra. So too, perhaps, Aeschylus deployed the stunning array of similitudes in his *Agamemnon* to ensure that the tale retained, albeit in adapted form, the status of archetypical comparandum that Homer assigned to it. Aeschylus may be putting the fate of Agamemnon at centre-stage, but in dramatizing this myth he employs similes and other structures of likeness to ensure that the tale still retains the essential character of its Homeric forebear.

Notes

1 An exact number is difficult to pin down. Even though similes have distinctive characteristics as compared to metaphor, certain formulations are nevertheless ambiguous as to whether they should be classed under this heading. Lists can be found in Earp (1948), 00 and Garvie (1969), 64; see also Rosenmeyer (1982), 121.
2 Wilson (2006).
3 Zeitlin (1978).
4 Knox (1952).
5 See in particular Goldhill (1984).
6 Hunter (2004), 5; see in particular the insightful discussion of Ford (2017), 12–14 exploring the importance of 'eikones' in Platonic thought.
7 My translation.

11

Agamemnon, Warfare and Its Aftermath

Isabelle Torrance

The extraordinary and grisly revenge plot dramatized in Aeschylus' *Agamemnon*, in which Clytemnestra murders her husband and his war captive the Trojan prophetess Cassandra, is, without a doubt, the most shocking and gripping aspect of the play. Beyond these acts of domestic bloodshed, however, it is important not to lose sight of the context of warfare and its aftermath, in which these murders play out. In many ways, the *Agamemnon* is a tragedy about warfare and its impact. It looks back to the beginning of the Trojan War in the lengthy opening choral song, and to Agamemnon's decision to put his military duty above his duty as a father when he sanctions the offering of his daughter Iphigenia as a human sacrifice to aid the launch of the military campaign. Avenging the slaughter of Iphigenia is Clytemnestra's primary motivation in plotting Agamemnon's murder. Moreover, the tragedy provides vivid details, through the reports of the Herald, of the miseries and horrors endured by ordinary soldiers both during the siege of Troy and on the return journey to Greece. The sufferings and humiliations of women in war are represented most poignantly through Cassandra, once a princess now a slave and a rape victim in a foreign land. The family of Agamemnon may well be cursed, as Cassandra's visions of the past and future confirm, but if the household (*oikos*) functions as a microcosm for the state (*polis*) in Greek tragedy, then even the internecine atrocities within the family's history can be mapped onto a broader social context.[1]

Fifth-century BCE Athenians had much experience of warfare and Aeschylus himself was a war veteran. He had fought in the Persian Wars, certainly at the Battle of Marathon in 490 BCE, where Herodotus reports that he lost his brother Cynegirus (*Histories* 6.114), and probably also at the battles of Salamis and Plataea in 480 and 479.[2] In 480, Athens was besieged by the Persians. Most of the citizens were evacuated but those who remained and had barricaded themselves into the Acropolis were slaughtered when the Persians took control of the Acropolis and burned its buildings (*Histories* 8.51–54). It was soon after this that the Athenian naval forces defeated the Persians at the Battle of Salamis, which was dramatized eight years later by

Aeschylus in his tragedy *Persians*. In 479, the Athenians decisively repelled the Persians at the Battle of Plataea. Athens and her allies then continued their military exploits by besieging Thebes in retaliation for Theban capitulation to the Persians and their failure to lend support to the defence efforts. The siege was resolved after twenty days (*Histories* 9.86–88), but these examples of Athenian military campaigns, both defensive and offensive, highlight the degree to which both Aeschylus and his audience were sensitive to the conditions and impact of warfare. In this chapter, we will examine the representation of warfare in *Agamemnon* and we will conclude by looking at adaptations of the *Agamemnon* story told in the context of modern warfare through Louis MacNeice's translation, Seamus Heaney's 'Mycenae Lookout' poems, and Colm Tóibín's novel *House of Names*.

Human sacrifice

There are a very small number of references to human sacrifice in historical sources relating to ancient Greece, but no archaeological evidence confirms that the ancient Greeks ever did practise human sacrifice. Classical Greeks seem to have believed that human sacrifices had occurred in their distant past, and the idea of human sacrifice as a concept was important throughout antiquity.[3] Certainly, the ancient Greeks were familiar with animal sacrifice in various forms. These included sacrifices made at religious festivals, which were consumed at a subsequent feast, as well as pre-battle sacrifices and sacrifices made in response to adverse weather conditions where the animal was not eaten but discarded.[4] In *Agamemnon*, the sacrifice of Iphigenia at Aulis functions both as a pre-battle offering and as a response to the difficult weather that prevents the naval fleet from sailing. As a human sacrifice, however, it is a horrific distortion of normative custom where the cultural language and imagery of animal sacrifice is applied to the murder of a human. The sacrifice of an animal followed a distinctive ritual pattern where an animal deemed to be a perfect specimen was led in a procession to the sacrificial altar. The sacrificial knife was hidden from the animal's view, and its head was sprinkled with water eliciting a symbolic 'nod' of assent to the sacrifice. An animal that struggled at the point of death was considered an ill omen.[5] It is in this context that we should consider Aeschylus' description of the sacrifice of Iphigenia. She is lifted above the altar on her father's orders 'like a yearling goat', face down, and gagged by force so that she cannot curse her father's house (232–38). Iphigenia's pleas for her life prove meaningless to the war-hungry army officers (228–30). These are men she knows by name, her father's friends, whom she has previously entertained with song at banquets in her father's halls (242–47). She is a young teenager, called 'unbulled with a pure voice' (245). The obscure term 'unbulled' (*ataurōtos*) seems to refer to a sacrificial heifer who has not mated, and the phrase equates Iphigenia with an unblemished and therefore ideal animal sacrifice. The purity of her voice creates an unsettling conflation in this image between a human and an animal sacrificial victim. Although she is gagged, she still manages to plead with her eyes albeit to no avail (240–41). The moment of Iphigenia's death is captured as a still frame for the audience as if she were 'in a painting' (242). It is very clear that the event is terribly ill-omened, and that Iphigenia struggled until the last moment to avoid her death.

This ominous pre-battle sacrifice, then, highlights how military duty and lust for war can work to betray basic human values. In resolving his dilemma, Agamemnon sets his martial role and his allegiance to the Greek army above his duty as a father. He acts in the interests of the army, whose soldiers are idle and starving (194), but the campaign is one of aggression launched on the questionable pretext of retrieving his brother's cheating wife. This pretext masks the true motivation for the war, which is a hardly concealed greed for Trojan wealth. Agamemnon's opening speech on his return from Troy evokes a grotesque image of the city's ashes blowing about and sending forth 'thick puffs of wealth' (818–20) even in its destruction. His desire to be like the wealthy Trojan king Priam is what persuades him to walk on the embroidered cloths set down by Clytemnestra as a psychological trap, an equivalent to the 'nod' of assent elicited from a sacrificial victim (918–49). Moreover, Agamemnon's sacrifice of Iphigenia is made in response to the interpretation of an omen by the army's seer Calchas, an omen which graphically foretells the slaughter of the innocent in the war to come. A pair of eagles feast on a pregnant hare and her unborn young, representing Agamemnon and his brother Menelaus on their ruthless destruction of Troy. The feast angers the goddess Artemis, who then ostensibly demands Iphigenia's sacrifice (105–37). This will lead to a successful campaign, but the prophet also refers to 'unforgetting, child-avenging Wrath, a guileful keeper of the house' (155), an allusion to Clytemnestra's future vengeance. She, too, will apply the language of animal sacrifice to her butchery of Agamemnon and Cassandra when she says that the 'sacrificial sheep' are ready for slaughter before killing the pair (1056–57).[6] The military expedition's success is assured by the sacrifice of Iphigenia, and by the army's soldiers who sacrifice their own lives (641), but its consequences are simultaneously devastating. We are asked to consider whether all the death and destruction was worth it. Yes, the Greeks won the war, but at what cost?

Ordinary soldiers

The Herald provides further evidence of the debilitating human cost of the war both at Troy and on the perilous return journey. He rejoices at his arrival home after ten years of believing he would never see his homeland again, but even this joy is marred by the many men lost (502–7). The army, as it previously existed, is no more; there is only what the war has spared of it (517). As a nameless stock character, a herald is a common feature in Greek tragedy, but the Herald in *Agamemnon* is also much more than simply a messenger. He is an unnamed soldier, the kind of rank-and-file infantry member whose low social status means that his deeds will not be remembered in song like those of the famous noblemen he serves such as Agamemnon. As a 'song' about Agamemnon, Aeschylus' tragedy in fact presents a complicated picture of the actions of so-called war heroes. The play zooms in on the plight of ordinary soldiers focalized through the Herald's experiences. These soldiers lack contact with home to such an extent that they are not even aware of how much they are missed by the locals even as they themselves yearn for home (544–46). Living conditions on land and on sea were equally miserable, with wretched narrow sleeping arrangements on the ships and a constantly sodden state of existence in their bivouacs on land. Moisture from the dew on the ground and drizzle from the sky caused their woollen clothes to be persistently infested with vermin (555–62). The winters were so cold that the birds could not survive them; the summers were so hot that the sea became a waveless and windless expanse (563–66). When the Herald catches himself and changes tack, proclaiming that misery is over, the gains outweigh the anguish, and it is proper to rejoice (567–79), he returns to his formal role as herald for the army's generals who must be praised and honoured in their victory (580–82). But the power of the Herald's revelations about the life of ordinary soldiers should not be underestimated. The theatre audience will have been primarily made up of Athenian male citizens who had trained in compulsory military service, and who had first-hand experience of warfare.

The Chorus tease out more details from the Herald, bringing him back to the loss of life caused by the terrible storm that wrecked the naval fleet on the homeward journey. Menelaus has vanished with his ship and crew (615–33). The Herald is reluctant to mix good tidings of victory with news of disaster by giving further details of the storm to a city which has lost so many men as 'sacrificial victims' to the war (636–49), but he continues with his narrative and describes a truly terrifying night on the high seas. Lightning, whirlwinds, squalls of driving rain caused ships to ram into each other. One ship would gore another which would then disappear in a whirlpool of waves. When the morning finally came, the open sea was a blooming field of bodies and wreckage with few survivors (653–60). Although the storm was not a part of the war, it nevertheless vitiates the triumphant homecoming of the military victors and demonstrates the anger of the gods against the Greeks for their war crimes. Similarly, Agamemnon's 'noble deeds' are exclusively destructive. We have already heard of Iphigenia's sacrifice under his command. We then hear from the Herald how he has destroyed the whole population of Troy (528). Ostensibly a cause of celebration, the imagery employed by the Herald casts Agamemnon's deeds as problematic. The Herald claims that Agamemnon brings 'light out of darkness' to the people (522–23), but light is a corrupted image in this play where it indicates doom. The beacon-fires announcing the downfall of Troy, and the sacrificial fires lit in the palace at Argos both signal Agamemnon's death (cf. 254, 265, 279, 1577). In another image used by the Herald, Agamemnon has 'cast a yoke on Troy' and has come home 'a happy man' (529–31), but the yoke is an overwhelmingly negative image in the tragedy, associated with Agamemnon's decision to kill his daughter (219) and with Cassandra's experience of slavery (953, 1071).[7] 'Heroic' deeds are thus called into question, while the suffering and sacrifices of ordinary soldiers are noted.

Slavery and rape

Greek tragedy is very clear on the fate of women from a conquered city – rape, slavery, and relocation in an enemy household. Agamemnon may not have been the worst captor. He asks Clytemnestra to treat his Trojan slave Cassandra kindly (951–52). Clytemnestra claims that she will, suggesting disingenuously while plotting Cassandra's murder that the Trojan is lucky to have been allotted a family of ancient wealth since those with new money are cruel to their slaves in every way (1042–46). Cassandra, of course, is no ordinary slave, but a gifted prophet who foresees her own death and walks knowingly into her own murder with the observation that a slave is an easy victim to kill (1326). Nevertheless, it is clear that her final hours are filled with terror. She is overwhelmed by the visions of horrors related to the family of Agamemnon. Babies murdered by Agamemnon's father Atreus are served as food to their own unsuspecting father, Agamemnon's uncle Thyestes (1096–97, 1217–22). A band of Furies remains in the house and drinks human blood (1186–97). Cassandra foresees the murder of Agamemnon and is as terrified as a mortally wounded warrior (1121–24), and laments for the utter destruction of her city and family (1167–72). Before entering the house, she recoils in horror at the smell of human blood and must steel herself to enter in spite of her terror (1309–17).

Through imagery referring to herself as being 'like a newly-wedded bride' (1179), Cassandra poignantly alludes to the union she has with Agamemnon. Her relationship with her captor is presented as a kind of perverse marriage, with traditional motifs and language normally associated with Greek marriage here applied to the slave Cassandra. Her entrance alongside Agamemnon in his chariot recalls the journey taken by the bride to the groom's home on marriage, and she is referred to as Agamemnon's 'select flower' (954–55).[8] Although the sexual violence experienced by Cassandra at the hands of Agamemnon is not directly mentioned, the attempted rape she suffered at the hands of the god Apollo, her resistance to that rape, and her subsequent trauma provide a framework through which to understand this kind of violence and its effects. Punning on Apollo's name, Cassandra addresses the god (*Apollon*) as her destroyer (*apollōn*) in a refrain (1080–81 = 1085–86). She recounts her shame at the sexual encounter with the god, and how Apollo offered her the gift of prophecy along with his sexual advances. He was 'a wrestler' and she consented at first but then rejected the god who punished her by making her prophecies fall on deaf ears (1203–12). As a result, Cassandra endures unanimous mockery by friends, and is forced to wander like an itinerant beggar, wretched and starving, with no one to help her (1270–76). Cassandra's life is ruined because she dared to resist an aggressive sexual act, instigated by an all-powerful male offering a reward whose value is sabotaged when his advances are rejected. This storyline is not unfamiliar in the age of #MeToo.

In death, Cassandra is viciously reduced by Clytemnestra to a 'cheap whore of the ship's benches' (1442–43; literally a 'mast-rubber', where 'mast' is a metaphor for a phallus), and one of Agamemnon's many Trojan sex slaves. Notwithstanding Clytemnestra's insult, Aeschylus portrays Cassandra with great pathos and dignity. She defies Clytemnestra by refusing to respond to the queen's requests and is the only character in the play who is immune to Clytemnestra's control. Indeed, this may explain Clytemnestra's particular vitriol for her at the end. Cassandra goes to her death on her own terms, having prophesied the ensuing vengeance that will see the death of her killer. Remarkably, she defies Apollo, first by resisting rape, and later by casting off the prophetic accoutrements, her staff and veil, that defined her subjugation by Apollo in an action that represents a 'semiotic death' in anticipation and acceptance of her actual death (1264–70).[9] Cassandra does not dwell on her sexual humiliations, which only elicit her sense of shame as a victim (cf. 1203). Her well-known rape by Ajax, son of Oileus, in the temple of Athena during the sack of Troy is not mentioned in the play, but it was one of the Greeks' major war crimes which elicited divine anger in the form of the devastating storm that battered the Greek fleet, as recounted by Agamemnon's

Herald. Aeschylus thus obliquely alludes to Cassandra's sufferings as a rape victim and war captive, all while presenting a dignified and sympathetic character caught up in the horrors that life has dealt her.

Looking at modern warfare through *Agamemnon*

Sexual humiliation and degradation is the plight of many women in war-ravaged countries, and one of the most shocking modern representations of Cassandra's experiences is the second poem in Seamus Heaney's 1996 five-poem set 'Mycenae Lookout'. Published in *The Spirit Level* collection the year after Heaney had won the Nobel Prize for Literature, the poems are inspired by the *Oresteia* trilogy and particularly by the first play *Agamemnon*. In the context of Heaney's oeuvre, the poems are unusually graphic and violent in their language. They express Heaney's rage at the decades of political violence in his homeland of Northern Ireland and, in the final poem, a hope for lasting peace. '2. Cassandra' casts Aeschylus' Cassandra as a young woman suffering the kind of punishment meted out by paramilitary groups on women accused of 'keeping company' with the 'enemy'. Her hair has been aggressively shaved off leaving her head scabbed. She looks 'camp-fucked / and simple' and is later called 'Little rent / cunt'.[10] The language shows her to be the victim of aggressive sexual violence, while the suggestion that she looks simple implies that it was easy to take advantage of her. She was a vulnerable target, depicted as frail, her speech compared to a bleating lamb. The presentation of the situation is highly complex. The poem's opening stanza seems to suggest that Cassandra was not completely innocent. It reads 'No such thing / as innocent / bystanding' with the first two lines repeated later in the poem where Cassandra's 'bewilderment' is called 'half-calculating'.[11] This implies that Cassandra must have known the repercussions she would face for the circumstances in which she finds herself, as she now consciously attempts to elicit sympathy for her plight. As the poem progresses, however, it becomes clear that this perspective is not objective. The not-so-innocent 'bystanders' are, in fact, the members of the community who watch her suffering and who feel roused to rape her as well.[12] Cassandra's punishment coincides with the return of Agamemnon and his 'drum- / balled, old buck's / stride'.[13] Reflecting Northern Ireland's culture of marches and parades across both sides of the political and ethnic divide, Agamemnon is a drum-beating leader but also a sexually aggressive one. He is a powerful man, a king who controls his community, as well as a child-killer. This is his world. In retrospect, then, the poem exposes how Cassandra, the victim, is both blamed and shamed by a complicit community conditioned to lust after violence and aggression. The precarious nature of life in such communities is captured at the end of the poem where Cassandra speaks and compares the extinction of life to the wipe of a sponge in an image taken directly from Cassandra's final words in *Agamemnon* (1328–29).

It is difficult to overstate the importance of this poem in exposing a part of the Northern Irish conflict that is commonly hidden from view. Cassandra's frailty, and that of the women she represents, is captured visually on the page by the very short lines and thin shape of Heaney's poem. It comes after '1. The Watchman's War' where the joy some felt at the recently launched war is contrasted with the grisly realities of the ensuing 'killing-fest'. Fire, the signal of triumph, is simply 'A victory beacon in an abattoir …' while references to the queen and 'the border' map the mythological war subtly onto the Northern Irish conflict.[14] The third poem '3. His Dawn Vision' presents the intransigence of both sides which leads to continued warfare, while the fourth '4. The Nights' illustrates how 'The war put all men mad' before the peace described in the last poem finally comes.[15] *Agamemnon* is the most important of the *Oresteia*'s plays for understanding the 'Mycenae Lookout' set, which opens with an epigraph quoting the striking claim by Aeschylus' Watchman that a great ox has stepped on his tongue (*Ag.* 36–37). The Watchman doubles as a persona for Heaney himself. As an observer of the Northern Irish conflict and a public figure who was under immense pressure to comment on contemporary politics, Heaney identifies with the Watchman who knows so much but is not able to speak for fear of repercussions.[16]

Heaney's 'Mycenae Lookout' poems are, in many ways, about the aftermath of warfare. They were written after the 1994 ceasefire when peace seemed, finally, to be almost within reach after three decades of horrific violence. It was a precarious time, and peace talks would fail until the 1998 Good Friday Agreement. Heaney's final poem '5. His Reverie of Water' reflects this anxiety when the poet can only 'nearly smell' the 'fresh water' that symbolizes peace.[17] The *Agamemnon* of Heaney's Northern Irish predecessor Louis MacNeice, first published in 1936, was also written in the aftermath of warfare and during a period of social anxieties concerning events in Europe that would lead to the outbreak of the Second World War in 1939. With the First World War still a recent memory, MacNeice's translation, which was written for performance, alluded both to traumatic experiences recognizable to First World War veterans and to alarming contemporary events. The raw material of Aeschylus' *Agamemnon*, which emphasizes the waste of human life and suffering caused by warfare, spoke directly to an audience familiar with such experiences. At the same time, choices made by MacNeice in his translation created a further layer of familiarity. Unlike Heaney, MacNeice was well-trained in Greek as well as Latin. From 1930 to 1936 he was a Lecturer in

Classics at the University of Birmingham, working alongside the illustrious Classicist and fellow Northern Irishman Eric Roberston Dodds. MacNeice acknowledges Dodds' friendship and advice in the preface to his *Agamemnon*, all the while conceding that the final product and choices made are his own responsibility.[18] Numerous references to 'God', as well as evocations of 'sin', 'holy water' and 'Hell' Christianized the ancient text for contemporary audiences.[19] The Herald's description of the soldiers' wretched experiences resonated strongly with reports on life in the trenches during the First World War, and MacNeice capitalized on this in his rendering of the Greek into idiomatic English: 'hard lodging', 'scanty blankets', 'rations that never reached us', and 'dews from the marshes / Rotting our clothes, filling our hair with lice'.[20] Ominous events are evoked when a member of the Chorus claims that Aegisthus and Clytemnestra 'are going to set up a dictatorship in the state'.[21] Allusion to Nazi Germany was amplified in performance through a Nazi salute given by Aegisthus' soldiers. Agamemnon and Cassandra were also to enter in chariots accompanied by martial music.[22] The 1936 production of MacNeice's *Agamemnon* was thus highly topical, as it was again in 1946 in the very recent aftermath of the Second World War when it aired on BBC Radio's Third Programme in a production by Val Gielgud. Audience figures for the Third Programme drama broadcasts imply that the production may have reached a staggering number of between 1.5 and 2.5 million listeners.[23] MacNeice's *Agamemnon* aired again on BBC's Third Programme in 1950 and on BBC's Home Service in 1953, in productions by Raymond Raikes. Falling numbers of listeners suggest a much lower figure for the later radio versions, around 90,000, but still a very large audience for an ancient Greek tragedy.[24]

From Heaney's poetry and MacNeice's theatre and radio, we come to the final and most recent of our case studies in the reception of *Agamemnon* as a war tragedy – Colm Tóibín's 2017 novel *House of Names*. Best known for his 2009 novel *Brooklyn*, which was subsequently adapted into an award-winning film of the same name, Tóibín frequently engages with themes of loss and identity in his work. *House of Names* alludes to a number of Greek tragedies that deal with the Trojan War and its effect on the family of Agamemnon, especially the surviving children Orestes and Electra. *Agamemnon* itself remains an important source, however, particularly in the first part of the novel, which is told from Clytemnestra's perspective. Iphigenia is gagged at her sacrifice to stop her cursing her father, as in Aeschylus, and in a detail that recalls Heaney's Cassandra her hair is cropped so roughly that her head is gashed. Clytemnestra kills Agamemnon in the bath on his return and he is compared to a lion in death, an image that recalls his military exploits in Aeschylus.[25] Unlike her Aeschylean counterpart, however, Tóibín's Clytemnestra does not believe the gods have any interest in or notion of human affairs. Iphigenia's sacrifice and all the other horrors are thus simply war crimes decided by men.

When Clytemnestra protests as her daughter is led off to be killed, she too is gagged, bound, and stuffed into a tiny underground crawl space covered by a heavy stone where she is left in a stress position for days without food or water. Occasional pitchers of water are thrown into the hole but she is unable to drink the water as it soaks into her clothes and mixes with her excrement. It is during this time that Clytemnestra loses her belief in the gods and determines to murder Agamemnon.[26] While Agamemnon is at war, Clytemnestra is a prisoner in her own home guarded constantly by Agamemnon's men. Aegisthus is a high value hostage and a prisoner in the palace from one of Agamemnon's previous wars, but he remains a dangerous and powerful figure with a loyal following. Although he should be chained up, he roams the palace at night quite freely and it is through his assistance that Clytemnestra dispatches Agamemnon's men and takes control, installing Aegisthus as her personal bodyguard. When Agamemnon returns, he is so enamoured with recounting his own valiance and triumph in battle that he does not sense any danger as Clytemnestra lures him to his death in the bath. Wrapping his head in a net, she stabs him in the neck and slices his throat; Cassandra is killed by Aegisthus. With Agamemnon dead, Aegisthus and his followers secure control by capturing and imprisoning Agamemnon's men. Leading men with experience of maintaining and consolidating the lands and riches taken in the wars are kept close to share their knowledge. The coup is effected according to plan, but Clytemnestra realizes that she is now under Aegisthus' control. It is he who has secreted Orestes away from the palace and, much to Clytemnestra's distress, it is he who will decide when Orestes should return.[27] As the novel progresses, we learn of Orestes' own experiences, of how he escapes from his place of entrapment thus depriving Aegisthus of power over him, and of the circumstances in which he eventually does return to the palace, killing his mother under the influence of Electra and taking control of the kingdom.

Tóibín's retelling of *Agamemnon* casts the original into a much broader complex of social and political intrigues, demonstrating how numerous different individuals and groups become drawn into the web of conflict. The brutality of this world is inspired not just by Aeschylus, but by the civil war in Northern Ireland and by the wars in Syria and Iraq. In Aeschylus' *Agamemnon* and its companion plays, as in the Northern Irish conflict, each atrocity is a retaliation for a previous atrocity in an apparently endless cycle of violence. A scene towards the end of Tóibín's novel was inspired by the 1986 Kingsmill massacre in Northern Ireland and by the 'image of a single figure still alive in a heap of dead bodies' that had haunted Tóibín for thirty years. As Tóibín was writing, the wars in Syria and Iraq raged on and the public was bombarded with constant images of human suffering and destruction from the war zones. Tóibín's Agamemnon and Clytemnestra were partly inspired by Bashar al-Assad and his wife Asma.[28] In Tóibín's novel 'evil comes in many guises', a notion that informed MacNeice's *Agamemnon* as well, when he refers in his preface to 'the principle of Evil which logic cannot comprehend' but which seems to drive the cycle of crimes.[29] Where MacNeice differs from Tóibín, and indeed from Heaney, is in his lack of focus on female suffering in war. MacNeice's Clytemnestra elevates herself to an obscenely god-like status after murdering Agamemnon, with the exclamation 'Mine is the glory' distorting the phrase 'Thine is the ... glory' from the Lord's Prayer.[30] In a drama where God is continuously evoked, this casts Clytemnestra in a particularly damning light. The negative portrayal of an adulterous wife may have been influenced by the fact that MacNeice's own wife had recently left him for another man (in late 1935). The draft for a prologue to his 1936 *Agamemnon* suggested that both Agamemnon and his brother had been 'ruined by their wives'.[31] Tóibín, on the other hand, stresses Clytemnestra's physical and psychological suffering in the motivations for her crimes while Heaney unveils the full horror of Cassandra's victimhood. All three authors, however, converge with Aeschylus in showing how warfare decimates both societies and families, regardless of wealth or of social class.

Notes

1 See Hall (1997), 104 on the relationship between household and state in the context of Greek tragedy.
2 For an overview of Aeschylus' military service, see Echeverría (2017), 74–76.
3 See Henrichs (1981), 232 and Hughes (1991), 185.
4 On these kinds of sacrifices, see Parker (2011), 155, 159.
5 For further details about the rituals of animal sacrifice in ancient Greece, see Burkert (1985), 55–59.
6 On the motif of corrupted sacrifice in *Agamemnon* and its companion plays, see Zeitlin (1965) and (1966).
7 On the intricate patterns of imagery of the *Agamemnon* and its companion plays, see Lebeck (1971).
8 Rehm (1994), 43–58 offers a detailed analysis of the complex representation of Cassandra's relationship with Agamemnon, and of other relationships presented as marriages in *Agamemnon*.
9 Wyles (2011), 65–66 uses the term 'semiotic death' in discussing the implications of Cassandra's removal of parts of her costume in this scene.
10 Heaney (1996), 31–32.

11 Ibid., 30–31.
12 Ibid., 32.
13 Ibid., 32.
14 Ibid., 29.
15 Ibid., 36.
16 For further discussion of Heaney's 'Mycenae Lookout' poems, see the insightful analyses of Vendler (2002) and Hardwick (2016), 292–302.
17 Heaney (1996), 36.
18 MacNeice (2008), 9.
19 MacNeice (2008). References to 'God' at 15, 17, 22, 25, 30, 32, 33, 35, 38, 43, 44, 45, 46, 47, 51, 61, 62; to 'sin' at 28 and 53; to 'holy water' at 48; to 'Hell' at 52.
20 Ibid., 31–32.
21 Ibid., 59.
22 These performance details are discussed by Sidnell (1986), 326–27.
23 Wrigley (2005), 224.
24 Ibid., 227.
25 Tóibín (2017a), 5–6, cf. *Ag.* 827–28, 1259.
26 Ibid., 33–36.
27 Ibid., 39–66.
28 Tóibín (2017b) discusses all these influences on his novel.
29 Quotations from Tóibín (2017b) and MacNeice (2008), 8, respectively.
30 MacNeice (2008), 61.
31 Quoted by Sidnell (1986), 325.

12

Revenge for Murder Seen through Modern Eyes: Recent Reception of Aeschylus' *Oresteia*

Betine van Zyl Smit

Aeschylus' *Oresteia*, the trilogy of which *Agamemnon* is the first play, has been a seminal text in Western cultural history and theatre performance since it was first produced in Athens in 458 BC. In Seneca's Latin adaptation, *Agamemnon* became an influential part of Renaissance drama. In subsequent centuries the trilogy, and especially *Agamemnon*, has inspired and challenged creators, in all fields of literature and performance.

This chapter examines how some modern playwrights have reimagined the story of Clytemnestra's murder of her husband Agamemnon on his victorious return from the Trojan War. The reception of Aeschylus' trilogy, and in particular of *Agamemnon*, has been widely studied. An invaluable resource is the edited volume *Agamemnon in Performance 458 BC to AD 2004*.[1] In eighteen chapters the performance history of the *Agamemnon* over the centuries is investigated and discussed. The volume deals not only with adaptation but also with translation. There is also critical consideration of the famous productions of the Aeschylean work by directors such as Peter Hall, Peter Stein, Karolos Koun, Ariane Mnouchkine and David Stuttard's 1999 and 2003 production with Actors of Dionysus. It seems superfluous to go over the same ground again, so this chapter will deal only with adaptations of *Agamemnon* which are not covered in the book or have been created since the volume's publication in 2005.

An attempt will be made to show the changes to the interpretation of this brutal killing and its aftermath as depicted in Steven Berkoff's *Agamemnon* (1976), Yael Farber's *Molora* (2008) and Zinnie Harris's *This Restless House* (2016). The discussion should reflect how the enduring preoccupation with one of the great tragedies of ancient Greece sheds light on the approaches to revenge and atonement in the modern world.

As the first part of a trilogy, the *Agamemnon* of Aeschylus has also often been reinterpreted as one play in a new trilogy, for instance *Homecoming*, the first play in Eugene O'Neill's trilogy, *Mourning Becomes Electra*. Two of the plays discussed in this chapter are independent works, while Zinnie Harris's

Agamemnon's Return forms part of her trilogy, *This Restless House*. As early as the first century AD already the Roman philosopher and tragedian Seneca wrote a play called *Agamemnon*. It is partly based on Aeschylus' eponymous tragedy.[2] To our knowledge he did not deal with the remaining plays in the trilogy, although his *Thyestes* has strong links with this tragedy in the sustained emphasis on the family curse.

Berkoff's *Agamemnon*

It is puzzling that *Agamemnon in Performance* does not deal with Berkoff's *Agamemnon*, as his adaptation clearly links his play to that of Aeschylus: he notes that it is 'freely adapted from the Aeschylus version'. This makes it plain that for Berkoff there is no single version of the shocking incidents on Agamemnon's victorious return from the Trojan War. Indeed, he explains that his *Agamemnon* is 'filtered through my own impressions of Greece and is rooted more in the elements of landscape, and sea . . . It is also about heat and battle, fatigue, the marathon and the obscenity of modern and future wars. Naturally it is also about the body and its pleasures/pains.'[3] Berkoff worked on his *Agamemnon* for several years. It was first performed as work in progress in 1973. The version that was published[4] was first staged in 1976. Berkoff's engagement with ancient Greek drama is above all associated with *Greek*, his adaptation of Sophocles' *Oedipus* which was first on stage in 1980. There are strong parallels in Berkoff's approach to the reworking of the ancient Greek dramas between the two plays. The similarities are especially in the language as well as in the physicality of the presentation.

Berkoff's *Agamemnon* starts with an account called 'Legend of the Curse' performed by the Chorus. In this play the Chorus is formed by the eight principal characters as well as three further actors. Their narrative, in the 'stream of consciousness' style which was to become typical also in *Greek*, gruesomely recaptures the sensations of Thyestes as he chewed his way through the 'pot of stew crammed with bits of human flesh' (p. 53). No name is mentioned, however, in this description, until the last words: 'The curse of the house of Atreus.' Thus, the curse, of which the meal of the slaughtered bodies of his children dished up to Thyestes by his brother Atreus is only one episode, is made prominent. This prologue is reminiscent of Seneca's opening of his *Agamemnon* with an appearance of the ghost of Thyestes. Seneca used an analogous opening in his *Thyestes* with the ghost of Tantalus pursued by a Fury coming to infect the house of Atreus with the curse. In his *Agamemnon* the ghost of Thyestes serves as prologue to the play evoking both the curse on the house and the cycle of revenge which will continue. Berkoff similarly prefaces the entry of the Watchman, modelled on the opening action of Aeschylus' tragedy, with an extensive and detailed repetition of the gruesome, cannibalistic meal served by Atreus. It prepares the audience for the revenge on Atreus' son Agamemnon by Thyestes' son, Aegisthus.

The setting and point where the action starts are succinctly indicated in a second preamble, 'Song of Lineage and Events' (p. 54). Noteworthy is the emphasis on death and killing and on the curse on the house of Atreus, which ends both the 'Legend of the Curse' and the 'Song':

> This is Argos / Argos is a clean city / this is Agamemnon's city / Agamemnon son of Atreus / ruler / husband of Clytemnestra / he sailed the seas to Troy / to kill that boy / Paris / who stole what wasn't his to take / Helen / Menelaus' mate / Agamemnon murdered his own child / a sacrifice / to calm the sea / so wild / for the Armada of death / Clytemnestra vows to avenge the bloody deed / and on it goes / without an end / the curse first laid on the house of Atreus.

The curse thus runs as a leitmotif through the play. When Cassandra learns that she has been brought to the house of Atreus, she immediately identifies it as cursed. Before her vision of Clytemnestra trapping Agamemnon inside the palace, she experiences the Thyestean meal: 'I hear them / screams / children / carved babies / the cries linger / flesh roasting / fathers cramming their own flesh in their hands / all here here here / Uuugh!' (p. 73). At the end Aegisthus recalls how Atreus tricked his father into consuming his own slaughtered children. He explicitly asserts that he planned the killing of Agamemnon as revenge for this monstrous deed. The Chorus also ascribe the outcome as due to the curse: 'Tarantula bitch has poisoned your life / but the curse of Atreus willed the knife' (p. 76).

Evident throughout as well is the stress on brutal realism which appears first in the prologue. It starts with the description of Thyestes eating his own children and covers every aspect of the dialogue. The Watchman muses that Helen, 'the young whore', 'must be old and poxy now' (p. 56). While Berkoff keeps the outline of the Greek tragedy, he fleshes out many scenes with additional dialogue that provides further perspectives on the characters. Thus, there are scenes where the thoughts of Paris as well as those of ordinary soldiers are voiced. The words of the dialogue and choral odes move the action in time and place. No sooner have the Watchman and Chorus announced the signal that Troy has fallen and the house of Priam been crushed, than the words of 'Two Brave Soldiers' give voice to the battle experience of either side: one 'fighting for Troy' and one 'fighting for Greece'. The Chorus sums up the harshness of war evoked in these words: 'Javelin / arrow / spear / sword /

axe / cut / thrust / bleed / hack' (p. 58). This scene has the title 'Battle One' and is immediately followed by one called 'Battle Two' where Clytemnestra and Agamemnon are the antagonists. This scene is typical of the anti-realistic presentation chosen by Berkoff. It takes place before the scene of Agamemnon's homecoming, but serves to clarify the deep differences between king and queen. This indicates that the war against Troy may be over, but another, domestic, war is still in progress. This scene evokes Agamemnon's struggle when he killed his daughter to ensure that his fleet could sail. He presents it as an impossible situation: 'Apollo show me a way / I drown in blood whichever way I turn / this web I cannot break /' (p. 61). Clytemnestra, on the other hand, gives different weight to the two sides: 'My daughter's life to help a war for a faithless wife!' (p. 60).

Berkoff uses flashbacks in a dialogue between the Chorus and Clytemnestra to recreate the whole of the Trojan War. The flexibility of time is complemented by a malleability in the composition of the Chorus. At moments they seem to be old men of Argos as in Aeschylus' version, and at others they become the Greek soldiers fighting in Troy, or travelling to the war, or on the homeward journey. Berkoff expands the application of the horrors of the war to the modern world. In the Herald's speech he inserts references to napalm, howitzers, bazookas and tanks into his account. Likewise, in the section titled 'The Celebration', the Chorus emphasize the dreadful results of war: 'widows / orphans / crippled / blinded' (p. 67).

Against this backdrop of the devastation caused by war is set the personal confrontation between Clytemnestra and Agamemnon. Berkoff emphasizes this by inserting another new scene between them. This takes place at the point where Agamemnon has already entered the palace, after having been persuaded by Clytemnestra to walk on the purple tapestries. The additional scene allows a further glimpse into the minds of the two characters. The stage directions stipulate that only the two of them should be present, seated on two chairs facing outwards. The physical separation thus created also signals the gulf between them. There is no dialogue between the two, but each has a monologue revealing their thoughts. Here Clytemnestra dwells on the lovemaking between Agamemnon and Cassandra. In this way a second powerful motive for her vengeance is stressed. Agamemnon expresses profound weariness which overwhelms every other feeling, even his helplessness because he realizes that he cannot regain the rapport he had with his wife. It is clear that there is no common ground between the two.

After Agamemnon and Cassandra have been killed, Clytemnestra's second motive comes to the fore again: she refers to their two bodies lying together 'as was his habit / bedded with his Trojan whore' (p. 76). In contrast, 'Aegisthus stands strong as a rock on whom I can rest my head' (p. 76). When he comes on the stage, he carries a bullwhip and threatens the Chorus. They are not cowed, but challenge Aegisthus' cowardice: 'sewer rat / sneaking out in the night / behind a woman's petticoat you bite' (p. 77). The confrontation between the Chorus and Aegisthus is much more succinct than in Aeschylus. The name of Orestes is not mentioned, although the Chorus's words 'The tale of blood is not over / it has only just begun' point to retaliation. Berkoff ends his version with Clytemnestra speaking last. As in the Greek tragedy, she addresses Aegisthus: 'you and I are in power darling / we shall order things well ...' (p. 77).

Berkoff has retold the ancient tragedy in a modern idiom, but preserved the ancient motifs of the Argive family torn apart, not only by the war, but by the curse on their house and by sexual jealousy on the part of the mother who is also embittered by the slaughter of her favourite child by her husband. Because this play stands alone, the ending with its indication of rule by Clytemnestra and Agamemnon, indicates another consequence of the war and its murderous aftermath, a tyrannical state.

Molora

A very different approach to the tale of the cycle of family murder is taken in the South African play *Molora*. It is one of what the dramatist Yael Farber calls her 'testimonial' plays. She defines this in the following way:

> To me, 'testimonial theatre' is a genre wrought from people bearing witness to their own stories through remembrance and words. Material culled from memory is crafted into a compelling yet true narrative, which is then brought to life through text, performance and the visual devices of the theatre. The essential component of this genre lies in its capacity for healing through speaking, hearing and being heard.[5]

Farber was also the director when *Molora* was performed, first in South Africa and then in other countries, before it was published in 2008.[6] This play is based on the entire *Oresteia*, but here I will highlight the parts which are adapted from *Agamemnon*. Farber acknowledges the translations she used for her version. They include renderings of Sophocles' *Electra* as well as the *Electra* of Euripides. For the *Oresteia* she relied on the translation of Robert Fagles and that of Louis MacNeice. The story of the myth on which the *Oresteia* is based has been adapted to transmit the testimony of characters bearing witness to their experiences and suffering as happened in the hearings of the Truth and Reconciliation Commission (the TRC) in South Africa.

Molora tells the story of the murder of Agamemnon and the quest for vengeance in the framework of the TRC. It was set up by a legal act in 1995, after the abolition of apartheid and the establishment of a constitutional democracy in 1994. The aim of the TRC was to publicly establish the truth about past atrocities, to recompense victims who would have the chance to tell their stories, and thus to prevent people from taking justice into their own hands. Thus, the tale of the murder of Agamemnon is presented in *Molora* as the testimony of Klytemnestra before the TRC. She is confessing to the murder of Agamemnon, but also setting out her reasons for her act. The cast is pared down to three characters, Klytemnestra, Elektra and Orestes, while the Chorus consists of six Xhosa women who dance and sing traditional songs and also form part of the audience at the hearing. Klytemnestra sits at a table giving her account and at a table facing her sits Elektra. The stage directions read: 'Perpetrator and victim face one another at last' (p. 20).

The murder of Agamemnon is presented as a flashback. Klytemnestra claims that she had justice on her side. She cites the two motives mentioned in Aeschylus' tragedy, but adds a third, that Agamemnon had killed her first husband and her child by him.[7] The killing of Agamemnon is presented onstage, unlike in the ancient drama. Klytemnestra mimes the action, striking the table with a pickaxe and then smearing her hands and face with blood from a dish. Elektra witnessed this execution as a child, ran to her father's body and tried to speak to him. She is pulled away by her mother and told not to look. Klytemnestra then proceeds to bury the body. When she has covered it, she proclaims: 'Here I stand ... And here I struck ... And here my work is done!'[8] In terms of the legal framework of the TRC, her confession serves as a full and frank disclosure of her past actions.

The role of Klytemnestra was played by the only white member of the cast. Her character represented the previous white government. The murder of Agamemnon became the symbol for the many acts of suppression and brutality of that regime. Klytemnestra claims to have justice on her side but fears the return of Orestes. Elektra, on the other hand, prays to her ancestors to send Orestes back to avenge the murder of their father.

The Chorus of Xhosa women have a dual function. They not only form part of the public at the hearing of the TRC, but they also comment on and even participate in the action of the play. Much of the dialogue and also the choral songs are in Xhosa. The words of the dialogue are translated into English by a Translator. This character represents the real-life role of interpreters at the TRC hearings where people could testify in their language of choice.

When Orestes returns there is an expectation that, as in the myth and in the ancient plays, he will kill his mother. Farber, however, creates a new tension: Elektra is determined that Klytemnestra must be killed as revenge for murdering their father, but Orestes starts to waver. When they confront Klytemnestra she calls for her 'man-killing axe' (p. 81), but Elektra manages to get hold of it and passes it to Orestes. Klytemnestra appeals to Orestes not to commit an act which will mean that he will never know peace. Orestes metatheatrically appeals to Elektra to 'rewrite this ancient end' (p. 83), but she is resolute not to abandon the vengeance she has been dreaming of for so long. She gets hold of the axe and rushes at her mother, but the women of the Chorus overpower her and take the axe away. They gradually calm her. The ordinary people, represented by the Chorus, have prevented the killing of Klytemnestra and stopped the cycle of revenge. Elektra and Orestes raise their cowering mother while the Chorus sing a song of praise that ends with a prayer for South Africa (p. 86). Klytemnestra then resumes her seat at the table. Her testimony ends in an apology on behalf of white South Africans for past wrongs and a promise of a new dawn of freedom. The hope provided by the end of the play is the result of the insistence of ordinary people that revenge killing does not provide a solution for injustices of the past. By boldly altering the mythical ending, Farber powerfully signalled how important reconciliation was for future peace. In terms of the myth it would imply that the cycle of revenge, provoked by the curse on the house of Atreus, would come to an end without further bloodshed.

Agamemnon's Return

While *Molora* focuses on the political as well as the human, *This Restless House* concentrates on the psychology of the characters and how they are affected by the brutal actions in which their family is involved. This trilogy, with the subtitle 'based around the *Oresteia* by Aeschylus', was first performed by the Citizens Theatre group in Glasgow in 2016 and published the same year.[9] The plays reveal how the mental states of the characters influence their deeds, but also the effect their deeds have on their minds. The progression of their mental affliction is clear in the three parts of the trilogy: *Agamemnon's Return*, *The Bough Breaks* and *Electra and Her Shadow*. The last play is actually set in a psychiatric hospital.

Zinnie Harris not only emphasizes the mental state of the characters, but also gives more prominence to the female members of the family. In Aeschylus' tragedy Agamemnon makes a very short appearance, and the male characters are the Watchman, the Chorus, the Herald and Aegisthus, who only appears in the last scene. In *Agamemnon's Return* Harris has kept these characters and expanded the roles of the Watchman and Agamemnon but has even more considerably enlarged the roles of Clytemnestra and Cassandra. She has added to the cast Electra as an eleven-year-old, a new character, Ianthe, in an extended Nurse/Nanny, confidante role. Ianthe is further involved in a subplot as the lover of the Watchman. Harris manages to incorporate into her play the events of Euripides' *Iphigenia at Aulis* which is often produced[10] as a preliminary to *Agamemnon*. She achieves this by extending the account of Agamemnon's struggle with the decision to kill his daughter in the words of her Chorus and by introducing the ghost of Iphigenia as a *dramatis persona*.

Harris has departed from the structure of ancient tragedy. *Agamemnon's Return* has three acts, and an interval is indicated between the second and the climactic third act. Like Berkoff, Harris has inserted new scenes at various points. These serve to give more detailed psychological portraits of the characters and also to create a new tension. Clytemnestra initially seems to have lost some of her iron resolve and control, and a softer side of Agamemnon is revealed.

The Chorus is retained, however. Their description is specific: 'old and dishevelled men'. They are social outcasts but are tolerated by Clytemnestra and even given an important role in 'welcoming' the king home. Their weakness ensures that they will not act against her when she executes her revenge. They further retain the established choral function of giving background information and commenting on the action. The play starts with the Chorus setting the scene and narrating the story of the origin of the Trojan War. The Thyestean meal is mentioned, but much more attention is given to how and why Iphigenia was sacrificed by her father. As they relate the story, the 'ghost' of Iphigenia appears on the stage. She is wearing the yellow dress described by the Chorus and carrying a little blue suitcase into which she is packing things she is bringing to keep her father safe and comfortable in the war. This new detail adds poignancy and enhances the pathos of her death. The Chorus reveal that Iphigenia appears every night and has been appearing for ten years. The ghostly visitation ends in her dying scream and the word: 'DADDY!' (p. 30). It is only at this point that the Watchman enters with the news of the fall of Troy. The Chorus's reaction to his wish to summon Clytemnestra suggests that all may not be well with her.

Most of the departures from Aeschylus' play serve to give more nuanced and detailed portrayals of the psyches of the two main characters. As the scene shifts to the interior of the palace where Clytemnestra is hosting a party, complete with karaoke, drink and drugs, it is clear that there is disorder in Argos. Clytemnestra's reaction to the trauma of losing Iphigenia has resulted in her constant partying and reliance on alcohol and drugs. An audience aware of the purposeful queen in Aeschylus' tragedy may well wonder whether this woman will be able to carry out her ancient role. Electra is also introduced in this scene. In her befuddled state, Clytemnestra mistakes her for Iphigenia as she is in a yellow dress identical to the one worn by her sister when she was killed. Electra has been told to wear the yellow dress when good news arrives. The good news, of course, is the fall of Troy and the return of her father. Iphigenia appears again but is visible only to Clytemnestra. This further highlights the fragile mental state of the queen. Electra is excited at the prospect of seeing her 'daddy' as she was a baby when the fleet left. Her anxious questions about her father evoke a description of Agamemnon from Clytemnestra. Her description hints at a charismatic and irresistibly charming man.

Harris's Agamemnon is a more rounded character than in the ancient tragedy. In addition to Clytemnestra's description of him to Electra, he appears in fresh scenes created by Harris. As in Berkoff's play, these inserted scenes provide more nuances to his relationship with Clytemnestra. Harris goes even further. Before his return, Agamemnon sends Clytemnestra a gift of an expensive, rather daring, silk dress. This is meant to be a gesture of goodwill towards her. When she is forced to send a reply, she at last comes up with: 'just come home sweetheart' (p. 60). This quickly becomes a slogan taken up by the Chorus but preserves the ambiguity understandable to anyone who knows the myth. The first appearance of Agamemnon follows on another new scene, between Ianthe and the Watchman. This scene is a sexual encounter where the Watchman's lack of success foreshadows Agamemnon's failure to return to his role as king and lover.

The very next scene, another addition, has Agamemnon on stage. On the pattern Odysseus adopts in the *Odyssey*, he appears alone and incognito. This shows a cautious king who sounds out the Watchman about the situation in Argos and also Clytemnestra's feelings. The Watchman is careful not to say too much. When he leaves, Clytemnestra arrives. This new scene also illustrates the vigilance of an Agamemnon who is by no means sure of how he will be received. He makes two offers to his wife: he can either not stop in Argos, but sail on somewhere else, or they can have the public welcome as expected, but live separately after that. Here the emotions of the two principal characters are revealed more fully than in the ancient drama. It is clear from the words of both, that they were once very much in love. Agamemnon in fact appeals to her on those grounds:

> if there is a tiny place where you think you can love me
> or understand at least what I had to do
> then please let me know of it
> a word would do, I am not asking for a kiss

just a simple word of kindness to me
everything will be on your terms, we will go as slow as you like.

pp. 72–73

Clytemnestra' reaction shows her suffering:

I would only have to half close my mind and
look at you broken and desperate I could take you in my arms
of course I could, love like we had doesn't die
but this other flame
this vengeful spirit
this other voice that leads me on
he killed our daughter
he killed our daughter
he killed our daughter.

p. 74

Agamemnon insists that he too is suffering, but that the gods compelled him. Clytemnestra retorts that she would have gone against the gods. This seems to imply that Agamemnon did have some freedom in the decision to sacrifice his daughter. Whether he has this freedom in Aeschylus' version has been disputed.[11] As the meeting progresses Clytemnestra concedes that Agamemnon is suffering too, and that the homecoming reception must not be cancelled. They start kissing each other when she notices a ribbon around his wrist. Persistent questioning on her part elicits that it was given to him by a woman. Clytemnestra realizes that, despite Agamemnon's saying that he had missed her, he had another lover. This breaks the more loving atmosphere. Agamemnon leaves, but they have agreed to meet tomorrow in the public welcome.

In yet another scene invented by Harris, Cassandra and Clytemnestra meet. It is gradually revealed that Cassandra is Agamemnon's concubine. When Cassandra predicts that Clytemnestra will kill her as well as Agamemnon, Clytemnestra protests that she is a kind and gentle person. When Cassandra perseveres and threatens to shout out her forecast, Clytemnestra gets hold of the scissors with which Cassandra has been cutting herbs and cuts out her tongue.

These additional scenes give the audience fuller information about the characters before the public arrival of Agamemnon. Agamemnon has unexpectedly soft sides to his character, while Clytemnestra seems dangerously volatile.

The third act commences with a scene of preparations for the public arrival. The Chorus have been invited by Clytemnestra to play a part in welcoming back their ruler. The Watchman has been given a new role as security guard in charge of crowd control. He is uneasy both about the role given to the Chorus and also about the instruction Ianthe has been given to keep Electra in her room so that she will not see or hear anything. In this tense atmosphere Agamemnon appears alone and is met by Clytemnestra. They rehearse what is to happen later, Clytemnestra directs Agamemnon, but her legs give way a few times. This physical frailty indicates her tension about what is to happen. Agamemnon is persuaded to walk on the purple cloths. He will enter the palace to spruce-up. Just before that, he announces that he has a gift for Clytemnestra, it is Cassandra, the prize given to him by the army. Cassandra's ability to speak has been restored by Apollo and she again maintains that Clytemnestra will kill her. Clytemnestra denies this and promises that Cassandra will not die by her hand.

When the Watchman announces that all is ready for the reception, Clytemnestra enters the palace indicating that she will ask Agamemnon to hurry. Then follows Cassandra's description of what is taking place inside, as Clytemnestra attacks Agamemnon in his bath. Harris transcends the boundaries of the ancient tragedy and has Agamemnon rush out onto the stage, naked and wounded. Now Clytemnestra openly confronts him and indicates she wants him to die in the same way he killed their daughter. Just as she is about to strike the death blow, Electra rushes in. Agamemnon recognizes her, but Clytemnestra proceeds to slit his throat. The ghost of Iphigenia appears and puts her hands over Electra's eyes. Clytemnestra holds Agamemnon's severed head up and proclaims to the Chorus who have been protesting ineffectually:

> behold your hero
> behold your vanquishing King.
> behold King Agamemnon, the butcher of children.
>
> p. 126

Clytemnestra is thus shown as a raging Fury, her mind disturbed by her suffering. Harris tempers this savagery by making it clear that she does not intend to kill Cassandra, but that she dies because she has been inadvertently struck by one of Clytemnestra's blows aimed at Agamemnon. This attempt to alter the ending thus fails. Clytemnestra has enhanced her revenge. Agamemnon does not even get public acknowledgement of his achievement in conquering Troy. He is killed while getting ready for it.

Aegisthus comes on after the deed and makes clear that he sees the revenge as retaliation for Atreus' monstrous tricking of his father. He intends to rule ruthlessly and his first act is to alter the truth about Agamemnon's death.

Ianthe is tortured and the Chorus forced to admit that 'the King fell in the bathroom he hit his head' (p. 131). Electra refuses to enter the palace with her mother and Aegisthus. She goes to her father's body and cradles it. The ghost of Iphigenia appears and cradles Electra. This last scene prepares for the way in which the mythical material will be presented in the further two plays. It will be Electra who kills her mother in *The Bough Breaks*.

In addition to the contemporary sensibility of the psychology of the characters, Harris's language is that of ordinary people in the contemporary world. She does not hesitate to use coarse terminology. For instance, the often-repeated phrase to announce Agamemnon's victory is 'he fucking nailed it'. Coupled with contemporary idiom is the use of anachronism to anchor the ancient events in the modern world. This consists of disparate touches, e.g. the blue suitcase, the karaoke machine, coffee, a big screen, the use of cocaine. In this way the opening play in the trilogy starts to pave the way for a more complete immersion in the modern world in *Electra and Her Shadow*, the third play set in a psychiatric hospital.

These are but three of the numerous later plays which have reworked Aeschylus' *Agamemnon*. Each of the plays has responded to the context and style of the playwright who has used their version of the ancient tragedy to shed light on aspects of their contemporary world.

Notes

1. Macintosh et al. (eds.) (2005). Another important source of information about *Agamemnon* and its reception is Barbara Goward's (2005) study, *Aeschylus: Agamemnon*. Her chapter on reception focuses on Seneca's tragedy as well as the influence of the tragedy on Shakespeare.
2. For discussion of Seneca's sources, see Braund (2017), 233–41.
3. Introduction to Berkoff (1977), 10.
4. Ibid.
5. Farber (2008a), 19.
6. Farber (2008b).
7. This is mentioned in Euripides' *Iphigenia in Aulis*.
8. Farber indicates that she has taken this from Fagles' translation of lines 1396–99 and 1379–80.
9. Harris (2016).
10. See Macintosh et al. (2005), 275–76, 316–17 for examples.
11. Cross-reference here to Chapter 2, 'Agamemnon at Aulis: Hard Choice or No Choice?'

Aeschylus' *Agamemnon*

translated by David Stuttard

The Characters of the Drama

In order of appearance

Watchman	Elderly member of Agamemnon's household
Chorus	Elders of Argos
Clytemnestra	Wife of Agamemnon, Queen of Argos
Herald	Solder in Agamemnon's returning army
Agamemnon	King of Argos, commander-in-chief of the Greek army at Troy
Cassandra	Trojan princess, priestess of Apollo, captive and perhaps lover of Agamemnon
Aegisthus	Agamemnon's cousin, lover of Clytemnestra

Non-speaking Maidservants of Clytemnestra; Attendants of Agamemnon; Attendants of Aegisthus

The scene: the courtyard outside the royal palace of Agamemnon at Argos, a flat-roofed structure with a central double door approached by shallow steps.

Agamemnon is the first play in the *Oresteia* trilogy, which was awarded first prize when it was first performed at Athens' City Dionysia in 458 BC.

Stage directions do not appear in manuscripts of *Agamemnon*, but to aid the reader some suggestions (printed in sans serif font) are given in the following translation. It should be noted, however, that these are pure conjecture.

Night-time. Crouching on the flat roof of the palace, the **Watchman** *gazes out into the darkness.*

Watchman   Gods! I beg the gods to end my suffering! A yawning year now I've been crouching like a watch-dog here on the Atreidae palace roof. Oh yes, I've got to know the patterns of the vastness of the stars, those which bring rain-storms, those which, like politicians, promise summertime to men. And so stars set, and others rise again.

And now I'm watching for the torch-light blaze of fire, the tongue of flame to bring the word from Troy, to tell us of its capture. She longs for that. Oh yes, she ordered this, the one who has a man's brain in a woman's body.   10

So me – sleep elbows me awake; dew soaks my bones; no dreams may come to soothe my bed. No. No! No sleep. But terror presses close beside me lest I close my eyes too heavily and sleep. And then perhaps I'll hum a bit or sing a song to conquer sleep, to slice through sleep in deep incision, and then tears flow and so I weep for all the ruin of this house once so well-tended, now so cruelly. So now I wish a happy ending to my suffering, the blaze of good news   20 slicing through the night.

Suddenly the **Watchman** *sees the beacon flare.*

It's there! There! There it is! The beacon! Night exploding into day! In thanks for this all Argos will be one big celebration. *Huzzah*!

Here's my report to Agamemnon's wife – get out of bed now! Now! And shout for all the house to hear and echo back the good news of the beacon light, if truly Troy is taken as the night fire tells. But me, myself, I'll lead the dancing,   30 mirroring my master's lucky throw, three sixes dancing in the fire-light all for me! If only he'd come home, my king, then I would clasp his hand in mine as I've so longed to.

As for the rest, I'm silent. A bull lolls leaden on my tongue. This house, this building, if *it* could speak, would say it all most clearly. To those who know, my words make sense; to those who don't, I've no more words to say.

Exit **Watchman**. *At the same time, the* **Chorus** *of Argive Elders enters.*

Chorus   Ten years. Ten years since, in their just pursuit of Priam, Menelaus   40 and King Agamemnon, sons of Atreus and joint commanders by the grace of Zeus, joint rulers joined unshakeable, led out the army in a thousand ships from Argos as a reinforcement to their claim, calling in their fury for a strong retaliation –

like vultures screaming in their lonely grief, which soar and circle high above the empty nest, their young all dead, their great wings dipping, rising in the sun like oars, now all their vigilance, their long hours caring for their growing chicks is gone; but there is one high on the mountain-crag – Apollo, Pan or Zeus – who hears the birds' lament, their piercing screaming tearing at the skies they share, and so in time against the one who did this thing, he sends the stalking demon of revenge, the wraith of retribution –

and so in power, greater than the power *they* wield, Zeus of the family, Xenios, the god of guests and friends, sends out the two Atreidae against Paris Alexandros; the cause, a woman manned and mounted by so many lovers

so many throbbing limbs, so many bodies writhing, locked together, knees that press hard, sinking deep into the dusty sand, spear-shafts shattered, bare blades broken as her marriage gift: this Zeus will send upon the Trojans and the Greeks alike.

It is now as it is, and what will be is destiny.

There are no sacrifices that a man can burn and no libations he can pour upon the earth, no, nothing raw and bleeding he can offer to the gods that might assuage their harsh unbending wrath.

We are the ones they left behind, the useless ones, the old,
and so we stay here tottering on sticks,
as weak as babies.

Feeble,
just like babies,
   that's what we old men are – no fighting spirit in us.

And great old age,
like late November leaves, all papery and dry,
crawls on, three-leggèd, shambling and hunched,
as weak as any baby,
a mirage shivering in the shimmering light of day.

Clytemnestra *appears at the palace door.*

Your majesty! Queen Clytemnestra, daughter of Tyndareus! What is the news? What's happened, what the reports or what intelligence that you've declared such sacrifice throughout all Argos? Yes! All the altars of the gods, the gods who keep the city safe, the sky-gods and the gods of earth, gods of

the home and of the market-place, the altars all blaze high with offerings. And 90
here and here and everywhere fire is exploding high into the heavens, flames
fuelled and fed by sacred balms, oil so long hoarded deep beneath the royal
palaces. So tell us what you can, what is not classified, and speak to salve our
schizophrenic cares, which plunge us now to bitter hopelessness, and then 100
Hope blazes from the firelight of your sacrificial flames to beat back the
foreboding, which is gnawing at my mind, of tragedy which threatens to
engulf me.

Clytemnestra *returns inside the palace.*

Authority and knowledge. I have the knowledge, the authority to tell the
journey's omen, the good omen of the road, which met our men in all their
strength and glory. Yes, I have power still to convince, a power that comes
from God, a power as venerable as my years, my battle-strength, my song of
how the screaming swooping bird sent forth the joint command 110
of all the youth of Greece, their leaders joined, one in their resolution, with
spear and muscle out to Troy –

*the eagles of the skies appearing to the eagles of the ships, bird-kings to the kings
of men, one purest black, the other its back streaked with dazzling white, in full
view of the palace, on the spear-side where the auspices are good, perched where
the army all could see, tearing, rending, glutting on a pregnant hare, her belly
bursting bloody foetuses, and all her running in the meadows stopped for ever.* 120

... chant the laments for sorrow, *may all turn out well* ...

*The army's prophet Calchas in his wisdom looked on the Atreidae, battle-ready
both and proud, and recognised in them the eagles glutting on the hare, saw
how they led the army, recognised the meaning of the omen there and said:*

In time, this great crusade will capture Priam's city, and Destiny will devastate 130
the groaning wealth of Troy, and all her flocks, and all her herds that graze
beneath her towers. But let no spiteful malice from the gods glower ugly on
the bridle-bolt that's clamped for Troy, flower for the army now before it's even
sailed. For in her pity, Artemis the Virgin lusts for retribution on the eagles, on
the mauling dogs unleashed to swoop down from the sky by Zeus, their
sacrifice, their slaughter of the pregnant mother, foetuses and all, and how she
trembles in the terror of her death. Yes, Artemis is sickened by the eagles' feast.

... chant the laments for sorrow, *may all turn out well* ...

Artemis in all her soothing loveliness smiles softly on the unweaned cubs of 140
mountain lions too weak yet, too unsteady, to follow to the kill. And suckling

young of beasts that roam the untamed tracts of nature all delight her. But
still she lets the omen run to its conclusion, visions promising success grim
with disaster.

Apollo, Healer, God, I call on you:
let her not stir the winds against the Greeks
to lash the ships to harbour, pen the fleet in port,
to close the sea-lanes and to hold back time itself
150   to hasten on another sacrifice,
a sacrifice barbaric, never sacrificed before,
a sacrifice no lips will ever taste,
the seed of anarchy and strife embedded in the house,
its tendrils clinging, wrapping round the very fabric of the house,
and no respect at all for any man there.

> It has not died, no, it breaks out afresh, the terror and the treachery, the governess that guards the house, the child-avenging Fury which will not forget.

This was the destiny that Calchas prophesied, this and the golden promises brought for the army by the birds to the royal household. And in response with one voice we

chant the laments for sorrow, *may all turn out well.*

160   Zeus. Zeus, whatever Zeus may be,
            if this name 'Zeus' finds pleasure with him,
      then as Zeus I name him now.
      There is no force, though I should weigh
      all others in my mind, can equal Zeus
      to exorcise the dull ache of foreboding from my brain.
      In the beginning was a mighty god,
      exalting in his battle-strength, his prowess, his invincibility.
170   But now he is consigned to history. We shall not think of him.
      Then came another. He was overthrown.
      And now, whoever like a zealot raises high the cry of victory for Zeus
      shall understand the meaning in all things.

Zeus set men on the path to knowledge,
setting firm this unequivocal command:

> *True understanding comes through suffering.*

And so, instead of sleep, the steady trickle to the heart,
180   the pain of suffering the mind cannot forget.

And so, although unwillingly, mankind
learns how to live within the bounds.
There is a kindness in the cruelty of gods
who sit as grim protectors in the hidden sanctum of the soul.

He did not blame him. No, King Agamemnon, elder brother, leader of the proud fleet of the Greeks, did not blame Calchas for his prophecies. No, but he swayed before the breath of destiny that had possessed him now the Greek army all was beached across the straight from Calchis, now that supplies were running out, now that starvation stalked the troops at Aulis where the rip-tides race.

And the gales swept down from Strymon, yes, and with them boredom, hunger and resentment. And the men began to drift away. And to the winds the ships, the hawsers were as nothing, and so, as time ebbed and flowed and swelled to an eternity, the winds tore, lacerated, shredded raw the flower of Greece. And then it was the prophet Calchas called aloud again, a second salve to soothe the storm-winds, baleful and more bitter for the generals. This was, he said, the will of Artemis. And when they heard him they could not hold back their tears, no, but they threw their sceptres heavy on the ground, the two Atreidae.

And then he spoke, King Agamemnon, elder brother, senior in command, and he said:

My demon will destroy me if I don't obey, but if I slaughter my own child, the jewel, the treasure of my household, if I pollute these hands, her father's hands, and drench them in her pure black blood before the altar, then my demon will pursue me too. Each way lies horror. How can I jump ship and fail my allies? No. In her fury, supernatural, untamed, the goddess lusts for sacrifice of virgin blood to stay the storm – and that is right and proper. And so now as it is, may all be well.

And so he clamped around his throat the leash of certainty – how could he fail to do what must be done? – and so he tacked his resolution to the evil breeze of blasphemy and sacrilege, and from that day his spirit changed and he would stop at nothing. Fanaticism gives men strength; it is unyielding and inflexible; it goads men on to cruelty and guides their path to ruin. So he submitted. He became the priest of sacrifice, and offered his own daughter as a bulwark in a war of vengeance for a woman's sake, first rites of passage for the fleet.

Oh, how she begged and prayed and how she called out for her father. They did not care, though, in their lust for war, the generals. They did not care for all her youth and innocence. Her father made the necessary prayer and told his men to hold her firm above the altar, like an animal, face-down, all wrapped close in the fabric of her robes. He told them too to gag her mouth, her lovely mouth, to muffle any words that might bring down a curse upon the house

by violence and the choking voiceless cord. Her yellow robes, dyed deep in purest saffron, fell heavy to the ground, and she shot glances at each man
240 there at the sacrifice, darting looks to melt the heart, lovely as a girl looks in a picture, wanting so to speak, as often in her father's halls she'd sung at banquet, her voice pure, lovely as a virgin's voice is pure, honouring in love and gentleness the third drink offering to god, the sacred hymn, the hymn of hope for her dear father.

What happened next I cannot say – I did not see it. But Calchas' visions come
250 to pass. Justice drags the balance down and so true understanding comes to those who suffer. What will be will be, and you will know it. Face it now, or (rather) weep. For it will come as clear as any dawn, which slices through the mists that rise with morning.

And so now, as it is, may all be well, as is her wish, Queen Clytemnestra, she, our sole protectress, she, the net that's fenced round Argos so to keep our city sure.

Clytemnestra *once more appears at the palace door.*

Clytemnestra, I have come, honouring your majesty. For when the throne is
260 empty of its man-lord, it is right and proper that we pay due honour to our ruler's wife. Has good news come? Has no news come? Are these sacrifices all in hope of a good resolution? I long with all my heart to hear. But, lady, if you're silent, I shall understand.

Clytemnestra There is a saying: may daybreak bring good news born from the blackest night. And I have news to tell you that you have not dared to hope. The Greeks have taken Troy.

Chorus No. No! It's unbelievable. I don't understand.

Clytemnestra Did I not speak clearly? I tell you, Troy has fallen. It is in Greek hands.

270 **Chorus** I never dared to hope...

Clytemnestra Your eyes, your tears, give you away, your loyalty.

Chorus It is a true report? You have the evidence?

Clytemnestra Oh yes. There is no doubt. Unless God tricked me.

Chorus Oh. So you had a dream; you saw a vision; you believed it.

Clytemnestra I'd not give credence to a dream.

Chorus No. But a rumour, maybe, insubstantial – did that feed your hopes?

Clytemnestra Don't speak to me as if I were a child.

Chorus When was the city taken then?

Clytemnestra Last night. Last night before the dawn.

Chorus How could the news have come so quickly? Who did you hear it 280
from?

Clytemnestra The god of fire, Hephaestus. He shot the blaze of fire first from Mount Ida, and then beacon passing torch to beacon, fire igniting fire, the race began, the relay race for home:

Ida on to Lemnos and the scarred peaks of Mount Hermes; third torch like a fire-ball arcing high onto Mount Athos and the sacred crags of Zeus; and then the sea – and as it skimmed the surface of the swelling waves, the torchlight swelled, exalted, grew in glory until golden as the very sun it shot its message to Macistus and the lookouts waiting there. Macistus did not 290
hesitate; alert, it played its part, and far away across Euripus' straits the watchmen on Messapion made out the beacon's flame. They plunged their torches in the pyre they'd built – the heather, sapless, dry – and so in answer that flame too leapt up and out and on. It never faltered in its strength, but like the purest moon leapt on across Asopus plain to forge the next link in the chain of fire to flare on Mount Cithaeron.

Its garrison embraced the flame and so a new blaze burst to life, a great 300
explosion shooting high, outleaping its command. The fire-burst streaked across the snake-pit marsh, Gorgopis, to the mountain, Aegiplancton, where the wild goats graze, and there it roused the watchmen and they scrambled to their task. And in their wild excitement there they raised their conflagration, their beard of flame, their comet, so it soared on past the headland, the Saronic Straits, the star-burst searing through the darkness till it came to Mount Arachne, only one more step to go.

And so it swooped low here to Argos, to the house of the Atreidae, the fire, the 310
true descendant of the fires that blaze at Troy. This was the relay I myself established for the torch-men, each passing on the beacon to the next until the race was done. And first and last the runners mount the rostrum crowned

with victory. This is the sign I give you, this the evidence, this message sent me by my husband out of Troy.

Chorus Gods! My lady, I'll give thanks now and forever to the gods. But, please!, give your report again – leave nothing out – that I might listen, that I might admire.

320 **Clytemnestra** Today the Greeks have Troy. I think I almost hear the shouting and the screaming and the dissonance that surges through the streets and lanes and splashes through the snickleways of Troy. Vinegar and oil walled in one bucket never mix – the enmity between them is so strong.

And so the voices of the victors and the victims are not one, the voices of their destinies discordant: women clinging to the corpses of their husbands; young men cradling their wives dead in their arms; children running to their grandfathers to save them, but the old men cannot help them, sprawled and slaughtered in the streets; and where they once knew freedom, love, they'll mouth forever pain.

330 But for our men, no more the night raids out to battle, no more grind, no, but they'll break their long fast, glutting on the city, each seizing what he can, no holding back for rank or order, no, but as each drew the token of blind chance, each man will settle in some Trojan's house, his captive now, his prisoner, now they have put behind them all the icy rains, the drizzle soaking through their dreams, and now like gods in gratitude unguarded they will sleep the whole night through.

And if they reverence the gods of Troy, the sanctuaries still sacred to the gods
340 though Troy is taken, the victors may yet stop the cycle and escape defeat. So let no lust enflame them, lest they trample what must not be touched, engulfed by greed, by gluttony. The journey home must yet be run, the last lap and the voyage home to safety. And if the army should return, still spotless in the sight of god, they may yet flee the wrath and retribution of the dead – unless some sudden ruin strike them unseen, unexpected.

These are my words, a woman's words, and you have heard them. So, may all turn out well. May it be seen most clearly. What I have now, I have; what need
350 have I for more?

Chorus Your words were like a man's my lady – a rational, judicious man's; your proof was unequivocal. And now I've heard it, I must first give thanks to all the gods for this deliverance, so dearly paid for with such suffering, such sacrifice.

Clytemnestra *returns inside the palace.*

Zeus, King,
gentle Night,
you who possess all things in cosmic order –

you cast the close-meshed net, drag-net of destiny,   360
taut on the towers of Troy,
that nothing might outleap its horror,
neither young nor old,
caught fast,
caught helpless in its cruelty.

And so I hold great Zeus in highest honour,
Zeus of the family, Zeus Xenios,
god of guests and friends,
for, all unhurried, he has stretched his bow-string taut
to calibrate a careful aim at Paris Alexandros,
so that his missile might not fall too short
nor shoot too high beyond the stars
but sink home solid, true.

So they can tell how Zeus engulfed them,
they can trace his tracks.
What he has done is done.
Zeus has achieved his purpose.

'I've heard men say gods do not care if men should trample the taboo – they   370
will not punish them. Whoever says this is a heretic. For Justice will crash
heavy on the covetous, their rasping breath, their homes which blossom
sickly with their greed. May no tears come, but to the man who has true
understanding may each day bring what each day needs and nothing more.   380
There is no wealth in all the world can shield a man from ruin, who has
trampled the great altar-stone of Justice under heel.

First, madness.
Then, conviction.
Absolute and cruel.
No going back.
No cure.

Not dormant, though, this plague, this virus –
blazing with a burning light –
the bad bronze burnished,   390

touchstone tarnished,
black beneath the surface,
scraped by Justice.

A little child is running,
chasing a wing'd bird,
and bringing plague and cancer to the city.

400 So Paris came to the Atreidae's house and in his cold contempt for friendship stole another's wife.

She left her city her inheritance –
imbroglio, confusion,
armies massing, weapons clashing,
boatmen press-ganged, soldiers now –
and so to Troy for dowry she brought holocaust;
between the gates she danced as if on air,
defying her destiny.

410 And in the houses, prophets wept; they mourned for homesteads, for the battle-line, for empty marriage-beds, for widows aching for lost loves, and said:

We see the emptiness of the bereft,
the silence, dull, no pride left,
no reproach, no understanding.

For she has gone beyond the sea,
and how he longs for her;
and soon her ghost will seem to fill the palace.
And yet, for all their beauty,
all his images of her bring only hatred.
His eyes are dull now.
All they love is gone.

420 *Dream-phantoms, so seductive,*
stretch out cool arms in incorporeal embrace.
Emptiness.
All emptiness.
He thinks he sees her, sees his love,
but then the dream dilates
and from his grasp the vision vanishes.
A dream like that will never come again.

Grief haunts the house,
this grief and grief more searing still,
and throughout Greece
for every man who sailed to Troy
no tears, no mourning yet, just emptiness.   430
There is so much can stop the heart.

They knew the men they sent away
but now in place of men
there comes to every house
an urn and ashes.

Ares, chancellor of war,
gold-dealer, dealing corpses in exchange for living men,
spear-shaft scales poised breathless in the balance of the battle,
sends home heavy gold-dust from the fires of Troy,   440
dry dust worth so many tears,
and where there once were men he packs their ashes
tidily, efficiently in urns.

And so they mourn them, and they praise them
this man had such skill in battle
this man fell so nobly,
    butchered for another's wife.

Such words as these are snarled in silence,
and so grief, cold and resentful, slithers,   450
coils against the two commanders, the Atreidae.

And others, brave and beautiful,
lie buried there beneath the walls.
The soil of Troy enfolds them,
and so they lie forever in an enemy's embrace.

Talk on the streets is dangerous when hatred fuels it.
Talk leads to discontent, and discontent to curses,
    and curses must be paid in full.

Fear haunts me lest I hear the voices in the darkness,   460
for gods do not ignore the man whose hands are steeped in blood.
Black demons watch him, wear him down,
this man so ruthless and so prosperous,
and so they rub his soul away;

they make him spectral, shadowy;
and when he has no shadow left,
what hope has any man?

470 A man who will hear only praise is dangerous for he attracts the eye of Zeus, the thunder-bolt. A lack of envy – that for me is wealth. *I* have no wish to sack a city, no, nor be a captive either, all my life destroyed.

The fire brought hope; it kindled rumour racing through the city. But if it's true – who knows? Perhaps it's just a trick that's played on us by gods. What man 480 is so naive, his brain so bruised he'd let his heart catch fire because some sparks had fizzled news he had not hoped to hear, and then when the report's reversed he's dashed? Premature jubilation – what can you expect when a woman's in control? Too plausible. A woman's gossip spreads like wildfire, but then, just like a woman, it lacks stamina; it loses interest; and it soon grows bored and jaded.

490 We'll know about the beacons and the ring of fire, the flames, the torches soon – if their report is true, or if like sweet seductive dreams the firelight crept on us to bilk our brains. Look! There! A man! He's coming, dappled through the olive trees, up from the sea, caked dry in dust as orange as the mud of Troy. *He* is no voiceless witness, no – *he* won't pile branches on some hill-top or rely on smoke-signs, no, or fire to give *his* news, no – he will either spit out his report that we might celebrate … I cannot face the other, the alternative. No. No. No, let his news be good that we might add it to the good 500 news we already have. And if there be a man or woman in the city prays the opposite, then may they drain the black and bitter gall of their disloyalty.

Enter the **Herald**.

Herald Sweet soil of home! Red soil of Argos! Ten years, ten years and in the dawning I've come home to you! So many hopes I had, all shipwrecked, but the anchor that I clung to most has held. I dared not dream I'd die at home in Argos or that I'd lie when I was dead in Argive soil. But now, my land, my own land, you – I look on you again – my sunlight and my Zeus, high god of Argos, yes, and you, Apollo, lord of Pytho, bow no longer bent nor shafts 510 unsheathed to shower on us – sufficient by Scamander's stream was your hostility. Now come to us as saviour, healer, lord Apollo.

I call on all the gods of battle and on you, my great protector, Hermes, spokesman's god whom spokesmen worship; heroes; demi-gods who sent us out – now welcome us back home to your embrace, the remnants of the army spared by war.

The palace, eh?! The royal court, so familiar. The sober benches and the gods who face the rising sun! – if ever once you welcomed him, our king, with dancing 520 eyes, give him his welcome now as he deserves, now he's come home at last and all our lonely years of exile are now ended. Yes, he has come with fire to thaw the velvet night-time now for you and you and everyone – King Agamemnon!

So, greet him gladly now as he deserves, now he has flattened Troy, destroying it with the mattock of the god of justice, Zeus, now he has harrowed all the plain, now all the seed of all the land of Troy is withering. This is the yoke that he has clamped on Troy, our king, the son of Atreus, the elder brother, and he's 530 coming now, and all the gods applaud him, of all men now alive most glorious. For neither Paris, no, nor Troy, his great accomplice, now can boast that what they did, the same and more has not been done to them. Guilty and convicted, rapist and thief, he has lost his prize and seen his house, his heritage, his very land laid waste, eradicated. So they have paid a double price, the sons of Priam, for their crimes.

Chorus *You* are the spokesman for the Greek army? I wish you well!

Herald Oh, I *feel* well! So much so that I could die today and still not bother!

Chorus You were so homesick? 540

Herald I could weep with happiness!

Chorus Such sweet sorrow!

Herald I don't understand.

Chorus Longing so for Argos, when Argos longed for you.

Herald You mean you wished the army was back home?

Chorus So much. We felt so helpless. Nothing *we* could do but grumble!

Herald Why? What was the matter?

Chorus I found this out a long, long time ago – the best way to dodge suffering is silence.

Herald What? When the generals were gone you lived in fear? Why? Who?

Chorus So much fear that, in your words, if I should die today my death 550 would be a blessing.

Herald Well, it has turned out well – yes, over any length of time a man might say, 'in such-and-such a thing the dice fell well', but then in such-and-such another he'll feel cheated. Only the gods live all their lives completely free from sorrow.

Oh, yes – if I told you of all *we* had to suffer, the aching billets, only narrow planks to sleep on, the damp and mildewed bedding – we had *cause* to grumble. And then we landed, and the torment multiplied.

Yes, we were fighting Troy and yet we pitched our tents beneath the *walls* of
560 Troy. And then, the never-ending drizzle, soaking, dripping, drenching, the mists that seeped and clung low to the sodden earth, and then the lice, the maggots everywhere in hair, in clothing. Yes, I could tell you of the icy winds, so cold that birds were frozen, snows that drifted on Mount Ida, no-one coming back, the baking heat, the sea at midday, molten, motionless, metallic, no breath, no breeze, a mirage merely, sleepless, shimmering.

570 Why worry now? It's over. It is over for us all – and for the dead, they need not rise again. For us, though, who remain, the Argive army, the prize is won, and nothing now can tip the balance. And so today, this shining day, this boast should skim the sea and soar high over all the earth: 'The Argive army once took Troy, and in accordance with the ancient rites, they nailed their booty in thanksgiving to the temples and the chapel doors of all the gods of Greece.' And
580 when they hear these words, they all will praise their city and their generals. And they will all give thanks to Zeus that in his grace he did such things.

There, now, I've done. I've finished. I have nothing left to say.

Chorus   You're right. You suffered more. I will admit it. Old men can learn – it keeps us young. I feel enriched by what you've said . . . and yet perhaps you should address your words to Clytemnestra and the royal house.

As if on cue, **Clytemnestra** *appears at the palace door.*

Clytemnestra   I raised the shout of victory long since when first the fire shot through the night to bring its news to me, to tell of Troy, how it was taken,
590 ground down bloody in the earth. Yet there were those who sneered at me: 'You put your faith in beacons, do you? You really think Troy's taken? Just like a woman to prematurely jubilate!' Oh yes, to hear them you would think I was so feeble-minded. But still they sacrificed and, like old women, here and here and everywhere throughout the city, croaked their cries of victory, 'may all turn out well', and in the chapels of the gods they lit their lullabying incense, lulling feral flames with musky balm.

So now – why bother telling me the rest? My master's coming. I'll learn
600 everything from him. My glorious husband. So. No more delay. I must do

everything I need that I can welcome him as he deserves. What day is sweeter for a wife to see than when her husband comes back home from war, kept safe by god, and she can spread the gates wide open and he enter?

Tell that to my husband. Tell him that the city pines for him. Tell him to come as quickly as he can. And when he comes, that he may find his wife at home as faithful as she was the day he left, the loyal obedient watch-dog of his house, the scourge of all who wish him ill, in all respects the same, her seal unbroken, even after all these years. I know no more of finding pleasure with another man or earning bad repute than I know how to plunge brute bronze into an icy bath to harden it. Such is *my* boast, a boast so pregnant with the truth there is no shame to broadcast it for such a woman, chaste and virtuous, as I. 610

Clytemnestra *returns inside the palace.*

Chorus So. She. Says. A pretty speech, whose subtlety you'd understand if you could see it. But tell me – what of Menelaus? Is he coming? Is he safe? All Argos needs him now.

Herald I can't tell lies convincingly enough, make bad seem good, that you'd enjoy their taste for long. 620

Chorus What if your news were good *and* true? That would be better. Discrepancy's discovered soon enough.

Herald He's disappeared. He and his fleet. They've disappeared. *That* is the truth.

Chorus You saw them sail from Troy, though? Did a storm blow up and separate his ships from yours?

Herald You're like a master bowman, you. You've hit your mark. You've summed up untold suffering with just one phrase.

Chorus Is he alive or dead? What news from any of the crew? 630

Herald No-one knows anything. There's no clear report. The only witness is the sun-god Helios, who looks down on us all.

Chorus How did the storm strike? How did it end? Was it the anger of the gods?

Herald Today's a day for celebration. Why blight it with grief? We should be giving thanks to all the gods, not *this*.

Look. A messenger comes to a city. Expression: grim. His news is this (the
640 opposite of what they've prayed): the army's decimated, city scarred, a septic
wound that will infect each citizen – so many men lost from so many families,
all whiplashed, scourged by Ares, mutilated, sprawling, skewered and bloody
in their slaughter. Such tragedy. How can his song not be a psalm of suffering,
all hallelujah to the demons of revenge?

But when he comes with *good* news, when all's well, when everyone is safe,
when he comes home and bells are ringing celebration through the streets –
why should I jumble good news up with bad and tell you of a storm whose
genesis could only be the anger of the gods?

650 Yes, fire and ocean, bitter enemies before, swore unity, and so, in token of their
faith, destroyed our army. Night-time, and the sea got up, black waves and
storm-winds lashing down from Thrace to smash ship shattering on ship, the
driving hurricane, the soaking spray, bows splintering on hulls, the maelstroms
and the whirlpools, warships rolling wildly, swamped and sinking, sucked
into the heaving sea, a demon driving them, down, drowning, disappeared.
And when the sun broke through at dawn, the whole Aegean sea was
660 blossoming with shipwrecks and the corpses of the dead.

But us, our ship: unharmed. A god's hand on the tiller, no man did it, guiding
us to safety, interceding on our ship's behalf. Fate smiled on us. Fate settled
softly on our ship and saved us. No need for *us* to ride the storm at anchorage,
no fear *we* would be driven on the rocks. And later, death behind us, sunlight
dancing on the sea, we still could not believe our luck, still trying to
670 comprehend disaster come from nowhere, all our army gone, wiped out so
cruelly. If any of the others live, they'll think *we're* dead. How not? That's what
we think of them. May all turn out for best.

But as for Menelaus, first and foremost, this: don't give up hope. Perhaps the
sun still shines on him, alive and safe and sound. If Zeus has no wish to wipe
out his family completely, he'll come home.

680 That's my report. That is the truth. You now know everything.

Exit the **Herald**.

Chorus   *Helen. Helen.*
So true a name. Who named her so?
   Helen. Helen.
Someone whom we could not see
yet could foresee so clearly
and tuned their voice with destiny.

Helen. Helen.
Spear-bride, spear-bedding,
wedding death to death. So true.
Helen. Helen.

Hell in ships and hell in men and hell in cities,   690
she stepped out from gauzy curtains.
Warm winds whispered,
filled the sails.
And so, so many shouldered shields and cast
like huntsmen for the vanished spoor of oars,
but they had landed
on the leafy shores of the Simoïs
and so war and slaughter came to Troy.

Raw anger works its will.   700
Raw anger brought the marriage rites,
last rites, so truly named,
to Troy (though late in time) for
    friendship flouted
    friendship taunted
    Zeus derided and all ties of hospitality
while they were bellowing
so brassily the bridal hymns,
his family, his brothers bawling loud
'here comes the bride!'

But that was soon forgotten –
they were learning other songs
in Priam's ancient city,   710
Priam's venerable city,
songs of sorrow, desolation,
songs of Paris and his marriage doomed to death,
songs of suffering, songs of the city,
songs of black blood
clotting with each rasping, dying breath.

There was a man once
reared a lion-cub in the palace.
All unweaned
it loved to suckle,
still so tame, so tender in its infancy.   720
The children loved it and the old men pampered it,

and in their arms they cradled it
just like a new-born child,
bright-eyed and purring,
feeding from their outstretched hands.

But gradually it grew
and it revealed its innate character.
It showed its gratitude
to those who'd nurtured it,
and of its own will, it
prepared a feast, insatiate,
a butchery, a shambles and
730 the house dripped viscous as an abattoir,
that no-one might outleap the horror or
escape the mutilation,
all the bloody devastation that engulfed it.

A priest of sacrifice,
an agent of obsession,
it had been reared by God's will in the family,
to cleanse the household.

I would imagine that at first there came to Troy
740 a mood of windless calm,
a soothing phantasm of wealth,
soft glances and seductive eyes,
a flowering of desire to sting the heart.
But then she changed –
and she contrived a bitter consummation, final marriage rites.
And so destruction stalked the city, trailing pestilence behind it,
devastation sent by Zeus against the proud young sons of Priam,
a demon of Revenge, a Fury,
and the young girls, newly-wedded, wept.

750 An old saying:
Great wealth grown fat does not die childless,
no, good fortune breeds destruction, all insatiate.
I don't agree.
760 I think that crime breeds crime in its own image, multiplied.
A house that's founded firm on justice
Will enjoy the justice in each generation.

Times are, ancestral arrogance can father

insolent young pride to join the evils of mankind.
The day comes, and the bud bursts,
black obsession blossoming,
a demon of revenge,
a rage so like her parentage, 770
impregnable, invulnerable. Diabolic.

But Justice can blaze bright in smoky cottages,
radiant for those whose lives are pure.
She turns her face from glittering prizes, superficial,
golden-plated, groped by grasping hands, and goes.
Modesty attracts her, never wealth,
so counterfeit, so fraudulent, so flattering. 780
So, Justice steers all things to their conclusion.

Enter **Agamemnon** *and* **Cassandra** *on a horse-drawn wagon reminiscent of the vehicle used at Greek marriages, bedecked with flowers.* **Cassandra** *is dressed in robes associated with a priestess of Apollo. They are accompanied by Agamemnon's* **Attendants**.

Agamemnon! King! Troy's taken! How should I address you now? How should I honour you so that my praise might not fall short nor shoot too high beyond the mark of modesty? For there are those (and many of them) honour superficial show, while shunning justice – all forced smiles, congratulations, rictus grins and sullen hearts, just like false friends, yawning their 790 commiserations, untouched ever by your tragedy. A good shepherd sees all things. He's not seduced by smiling eyes which seem so loyal and so solicitous; but they are fawning merely, watery with friendship. Once, when you led the army out to Troy, all for the sake of Helen (I will not hide it now) I formed an 800 image of you in my mind all ugly, corrupt, not steering well the tiller of the soul, too hasty, over-confident to lead our men to death. But now, I honour you with all my heart unstintingly, now all has turned out well. In time, tribunals of the citizens will tell who managed your affairs here well, and who maliciously.

Agamemnon Justice dictates that my first words should be to Argos and its 810 gods, with whose help I have now come home, with whose help too I have exacted the full sentence that the laws demand on Priam's city. Oh, yes – the gods held no debate. They did not hesitate but placed their votes for death, for Troy's destruction in the ballot-box for blood, and only Hope stretched out her hand for Troy's acquittal; but no vote fell. And still the smoke-pall fills the air where Troy once stood; black anger fans and billows still; but Troy is

820 dying, choking in its ash and dying embers, gushing gold-dust gasping with each rasping dying breath.

And so I must give thanks to all the gods, now and forever. We have exacted payment for a crime, a vicious crime, a rape, and for a woman's sake, and as the Pleiades sank low the beast of Argos ground their city in the dust our foal, our wooden horse, our army shouldered shields, launched its attack to storm the city. It leapt the towers, and like a mauling lion it glutted on the blood of kings. Such are my words, my first words, given at some length to all the gods.

830 As for your thoughts and your intentions, I have heard them and I shall remember. Your thoughts are mine and I shall not abandon you, for it is rare to find a man who can respect a friend's good fortune without envy. How well I know it! Yes, the reports that I could give! I looked hard into the glass of friendship and I saw that where I once had seen my staunchest allies I now
840 saw but the merest shadow of a dream. Only Odysseus, and he had not sailed willingly – when he had come on board he was more loyal and more reliable than any man. And even as I speak of him I do not know if he's alive or dead.

As for the rest, as for the city and the gods, we shall debate all things in full assembly, and where they're sound we must debate how they shall stay so. But where there's need for remedy, for cure, then we shall try to stop the cancer
850 spreading – with the surgeon's knife or cauterising fire.

Now I shall enter my own house, and there give thanks to all its gods for that they sent us out with godspeed on our voyage, yes, and brought us home again. And now that victory is ours, may it stay so forever.

*As **Agamemnon** is about to climb down from the wagon, **Clytemnestra** appears at the palace door. **Agamemnon** remains in the wagon.*

Clytemnestra (*to* Chorus)   You, gentlemen! You, citizens! You, Argive elders, you! I'll feel no shame to speak before you as a loving wife. Reticence recedes with time.

I've not learned sorrow second-hand; no – listen to the life I led while he, my
860 husband, was at Troy, a woman sitting all alone at home without her husband, worrying, worrying, and someone comes and then another, and his news is worse than all the terror come before, and so the nightmares rattle in the corridors. And if my husband had sustained as many wounds as their reports came home to me, I swear he'd have more gashes in him than a hunting net. And if he'd died as many deaths as men reported, he would be another

Geryon, a second Trinity, so often resurrected, slain, that he might boast he'd 870
got himself a three-fold coat of earth, killed once for each of his three aspects.
And every time those ugly rumours came, they had to cut me struggling
wildly down and free my neck, though I resisted, from the rasping noose.

(to *Agamemnon*) And so our child is not here now beside me, our child who
sealed our love-ties, yours and mine, our child who should be here, Orestes –
don't look so perplexed. He's being cared for by our friend and ally, Strophius, 880
in Phocis. I took advice from him. He warned me of the several disasters that
could strike, the danger you were facing out at Troy, the danger too (with you
not here) that public discontent might lead to anarchy and overthrow our
government. For it is human nature, as he said, to kick a man who's down.
And that is why. That is the truth. There is no need to hide it.

But as for me, the wellsprings of my tears, which used to flow so readily, are
all dried up – not one tear left me. No. My eyes are raw from all the sleepless 890
nights of weeping for you, waiting for the torch-light blaze which would not
come. And then I'd sleep so lightly that the softest sounds, the droning of a
gnat's wing, seemed to scream aloud. But I'd already seen you suffer so, so
many sufferings compressed in a such a little sleep.

(*to* Chorus) But now, all that is in the past, my grief is done, and I should
speak of him, my husband, as the watchdog of our house, our saviour,
mainstay of his ship, the deep-set pillar shouldering the vaulting roof, the
only son, the dry land seen by sailors, when all their hope is gone, the sun's
rays breaking out in stormy weather, the cool spring splashing on the stones 900
for thirsty travellers. Such are the images I see him in. Let them incur no
jealousy. We have endured sufficient suffering already.

(*to* Agamemnon) But now, my love, my darling, come down from your
carriage – don't set your feet, the feet that trampled Troy, on bare earth, king!
Girls! Quickly! As I taught you – spread the fabrics on the ground for him to
walk on. Now, let a path appear, a blood-red river, a triumphal way, and Justice 910
lead him to a home he had not hoped to see.

Clytemnestra's **maidservants** *lay fabrics leading from the wagon to the palace door.*

As for the rest, conviction, wakeful, vigilant, shall win, and with god's will and
Justice lead to destiny.

Agamemnon   Clytemnestra – keeper of my house, my chatelaine – your
speech matched well my absence: both were much too long. Praise has its

proper place but eulogies like this should come from others, not from you. And as for these, I'm not a woman, so don't pamper me like one. I'm not a pasha either, so no genuflections, no salaams, no perorations, no, no fabrics scattered on the ground to trace a path which cannot but attract the jealousies of gods. The gods *deserve* such shows of adoration, but for me, a man, to trample on such beautiful brocade brings only fear. I tell you: honour me – but as a man not as a god. These are not carpets, no, but sacred vestments, in no way the same. Deliverance from evil is the greatest gift the gods can give, and for a man the only truly prosperous life's a life that ends before it's met disaster. There. That's my policy and I have spoken. That is the policy by which I'd live and be secure.

Clytemnestra But tell me this, in all truth . . .

Agamemnon In all truth, I tell you this – I shall not compromise.

Clytemnestra But all I ask . . . is there no circumstance, no fear perhaps, would make you vow to do this for the gods?

Agamemnon If some wise, holy man prescribed this course of action, I'd do it, yes.

Clytemnestra And Priam, what would *he* have done if victory were *his*?

Agamemnon I know without a doubt what *he*'d have done. He would have walked on them.

Clytemnestra Well, then, why hesitate? What are you frightened of?

Agamemnon The people. Public discontent can lead to riots and rebellion.

Clytemnestra No – envy's good – it makes a man ambitious.

Agamemnon A woman should not revel so in conflict.

Clytemnestra Yet even for a victor there are times it is more gracious to surrender.

Agamemnon To have your way in this means so much to you?

Clytemnestra Give in. If it's by *your* will that you submit, yours is the victory truly.

Agamemnon Well. As you wish.

(*to* Attendants) Come, someone, quickly now, take off my boots; they've served me well.

And as I bruise these blood-red robes, this sacred damask here, may no-one shoot the glance of envy at me from afar. I feel contrition so to trample on this house's wealth, to waste our riches, waste these webs with so much silver woven in their warp and weft.

(*to* Clytemnestra) Enough of this. This girl, our guest, take her inside and show her some respect. Even from far, the gods look kindly at the man who uses his power gently, and no-one *chooses* slavery. But she was chosen for me from the wealth of all our plunder, my flower, my blossom, the gift the army gave me, that she might come with me. 950

Agamemnon *steps down from the wagon onto the fabrics.*

There, I have heeded you. I'm down.

So this is how I come home – treading grape-red tapestries, a path of blood!

Agamemnon *walks slowly towards the palace.*

Clytemnestra The sea is there forever; who could drain it? It breeds the dye which oozes blood-red always, sempiternal, so much silver spent to steep the weave in. But by god's grace this house *has* silver, king, much of it – poverty's a thing this house knows nothing of. And I'd have vowed to trample clothes for ever if an oracle had told me that this way I'd bring him home alive. 960

It needs a little root just for the leaves to come again to thatch the house and shade it from the dog-star's parching heat. And now you're home like warmth in winter thawing out our house to make it blossom. When Zeus treads down the vintage, trampling the bitter grapes, chill winds sigh through the corridors, the master moving back and forward deep inside the house. 970

Agamemnon *enters the palace.*

Zeus, Zeus, you who bring all things to fulfilment, now fulfil my prayers! Consider now, give thought, I pray, to their fulfilment!

Clytemnestra *enters the palace, leaving the* **Chorus** *and* **Attendants** *still on stage and* **Cassandra** *still in the wagon.*

Chorus Why is this horror with me always, roosting, glowering, grim, and beating its black wings against my heart to lash my prophecies? And all unbidden, unrewarded too, it moans its horoscopes in mantras. I can't 980 dislodge it like a dream I can't divine; I can't let courage come to comfort me, to take command, to commandeer my mind. Time has grown old since they slung the hawsers on the ships so hastily (and the sand sprayed as they slung them) and the Greek armada sailed to Troy.

They have come home, and I have seen them. Still, my soul stirs deep within me all untaught and all untutored, moaning plainchants *a cappella* for the demons of revenge. And the confidence that hope brings has all left me. Gut feelings don't deceive, and the irrational engages with the rational, the seat of Justice, spinning round, gyrating in a great maelstrom, a vortex, sucking in its weltering waves until they reach fulfilment. I pray that my forebodings never come to pass, but fall like barren seed, unblossoming.

The circle closes with its opposites. The balance tips. The mould of sickness mildews on the mansion walls. Man's destiny, which seemed to sail so smooth, so true, snags on a hidden reef and founders. Then a judicious captain throws some cargo overboard – but just enough – and so, by sacrificing some, he saves the rest. His whole house will not sink then, groaning with the weight of too much wealth, nor will he waterlog his vessel. And year by year Zeus in his generosity makes grain to grow across the furrowed land and so staves off for us the murrain of starvation.

But once a man's black blood, man's dying blood, has fallen on the earth, what cures are there, what chants can call it back again? There was a man once knew a secret: how to resurrect the dead. Zeus put an end to him. No harm was done. And if my destiny were otherwise ordained, not ordered by my destiny from God, my tongue could not contain my heart, my heart would sing so clear. But as it is, all I can do is grumble in the dark, all gloomy, grim, and no hope left me that the time will come, the black thread break. My mind's a furnace and my brain ablaze.

Clytemnestra *appears at the palace door.*

Clytemnestra Cassandra! Cassandra, come inside now, too, since in his kindness Zeus has given you to us to share our house, our stoups of holy water, as you stand with all our slaves before his altar. Come down now. Put away your pride.

They say that even Hercules was sold once into slavery, to eat with slaves, to break their bread. And if it is your destiny to suffer such a fate as this, give thanks your masters come from an old family. The *nouveaux riches* treat slaves unconscionably badly, but we appreciate the worth of each and so treat each as each deserves. That's my philosophy – you know it now.

Chorus (*to* Cassandra)   She's stopped speaking to you now. An ingenuous speech. And so, since you've been taken, netted in the toils of destiny, obey her, if you would obey. Perhaps, though, you are disobedient.

Clytemnestra (*to* Chorus)   If she can comprehend, yes, if her language is   1050
not primitive, barbarian, unstructured as a swallow's rasping scream, I shall persuade her.

Chorus (*to* Cassandra)   Go with her. As things are, she's speaking for the best. So listen to her. Come down from your carriage, from your throne.

Clytemnestra   I can't waste time out here. The sheep are there already by the navel-stone; the fires are ready and the sacrificial blade, an act of closure I had never hoped to see. And if you'd have a part in this, no more delay.

(*to* Cassandra) Look. If you're deficient, chuckle-headed, if what I say can't reach you, well – don't try to speak. No, use your hands, communicate in   1060
signs. That's what the primitive tribes do.

Chorus   I think our friend needs a translator, yes, a dragoman. She's like an animal just taken from the wild.

Clytemnestra   She's mad, moronic, gormlesss – she can't understand. Her city's just been taken. Now she's here. She doesn't have the wits to bear the bridle easily before she lets her life's blood bubble from her. I've no more words to waste, and I won't be insulted.

Clytemnestra *returns inside the palace.*

Chorus (*to* Cassandra)   I won't be angry with you. No. You have my sympathy. Come down, my dear, down from the carriage. It's all so new for   1070
you. What you can't change, you must put up with.

As **Cassandra** *steps down from the wagon, she suddenly sees spectral shapes hovering around the palace, and utters a blood-curdling scream.*

Cassandra   *otototoi popoi da!* Apollo! Apollo!

Chorus   Apollo? What? Why call on *him* in such a voice? He has no part in death-songs.

Cassandra   *otototoi popoi da!* Apollo! Apollo!

Chorus   She's calling him again. It's blasphemy! It's not right to involve him in such choking cries.

1080 **Cassandra** Apollo! Apollo! My liminal Apollo! Eliminating me again, this time completely!

Chorus I think she's going to prophesy about what's plaguing her. The god's gift doesn't leave you, not even in slavery.

Cassandra Apollo! Apollo! My liminal Apollo! What have you brought me to? What is this house?

Chorus It's the house of the Atreidae – Agamemnon and King Menelaus. If you don't know that, well, I can tell you – it's the truth, no lie.

1090 **Cassandra** The gods abominate this place, this house, its cruel complicity – the killing, so much killing in one family, beheading – this, this charnel-house, this abattoir, this baptism of blood.

Chorus This girl, she's like a hunting-dog, keen-scented, casting for the spoor of slaughter, and she'll find it.

1100 **Cassandra** Yes, yes, the signs are here! I see them! Babies bawling, butchered, roasted; father gorging on their flesh.

Chorus We'd heard you were a famous prophet, but we don't look for clairvoyants here.

Cassandra *io popoi!* What are they doing? What's this conspiracy? This agony? It's breaking out afresh. The house. The house. Evil conspiracy. The household – no! It can't be borne, and there's no cure now. Help is far away.

Chorus This new clairvoyance baffles me. I understood the rest, though – the whole city throbs with it.

Cassandra So *this* is what you mean to do? *Talaina!*
Cleansing your bed-mate, your husband, with ritual ablution –
how shall I speak of the end, though? Sudden! So sudden!
1110 Hands stretching out, and hands stretching after in ritual oblation.

Chorus I'm still no wiser. My mind's clouding over. Riddles, enigmas – I can't understand them!

Cassandra *è, è, papaï! Papaï!* What's taking shape now?
A drag-net of death? But the net is his bed-mate,
accomplice in killing. So let strife insatiate
raise for the family the triumph of victory
where death comes by stoning.

Chorus What's this? You're calling the demon of vengeance here to our house now? I find your words chilling, and in my heart bubbles the mucous of terror, as yellow as saffron, dyed deep with the crocus, the mucous men swallow when struck by the spear-shaft, and life's fading rays sink below the horizon. Disaster comes quickly. 1120

Cassandra Look! Look! Keep the bull from the heifer.
She's snaring him fast in the webs of her weaving,
the black horns are goring, the weapon sinks home.
And he's sliding back in the bath, in the water,
the purifying bowl of adulterous death. –

Chorus I won't boast and say I'm an expert in visions, but *this* I can work out: it won't turn out well. What good ever comes of an oracle anyway? Fear of the future is all their rhymes tell. 1130

Cassandra *Ió, ió, talaina!* My own evil destiny!
This is my tragedy now I'm lamenting,
pouring my fate in the same cup of death!
Why did you bring me here, me, me, talaina,
nothing to do now but share in his death.
Why?

Chorus You're possessed by a god, you are spell-bound. It's *your* death you're mourning – your own rasping death song – just like a nightingale, xanthus and blossoming, death all around her, her death dirge insatiate, 'Itys' and 'Itys', her trembling lament. 1140

Cassandra The nightingale died, and her songs have died with her,
a quiet death – the gods wrapped her body in feathers
and made her immortal and untouched by grief.
But me – what awaits me's the cleaver,
my limbs hacked, dismembered, the blood and the pain.

Chorus Where have they come from, these pains pressing on you, god-given and empty, the terrors you tell of, the animal voices, the ear-splitting screams? Where have they come from, these pathways to prophecy ending in death? 1150

Cassandra The marriage of Paris! The death of my family!
The streams of Scamander that snaked below Troy!
I used to walk by your shores in my childhood,
talaina, I spent all my girlhood with you.
But now I am going to Cocytus and Acheron, 1160

rivers of death, and I'll prophesy there.

Chorus Why are you saying this? The meaning's too clear. Even a small child could tell it. It's like it's tearing me, bloody and rasping, your sobbing, your tears. They so pain me to hear.

Cassandra Troy's gone with its spasms and death-throes –
and all of his slaughter of beasts was in vain –
my father, his sacrifice under the towers –
1170 but nothing could ward off its fate from the city,
nothing could stave off its suffering then.
And so I shall die in a little and join them,
drenching the earth with my ebbing black blood.

Chorus Just like your last words. A demon is riding you, black and malignant, making you tell of your death and your pain. I see no end to it.

Cassandra *begins to vacillate between periods of distress and calmness.*

Cassandra No. No. It's over. My vision won't blush coyly out from gauzy
1180 veils like some new bride, but like a fresh breeze it will fan and race to meet the sun-rise, and the dawn will break and with it a great deluge more devastating yet than any you have known.

I'll tell you now, and no more riddles. But you now – be my witnesses! Join with me in the hunt, track down the scent, the spoor of all these horrors done
1190 so long ago. It never leaves this house, the chorus, chanting its cabbala in a unison, cacophonous, words so diabolic, and they've drunk human blood, and so their power is growing and they're haunting all the house now with their ghostly tarantella and they cannot be dislodged – they're in the blood, congenital, the demons of revenge. They are roosting in the palace, chanting psalms of blinding madness, of the passion that began it, a polyphony of loathing for a brother's wife debauched, detestation for the man who so seduced her.

Am I wrong? Or, like a marksman, have I hit my mark? *Am* I just some gypsy sham, some drooling lunatic just scratching at the door? Bear witness now upon your oath. Have you no evidence, no knowledge of the sins this house has harboured for so long?

Chorus What difference does it make how firm or fast an oath I swear? It won't cure anything. But you amaze me. You've come here from abroad, a
1200 foreign country, yet you speak so clear, as if you'd lived here all your life.

Cassandra Apollo, the prophet, ordained me in these orders.

Chorus But he's a god! Was he smitten by you too?

Cassandra I've not told anyone before. I've been ashamed.

Chorus We can all afford our scruples when our life's going well.

Cassandra Oh, how he fought to have me, breathed the hot breath of his grace upon me!

Chorus Did you bed him, then? That usually comes next.

Cassandra I promised him I would, and then I broke my word.

Chorus With his power already in you?

Cassandra Yes. Already I was prophesying all that would happen to my people. 1210

Chorus But you escaped Apollo's anger?

Cassandra After my shortcomings, no-one would believe a word I said.

Chorus But *we* believe you. *We* believe your prophecies.

Cassandra *once more becomes possessed.*

Cassandra *ioú! ioú!* No! No! The horrors! Pressing pain!

Truth's terror clutching, gripping; spasms spinning round my brain; the prelude . . . look!

Do you see them, roosting, huddled close beside the house, the young – dream-phantoms, arms outstretched – the children killed – no! can it be?! – by their own family, clutching in their hands their flesh, their guts, their 1220 entrails, sweetmeats in a feast for their own father, no! No! Such sorrow!

So, for them, this is my prophecy! A listless lion is lolling on his bed, effeminate and pampered, plotting vengeance on the king when he comes home.

The bitch's blandishments, her lolling tongue, her long-drawn dancing words of welcome all seduced him and he cannot see, the general, the scourge of Troy, he cannot see how like a black malignant demon she will work her will and viciousness will favour her. Such outrage this – the female slaughtering 1230 the male!

She is – how should I name her for her butchery insatiate, this beast, this amphisbaena, this, this Skylla crouching in her cave, this gorgon drowning sailors, this, this mother spawning death, her hot breath fetid for her family, the breath of Ares, god of battle, stirring fighting into death.

Oh, how she raised the cry of victory, all boasts, bravado like a general who's turned a battle into rout. And she pretends she's glad he's come home safely.

1240 And if you don't believe me, well, what does it matter anyway? What will be will be, and in a little, such a little, you will speak of me in pity as too true a prophetess.

Chorus Thyestes feasting on his own sons' flesh – I follow you. My neck is bristling. Fear clutches me to hear you speak so true, not masked in images. But all the rest – I heard it but I'm wide of understanding.

Cassandra I tell you: you will look on Agamemnon dead.

Chorus No malediction, no, *talaina*! Hush what you're saying now.

Cassandra No cure will come to cicatrize my prophecy.

Chorus Not if it is as it will be. But I say, let it not be so!

1250 **Cassandra** They're bent on slaughter and you're mouthing prayers!

Chorus Who is he then? What man is scheming so much suffering?

Cassandra So, you've not understood my prophecies.

Chorus I've no idea who'll do it.

Cassandra Yet I speak your language all too well.

Chorus So does the oracle at Delphi – it's still hard to understand.

Cassandra *papaï!* The flames are licking, blazing! *ototoï!* Lycean Apollo! Wolf-god Apollo! *Oi, egó, egó!*

The lioness, two-leggèd, is bedding with the wolf,
   when the lion has left his lair.
1260 And she'll kill me, me, *talaina*.
Like a witch, who works her poison,
she will stir my wage, my wormwood!
And she revels as she whets the sword
and boasts that it's because he
brought me home that she will kill him
with our slaughter as his payment.

So why keep these symbols still of my disgrace, this sceptre and this garland? No! Damnation take them!

Cassandra *tears off her robes, and as she does so gradually becomes calmer.*

There's my response to you, there on the ground! Go, give some other girl your wealth of ruin – not me. Look! Look! Apollo himself's stripping me of my prophetic costume. He watched me mocked in these robes by my family, my enemies, all their conviction empty, and they called me names, *talaina*, like a gypsy sham, a refugee; I bore their taunts of beggar, pauper, tramp. 1270

And now the circle closes, and the prophet's done with me, his prophetess, and so he's brought me here to die. No more my father's altar, just the chopping block – it's waiting, steaming bloody with my death and with my sacrifice.

Yet our deaths won't go unhonoured by the gods or unavenged, for there shall come another to avenge us, a son to kill his mother and to take his vengeance for his father's death. An exile and a wanderer, a refugee from his land, he'll come home and so cement the coping-stone of ruin for his family. His father's corpse sprawled supine on the earth will call him home. 1280

Why such self-pity? Why these tears? I saw my city, I saw Troy endure all it endured; I saw the men who raped my city taken as the gods decreed in retribution. And so I too shall go. I too shall die. 1290

This house – it is as if it is the house of death, of Hades.

But I pray the first stroke kills me outright, that with no convulsions, as my blood drains from me, I might close my eyes in gentle, welcome death.

Cassandra *begins to walk slowly towards the palace.*

Chorus   Poor girl, such sorrow and such knowledge, too! You've said so much. But if you really know your death, how can you go so bravely like a beast to sacrifice?

Cassandra   There's no escape. No more. Time has run out for me.

Chorus   And yet our last day demands due respect. 1300

Cassandra   That day has come. There's little to be gained in trying to escape.

Chorus   You are a brave girl and courageous.

Cassandra   You'd not have said that if all this had turned out well.

Chorus   Yet there's some consolation to be had in death with honour.

Cassandra   My father and my family!

Cassandra *suddenly turns from the palace, horrified.*

Chorus What's wrong? Why are you turning back? What's scaring you?

Cassandra The house – it's breathing – exhalations heavy with the stench of death. Its walls are dripping blood.

1310 **Chorus** No, no – it's just the sacrifices from the altars.

Cassandra No, it's like the stench that issues from the grave.

Chorus No, that's the incense you can smell. They're burning it inside.

Although she knows the truth, **Cassandra** *becomes calm once more.*

Cassandra Well, I shall go inside the house and there lament my death and Agamemnon's. Enough of life.

ió, ió, xéni!

No, it's not terror makes me tremble like a bird caught in the woods. No. No.

I only pray that when I'm dead you'll be my witness, when she dies for me, a woman dying for a woman's sake, and when a man falls for a man so cruelly
1320 wedded. I ask you in my hour of death for this, my only grave gift.

Chorus My heart breaks. You can see your death so clearly.

Cassandra I've one last word, my own one final death song. I pray to Helios, the Sun God, to this last light I shall ever see, that for the guilty, for my murderers, what they shall do, the same be done to them, even for a slave's death, killed so easily.

Look at us human creatures, and look at our achievements, look at us all and weep, for we are impotent. We prosper – and a shadow passes and the balance tips. We suffer – and a sponge thrown angrily against a canvas blots the image,
1330 washes it away. And now all this; and, more than anything, I look on all of this and feel such sorrow.

Exit **Cassandra** *into the palace.*

Chorus Prosperity. Success. No-one ever feels he has too much. No. No-one jabs a finger at success and tells it to 'get out and don't come back'.

The gods bestowed their grace on Agamemnon and he captured Priam's city, Troy, and so came home in honour. But if he now must pay in blood for blood

spilt long ago, if he must pay the dead their recompense for death by dying 1340
himself, what man can boast that he's born free from danger, who has heard
of Agamemnon?

Suddenly blood-curdling screams are heard from within the palace.

Agamemnon (*offstage*)   No! Murder! No! They're killing me!

Chorus   Shh! Who's that shouting? Who's been wounded? Who's being killed?

Agamemnon (*offstage*)   No! No! Again! They're killing me!

Chorus   I think it's done. Those are his death cries. We must unite now, think how we can save the situation.

*The **Chorus** severally propose a course of action.*

- I'll tell you what *I* think – that we should get this message to the people: come here quick and help.
- *I* think that we should burst in now, not waste time, but catch them while the evidence is fresh!
- Yes. I agree. That's my vote too. No time to lose! 1350
- The situation's clear enough. This is the first step to dictatorship.
- We're wasting time – *they're* not. They're trampling caution underfoot. Their hands are busy.
- *I* don't know what advice to give. No. Those responsible for acting must make their own decisions.
- Yes, I agree. I can't see how, for all our words, we can bring back the 1360 dead.
- So, must we drag the rest of our lives out kow-towing before tyrants who have held our constitution in contempt?
- It can't be borne. No. Death is better. Death's more gentle than dictatorship.
- Look. All we've got to go on is some shouting. Why should we conclude he's dead?
- Yes. We need more information before we can debate this any further. Speculation's not the same as solid facts.

1370 – I agree with the consensus. I approve the view: we should confirm more clearly what the situation is with Agamemnon.

The palace doors open. Enter **Clytemnestra** *on the ekkuklēma. A sword in one hand and a net in the other, she stands blood-spattered over the bodies of* **Agamemnon** *and* **Cassandra**.

Clytemnestra   I have mouthed many speeches in the past to marry with the moment, and I shall feel no shame to contradict them now. For in the care and preparation of cruel vengeance on those enemies who masquerade as family and friends, how else to hem around the hunting-nets so high that nothing might outleap their horror? For me, this struggle spans so many years, so much contriving, but now in time and with eternal Justice it has flowered to its fulfilment.

1380 I stand here where I struck. I have achieved my purpose. What I have done is done, and I shall not disown it. And he could not escape or ward off his destruction.

The all-enclosing net, drag-net of destiny – I cast its fabric and its wealth of cruelty around him. I strike two blows and with two groans upon this very place he lets his limbs fall limp. And on his fallen body I bestow a third, an offering of thanks long prayed-for to Zeus the Guardian of the Dead, who rules beneath the earth.

And so he lies there, ebbing out the vomit of his very life, and gasping forth a
1390 frothing arc of blood he spatters me with dark dank droplets of his bloody dew, while I exalted as the growing corn exalts, in labour with the bursting seed, when Zeus sends down his rain.

And so, as things are so, rejoice, you Argive elders, if you would rejoice. For I – I revel in my deed. If ritual did not forbid, then I would pour libations on the dead man's corpse, an offering most just, surpassing justice.

In his own house, he filled a mixing-bowl that brimmed with such cruel curses, and now he has come home and drained it to the dregs.

Chorus   How can you speak like this, so brazenly. How can you boast that
1400 you've killed your own husband?

Clytemnestra   You question me as if I were some brainless *woman*! I tell you this – from one who's not afraid to one who's wise: praise me if you wish, or criticise. It makes no difference. *This* is Agamemnon; *this* is my husband; *this* is the corpse created by my hand; and this is how things are.

Chorus What mess of evil writhing from the earth, what drug mixed from the snaking sea – what have you devoured, my lady, to make you care so little for the city's curse and your pollution? No, you've cast off your line, cut off your life, and you will go in exile from your city, weighted heavy with the hatred of the citizens. 1410

Clytemnestra Is this your judgement: exile and the city's curse, the hatred of the citizens? Is this the Justice that I get from you? Oh, but you showed no opposition to my husband when he broke our faith, when – like it was a sheep he killed, picked for its fleece from all the flocks we own – he sacrificed his daughter, my baby I loved more than anything, a lullaby to soothe the winds from Thrace. Should you not have exiled *him* in retribution for unleashing such pollution? No? Yet when you hear what I've done you're the harshest judge. 1420

I tell you: threaten all you like, but know I'm ready to match force with force, for only force can master me. But if God grant me victory, you'll learn your lesson despite all your years, that to be circumspect is to be truly wise.

Chorus You're overconfident. Your words are all bravado. The blood's dripped in your brain and maddened you. Your eyes peer glutinous through bloody cataracts. You have no friends, no allies, only punishment, death given as a due for death. 1430

Clytemnestra Listen, too, to this, the sacred power of oath: by Justice done for my own daughter, and by the fury, by the demon of revenge, for whom I killed him – I am not afraid, no. I feel only confidence while he keeps my fire burning in my grate, Aegisthus, who supports me now as he has always done. He is my shield, my courage, my defence.

But *Agamemnon*? I have laid him sprawling on the ground, my ruin, my ... my Casanova with his harem and his whores at Troy, and she, his bondage-slave, so good with crystal balls, his faithful little bed-mate, tugging on his oar, kneeling by his bench below the main mast. 1440

It's not gone unrequited. No. His death was as it was, and his lover lies beside him, and her last song was the death song that a swan sings at its dying, a song to savour, to let linger on the tongue, to add spice to my appetites in bed.

Chorus I wish *my* death would come now quick and with no pain, no wasting sickness, only sleep that lasts for ever, no awakening; dead, now our guardian is dead, King Agamemnon, dead, who cared for us so 1450 kindly, who suffered so much for a woman's sake; and at a woman's hand he perished.

Helen. Helen.
Alone, in blind infatuation, you consumed so many men,
so many souls at Troy,
and now, yes and forever,
you have flowered to your fulfilment in a bloody dew
that will not wash away.
Imbroglio was in the house, embedded in the soil,
1460 and for her husband came the nightmare of his sorrow.

Clytemnestra Don't pray for death, for all your megrims, no, don't turn your wrath on Helen. No. Don't call her murderess or claim she stood alone and so consumed so many men, so many Greeks, so many souls and sowed such grief which cannot be endured.

Chorus A demon's flapped down raggèd on this house and on the family of
1470 Tantalus. It sucks its strength from women's souls; it gnaws my heart; it governs everything. It's settled on me like a black crow rasping its hoarse tuneless hymn of exaltation.

Clytemnestra Your mind has cleared. You see it now for what it is, the demon which has gorged itself three times upon this family. It feeds the craving in the guts to glut on blood, a new discharge of pus, a fresh infection
1480 for the wound before the scab has healed.

Chorus You've brought the demon to the daylight, so dangerous to name it, a plague on the household, a deep-rooted violence, a virulent cancer insatiate. This comes from Zeus, the architect of everything, the source of all that is. For nothing mortal reaches its fulfilment without Zeus and nothing here has not been sent by God.

1490 My king, my king, how shall I weep for you?
My spirit's so loyal, but what can I say?
You're caught fast, cocooned in the threads of the spider's web,
gasping your life out in blasphemous death.
And now you've been laid like a slave snared in treachery,
slain by your wife and the razor-sharp blade.

Clytemnestra Are you so sure that I *am* Clytemnestra? Are you so sure I
1500 was his wife? Are you so sure I did it? No. The atavistic demon of revenge, the wraith, has become flesh, incarnate as this corpse's wife, in retribution for the

fleshy feast of Atreus, to sacrifice a grown man for the little children as a closure, a last offering.

Chorus What? Are you guiltless of his murder? Who'll support your cause? How could it be? How? How? Perhaps a demon of revenge, a revenant regenerated by a father's crime, *might* come as an accomplice.

Black Ares, god of violence, forces through in drenching deluges of blood, 1510 disgorging from one generation to the next. And where he goes, the blood clots, feasting on the children's flesh.

My king, my king, how shall I weep for you?
My spirit's so loyal, but what can I say?
You're caught fast, cocooned in the threads of the spider's web,
gasping your life out in blasphemous death.
And now you've been laid like a slave snared in treachery,
slain by your wife and the razor-sharp blade.   1520

Clytemnestra No, not like a slave; he did not die unworthily, not snared by treachery. I was ingenuous, open as he was, when he unleashed madness on his house, his family – and he took our child, the child that I bore him, our Iphigeneia, and so became the priest of sacrifice and there at Aulis killed our child. And what he did, the same was done to him in equal measure. So now he can no longer boast, now death has come, now retribution has been paid in full for his transgressions.

Chorus I can't think straight. I don't know where to turn. The house is 1530 crumbling; I'm cowering and the thrumming thunder of the deluge of black blood is battering the house. No drizzle now, no spattering. Already Destiny is grinding sharp the sword of Justice for a new revenge.

Earth. Earth.
    I wish you'd taken me in your embrace
    before I'd seen him laid out in this *bath*, this silver coffin.   1540
Who now will bury him?
Who will lament him?
Will *you* dare to do it,
    to rasp out a death song for the husband you killed?
Will *you* dare discharge the obsequies?
Will you perform the last rites for his soul – unrighteously –
    a jarring gratitude for all he did?
Who'll praise him, his achievements?
Who'll give the speech of honour?

1550 Who'll shed the true tears a hero deserves?

Clytemnestra Don't worry. No. These duties are not your responsibility. I killed him; I shall bury him. And as for tears, there will be none in this house, no – Iphigeneia: she will welcome him, a daughter welcoming a father, stretching out her arms, cool, incorporeal, kissing him in lingering embrace: sublime reunion beside the racing streams of death.

1560 **Chorus** Recrimination's answered by recrimination and the truth is hard to judge. The robber's robbed, the killer killed. As long as Zeus sits on his throne this shall be so, for this is *his* law, the law of Zeus: that which you do, the same shall be done unto you. Who can gouge out the curse's seed embedded deep within the house? Destruction claws close, clinging to the family.

Clytemnestra You're wise, far-sighted; you have recognised the truth. But me, my wish is this: to reach an understanding with the demon of revenge
1570 that haunts this house, the house of Pleisthenes, to swear an oath that I shall live with what I've done, hard though it be, if for all future time it leaves this house, unleashing its incestuous slaughter for some other family. And if I only have a little, I shall have enough, if I have closed the circle, if I've driven out this slaughter from my family.

Enter **Aegisthus** *from the palace.*

Aegisthus See how the sunlight blazes so benignly on this day now Justice is restored. Today now I can truly say the gods look down from sky to earth
1580 to take their vengeance for the sufferings of men, now I have seen him sprawling in the net, the webs close-woven by the wraiths of retribution, a sight so sweet, a gift of vengeance for his father's workmanship.

Yes, Agamemnon's father Atreus ruled Argos and (to put it bluntly) turned Thyestes, his own brother and my father, from his city and his house because he'd questioned his authority. Thyestes was unhappy though, and came back home to try to smooth things over, and he found that he was safe. He wasn't killed. No blood was spilt.

1590 But Atreus, Agamemnon's father, was a godless man. He made a fuss of him, and with unnatural haste invited him, *my* father, to a banquet (making out it was a feast, a holiday) – a banquet of his children's flesh. He'd cut their fingers and their toes up small and sprinkled them on top as garnishes. My father sat with Atreus, suspecting nothing, and so helped himself enthusiastically to meat – it looked so unremarkable – the cannibal ragout to wreck the family.

But when he knew what he had done, he wretched, he vomited, he fell back, kicking at the table, spitting out a curse so cruel, so apposite: 'Thus perish all the race of Pleisthenes!' 1600

And so now Agamemnon's dead. And so it was with Justice that I wove the warp and weft, the scheme of slaughter. You see, he drove me out, the thirteenth child, with my poor father, though I was a baby. But I grew up and Justice brought me home again.

And though I did not kill him, it was my hand struck the blow, since all the planning, all the plotting, all the vengeance all was mine. So I can die content now I've seen Agamemnon taken in the mesh of Justice. 1610

Chorus Aegisthus – it's not my way to brag when others suffer. No.

Now – do you say you killed him unprovoked, that you and only you planned Agamemnon's murder?

I tell you this: you won't escape the sentence all the citizens will pass when they take you out – no, listen! – when they take you out to stone you with their curses.

Aegisthus Is this how you'd address me? Is this how galley-slaves address their masters? Old man, you'll learn how painful it can be to take instruction at your time of life on how best to be circumspect. Chains and starvation are extraordinary cures for troubled minds, even for old men like you. Have you not eyes? Can you not see? It's best not to resist the cattle-prod, for, if you do, you might get hurt. 1620

Chorus You coward, you! You woman! How could you do this when they'd just come back from war? Not you, though. No! You stayed at home, the little housekeeper, committing your adulteries in his own bed. How could you plan a death like this for Agamemnon?

Aegisthus The more you say, the more you'll suffer later. But you're no Orpheus, no – *he* sang so enchantingly that all things followed him, but you? I find your bleating so banal, so rasping, that I'll have *you* led away. I'll break you yet; I'll tame you. 1630

Chorus You think we'll let you rule in Argos? No! You might have plotted Agamemnon's death – you couldn't *kill* him though!

Aegisthus No. It was obvious. To snare him was the woman's work, but me – I'd been his enemy too long. He'd have suspected me. I'll use his wealth. I'll try to rule. And any who does not obey, I'll clamp the bridle on him hard, 1640 no life of clover for him, no, but darkness and starvation will soon see him softened.

Chorus   Why did *you* not do it? Coward! Why did *you* not kill him? Why did it have to be his wife, when that would bring pollution on the land of Argos and the gods? Somewhere Orestes is alive, and some day he'll come home, and so in victory and with good fortune he will kill them both!

Aegisthus   If this is how you mean to act, if this is how you mean to speak,
1650   it's time to learn your lesson. *Eiá!* Comrades! Guards! To work now!

Aegisthus' guards pour onto the stage armed with clubs.

Chorus   *Eiá!* To arms and forward!

Aegisthus   To arms, yes! I am ready to face death!

Chorus   Death? Yes – we accept your challenge and we'll take our chance!

*The **Chorus** and **guards** are ready to fight. **Clytemnestra** stops them with the merest gesture.*

Clytemnestra (*to* Aegisthus *soothingly*)   No! No! My darling! No! No, this is wrong – no more of this. No! Even these would be too many for our scythe, too hard a harvest. No. There's been enough of suffering, so no more blood.

(*to* Chorus) Go home now, you, you elders; go with our honour and respect, before what you would do is done to *you*.

What's done is done – we must accept it. If there could be an end to all this
1660   suffering, I'd welcome it most gladly. The wraith of retribution, yes, the demon of revenge has struck us with his hoof and we've all suffered.

These are my words to you, a woman's words, if you would hear them.

Aegisthus   No! They've insulted me with all their threats, their jabbering. I am their master. They've no sense of decency.

Chorus   We Argives don't kow-tow to criminals.

Aegisthus   We shall meet later, you and I.

Chorus   Not if the spirit of revenge should bring Orestes home.

Aegisthus   I know the empty hopes that exiles feed on.

Chorus   Gloat all you will! Grow fat! Soil justice while you have the chance!

Aegisthus   Know this, the time will come you'll pay for this stupidity.   1670

Chorus   Go on, go strut with your woman, strut and crow, just like the cock you are!

Clytemnestra (*to* Aegisthus)   Ignore them – it's all empty yammering. We rule now, you and I, and we'll arrange all well.

Exeunt **Clytemnestra** *and* **Aegisthus**. *Exit* **Chorus**.

Bibliography

Alexopoulou, M., *The Theme of Returning Home in Ancient Greek Literature: The Nostos of the Epic Heroes*, Lewiston, 2009.
Bakewell, G., 'Aeschylus: Gods, fate, and necessity', in H. M. Roisman (ed.), *The Encyclopedia of Greek Tragedy*, vol. 1, 33–35, Oxford, 2014.
Bakola, E., 'Crime and punishment: Cratinus, Aeschylus' *Oresteia*, and the metaphysics and politics of wealth', in E. Bakola, L. Prauscello and M. Telò (eds.), *Greek Comedy and the Discourse of Genres*, 226–55, Cambridge, 2013.
Balot, R. K., *Greed and Injustice in Classical Athens*, Princeton, 2001.
Bednarowski, K. P., 'Surprise and suspense in Aeschylus' *Agamemnon*', *American Journal of Philology*, 136.2 (2015), 179–205.
Berkoff, S., *Agamemnon: The Fall of the House of Usher*, in *EAST*, 51–77, London, 1977.
Bollack, J. and Judet de La Combe, P., *L'Agamemnon d'Eschyle: le texte et ses interprétations*, 3 vols. (Ii, Iii, II), Lille, 1981–82.
Braund, S., 'Introduction' to her translation of *Agamemnon*, in S. Bartsch (ed.), *Seneca, the Complete Tragedies*, vol. 2, 233–41, Chicago, 2017.
Burkert, W., *Greek Religion*, trans. J. Raffan, Cambridge, MA, 1985.
Cairns, D. L., '*Hybris*, dishonour, and thinking big', *Journal of Hellenic Studies*, 116 (1996), 1–32.
Clay, D., 'Aeschylus' Trigeron Mythos', *Hermes*, 97 (1969), 1–9.
Collard, C., *Aeschylus: Oresteia*, Oxford, 2002.
Conacher, D. J., *Aeschylus' Oresteia: A Literary Commentary*, Toronto, 1976.
Conacher, D. J., *Aeschylus' Oresteia: A Literary Commentary*, Toronto, 1987.
Dalzell, J. O., 'Pleisthenes in the "Agamemnon" of Aeschylus', *Hermathena*, 110 (1970), 79–80.
Debnar, P., 'The sexual status of Aeschylus' Cassandra', *Classical Philology*, 105 (2010), 129–45.
De Jong, I. F., *A Narratological Commentary on the Odyssey*, Cambridge, 2001.
Denniston, J. D. and Page, D. L., *Aeschylus: Agamemnon*, Oxford, 1957.
de Romilly, J., *Time in Greek Tragedy*, Ithaca, 1968.
Dodds, E. R., 'Morals and politics in the Oresteia', *Proceedings of the Cambridge Philological Society*, 6 (1960), 19–31. Reprinted in Dodds, E. R. (ed.), *The Ancient Concept of Progress*, Oxford, 1973, and in Lloyd, M. (ed.), *Aeschylus*, Oxford, 2007.
Dover, K. J., 'Neglected aspects of Agamemnon's dilemma', *Journal of Hellenic Studies*, 93 (1973), 58–69.
Earp, F. R., *The Style of Aeschylus*, Cambridge, 1948.
Easterling, P. and Hall, E. (eds.), *Greek and Roman Actors: Aspects of Ancient Profession*, Cambridge, 2002.

Echeverría, F., 'Greek armies against towns: Siege warfare and the *Seven against Thebes*', in I. Torrance (ed.), *Aeschylus and War: Comparative Perspectives on Aeschylus' Seven against Thebes*, 73–90, London, 2017.

Edwards, M. W., 'Agamemnon's decision: Freedom and folly in Aeschylus', *California Studies in Classical Antiquity*, 10 (1977), 17–38.

Eidinow, E., 'Popular theologies: The gift of divine envy', in E. Eidinow, J. Kindt and R. Osborne (eds.), *Theologies of Ancient Greek Religion*, 205–32, Cambridge, 2016.

Elata-Alster, G., 'The king's double bind: Paradoxical communication in the parodos of Aeschylus' *Agamemnon*', *Arethusa*, 18.1 (1985), 23–46.

Farber, Y., *Theatre as Witness. Three Testimonial Plays from South Africa*, London, 2008a.

Farber, Y., *Molora*, London, 2008b.

Ferguson, J., *A Companion to Greek Tragedy*, Austin, 1972 (2001, 2013).

Fisher, N. R. E., *Hybris: A Study in the Values of Honour and Shame in Ancient Greece*, Warminster, 1992.

Foley, H., *Female Acts in Greek Tragedy*, Princeton, 2001.

Ford, A., 'Alcibiades' Eikôn of Socrates and the Platonic text', in P. Desrtrée and R. Edmonds (eds.), *Plato and the Power of Images*, 11–28, Leiden, 2017.

Fraenkel, E., *Aeschylus: Agamemnon*, 3 vols., Oxford, 1950.

Franco, C., *Shameless: The Canine and the Feminine in Ancient Greece*, Berkeley, 2014.

Gagné, R. and Hopman, M. G., 'Introduction: The chorus in the middle', in R. Gagné and M. G. Hopman (eds.), *Choral Mediations in Greek Tragedy*, 1–34, Cambridge, 2013.

Garvie, A. F., *Aeschylus' Supplices: Play and Trilogy*, London, 1969.

George, A. R., *The Babylonian Gilgamesh Epic*, vol. 2, Oxford, 2003.

Goldhill, S., *Language, Sexuality, Narrative: The Oresteia*, Cambridge, 1984.

Goldhill, S., *Reading Greek Tragedy*, Cambridge, 1986.

Goward, B., *Aeschylus: Agamemnon*, London, 2005.

Gruber, M. A., 'Reichtum und Familie im "Agamemnon" des Aischylos: ein ökonomischer Ansatz zur Interpretation der Tragödie', in I. De Gennaro, S. Kazmierski and R. Lüfter (eds.), *Wirtliche Ökonomie: philosophische und dichterische Quellen*, 307–42, Nordhausen, 2013.

Güterbock, H. G., 'The Hittite version of the Hurrian Kumarbi myths: Oriental forerunners of Hesiod', *American Journal of Archaeology*, 52.1 (1948), 123–34.

Hall, E., *Inventing the Barbarian*, Oxford, 1989.

Hall, E., 'The sociology of Athenian tragedy', in P. Easterling (ed.), *The Cambridge Companion to Greek Tragedy*, 93–126, Cambridge, 1997.

Hall, E., 'Clytemnestra's manly heart in the *Agamemnon*', *Omnibus*, 36 (1998), 27–90.

Hall, E., 'Aeschylus' Clytemnestra versus her Senecan tradition', in F. Macintosh, P. Michelakis, E. Hall and O. Taplin (eds.), *Agamemnon in Performance*, 53–76, Oxford, 2005.

Hall, E., 'Why are the Erinyes female: or, what is so feminine about revenge?', in L. Dawson and F. McHardy (eds.), *Revenge and Gender from Classical to Renaissance Literature*, 33–57, Edinburgh, 2018.

Hall, E., 'Black Sea back story: Euripides' *Medea*', in D. Braund, E. Hall and R. Wyles (eds.), *Greek Theatre and Performance around the Ancient Black Sea*, 267–88, Cambridge, 2019.

Hall, E., 'Aristophanes' *Birds* as satire on Athenian opportunists in Thrace', in R. M. Rosen and H. P. Foley (eds.), *Aristophanes and Politics*, 187–213, London, 2020.

Hardwick, L., 'Voices of trauma: Remaking Aeschylus' *Agamemnon* in the twentieth century', in S. Constantinidis (ed.), *The Reception of Aeschylus' Plays through Shifting Models and Frontiers*, 280–303, Leiden, 2016.

Harris, Z., *Agamemnon's Return*, in *This Restless House*, 15–136, London, 2016.

Heaney, S., *The Spirit Level*, London, 1996.

Heath, J., 'Disentangling the beast: Humans and other animals in Aeschylus' *Oresteia*', *Journal of Hellenic Studies*, 119 (1999), 17–47.

Hedreen, G., *Capturing Troy*, Ann Arbor, 2001.

Henrichs, A., 'Human sacrifice in Greek religion: Three case studies', in J. Rudhardt and O. Reverdin (eds.), *Le Sacrifice dans l'Antiquité*, 195–242, Geneva, 1981.

Herington, J., *Aeschylus*, New Haven, 1986.

Hogan, J. C., *A Commentary on The Complete Greek Tragedies, Aeschylus*, Chicago, 1985.

Hughes, D., *Human Sacrifice in Ancient Greece*, London, 1991.

Hunter, R. L., *Plato's Symposium*, Cambridge, 2004.

Jones, J., *On Aristotle and Greek Tragedy*, London, 1962 (reissued 1980).

Kakridis, J. T., 'Pleistheniden oder Atriden? Zu Hesiods frg. 195 M.-W.', *ZPE*, 30 (1978), 1–4.

Keith, A. L., 'The taunt in Homer and Vergil', *Classical Journal*, 19 (1924), 554–60.

Knox, B. M. W., 'The lion in the house (*Agamemnon* 717–36 [Murray])', *Classical Philology*, 47 (1952), 17–25.

Knox, B. M. W, 'Aeschylus and the third actor', in B. M. W. Knox (ed.), *Word and Action: Essays on the Ancient Theater*, 39–55, Baltimore, 1979.

Kovacs, D., *Euripides*, vol. IV, Cambridge, MA, 1999.

Kyriakou, P., 'Warrior vaunts in the *Iliad*', *Rheinisches Museum für Philologie*, 144 (2001), 250–77.

Langwitz Smith, O., 'Once again the guilt of Agamemnon', *Eranos*, 71 (1973), 1–11.

Lather, A., 'Olfactory theater: Tracking scents in Aeschylus' *Oresteia*', *Arethusa*, 51.1 (2018), 33–54.

Lawrence, S., 'Fate and chance', in H. M. Roisman (ed.), *The Encyclopedia of Greek Tragedy*, vol. 1, 502–6, Oxford, 2014.

Leahy, D. M., 'The role of Cassandra in the *Oresteia* of Aeschylus', *Bulletin of the John Rylands Library*, 52.1 (1969), 144–77.

Lebeck, A., *The Oresteia: A Study in Language and Structure*, Cambridge, MA, 1971.

Lesky, A., 'Decision and responsibility in the tragedies of Aeschylus', *Journal of Hellenic Studies*, 86 (1966), 78–85.

Ley, G., *The Theatricality of Greek Tragedy: Playing Space and Chorus*, Chicago, 2007.

Lloyd, M. (ed.), *Aeschylus*, Oxford, 2007.

Lloyd-Jones, H., 'Zeus in Aeschylus', *Journal of Hellenic Studies*, 76 (1956), 55–67.

Lloyd-Jones, H., 'The guilt of Agamemnon', in E. Segal (ed.), *Oxford Readings in Greek Tragedy*, 61, Oxford, 1983. Originally published in *Classical Quarterley*, 12 (1962), 187–99.

Lloyd-Jones, H., 'Ten notes on Aeschylus' *Agamemnon*', in R. D. Dawe, J. Diggle and P. E. Easterling (eds.), *Dionysiaca: Nine Studies in Greek Poetry*, 45–61, Cambridge, 1978.

Lloyd-Jones, H., *Aeschylus: The Oresteia. Agamemnon*, London, 1979.

Macintosh, F., Michelakis, P., Hall, E. and Taplin, O. (eds.), Agamemnon *in Performance 458 BC to AD 2004*, Oxford, 2005.

MacNeice, L., *The Agamemnon of Aeschylus*, London, 2008. Originally published 1936.

Medda, E., *La saggezza dell'illusione. Studi sul teatro greco*, Pisa, 2013.

Nappa, C., '"Agamemnon" 717–36: The Parable of the Lion Cub', *Mnemosyne*, 47 (1994), 82–87.

Parker, R., *On Greek Religion*, Ithaca, 2011.

Parks, W., *Verbal Dueling in Heroic Narrative. The Homeric and Old English Traditions*, Princeton, 1990.

Peradotto, J. J., 'Some patterns of nature imagery in the *Oresteia*', *American Journal of Philology*, 85 (1964), 378–93.

Peradotto, J. J., 'The omen of the eagles and the *ethos of* Agamemnon', in M. Lloyd (ed.), *Aeschylus*, Oxford, 2007. Originally published in *Phoenix*, 23 (1969), 237–63.

Potamiti, A., 'To chase a flying bird: Aeschylus, *Agamemnon* 393–5', *Classical Journal*, 110 (2015), 303–31.

Raeburn, D. and Thomas, O., *The* Agamemnon *of Aeschylus. A Commentary for Students*, Oxford, 2011.

Redfield, J., *Nature and Culture in the Iliad: The Tragedy of Hector*, expanded edition, Durham, NC, 1994.

Rehm, R., trans., *Aeschylus' Oresteia: A Theatre Version*, Melbourne, 1978.

Rehm, R., *Marriage to Death: The Conflation of Wedding and Funeral Rituals in Greek Tragedy*, Princeton, 1994.

Rehm, R., '*Antigone* and the Rights of the Earth', in D. Stuttard (ed.), *Looking at Antigone*, 93–106, London, 2018.

Roisman, H. M., *Loyalty in Early Greek Epic and Tragedy*, Hain: Beiträge zur Klassischen Philologie, 1984.

Roisman, H. M., 'Clytaemenstra's ominous words, Aeschylus, *Agamemnon* 345–347', *Zeitschrift für Papyrologie und Epigraphik*, 66 (1986), 279–84.

Roisman, H. M., 'Like father like son, Telemachus' *kerdea*', *Rheinisches Museum für Philologie*, 137 (1994), 1–22.
Roisman, H. M. (ed.), *The Encyclopedia of Greek Tragedy*, 3 vols., Malden, 2014.
Roisman, H. M., 'Loyal Clytemnestra: γυναῖκα πιστήν (Aeschylus, *Agamemnon* 606)', *Giornale Italiano di Filologia*, 70 (2018), 11–18.
Roisman, H. M., *Tragic Heroines in Ancient Greek Drama*, London, 2021.
Rose, P. W., *Sons of the Gods, Children of Earth: Ideology and Literary Form in Ancient Greece*, Ithaca, 1992.
Rosenmeyer, T. G., *The Art of Aeschylus*, Berkeley, 1982.
Rutherford, R. B., *Greek Tragic Style*, Cambridge, 2012.
Schein, S. L., 'The Cassandra scene in Aeschylus' "Agamemnon"', *Greece & Rome*, 29 (1982), 11–16.
Scott, W. C., 'The confused chorus (*Agamemnon* 975–1034)', *Phoenix*, 23.4 (1969), 336–46.
Seaford. R., *Money and the Early Greek Mind: Homer, Philosophy, Tragedy*, Cambridge, 2004.
Seaford, R., *Cosmology and the Polis: The Social Construction of Space and Time in the Tragedies of Aeschylus*, Cambridge, 2012.
Sider, D., 'Stagecraft in the *Oresteia*', *American Journal of Philology*, 99 (1978), 12–27.
Sidnell, M., 'Another "Death of Tragedy": Louis MacNeice's translation of *Agamemnon* in the context of his work in the theatre', in M. Cropp, E. Fantham and S. Scully (eds.), *Greek Tragedy and its Legacy: Essays Presented to D.J. Conacher*, 323–35, Calgary, 1986.
Simpson, M., 'Why does Agamemnon yield?', *La Parola del Passato*, 26 (1971), 94–101.
Solmsen, F., *Hesiod and Aeschylus*, Ithaca, 1949.
Sommerstein, A. H., *Aeschylean Tragedy*, second edition, London, 2010. Originally published Bari, 1996.
Sommerstein, A. H., *Aeschylus Oresteia*, Cambridge, MA, 2008.
Sommerstein, A. H., *The Tangled Ways of Zeus and Other Studies In and Around Greek Tragedy*, Oxford, 2010.
Sommerstein, A. H., '*Atē* in Aeschylus', in D. L. Cairns (ed.), *Tragedy and Archaic Greek Thought*, 1–15, Swansea, 2013.
Taplin, O., *The Stagecraft of Aeschylus*, Oxford, 1977.
Taplin, O., *The Oresteia*, Norton Critical Edition, ed. O. Taplin and J. Billings, New York, 2018.
Thiel, R., *Chor und dramatische Handlung im 'Agamemnon' des Aischylos*, Stuttgart, 1993.
Thomas, O., 'Nine passages of Aeschylus' "Agamemnon"', *Classical Quarterly*, 63.2 (2013), 491–500.
Thomson, G. D., *The Oresteia of Aeschylus*, new revised and enlarged edition, Amsterdam, 1966. Originally published Cambridge, 1938.
Tóibín, C., *House of Names*, London, 2017a.
Tóibín, C., 'How I rewrote a Greek tragedy', *The Guardian*, 20 May, 2017b. https://www.theguardian.com/books/2017/may/20/colm-toibin-rewrites-greek-tragedy

Tyrrell, W. B., 'Agamemnon at Aulis', *Classical Journal*, 71 (1976), 328–34.
Vendler, H., 'Seamus Heaney and the *Oresteia*: "Mycenae lookout" and the usefulness of tradition', in M. McDonald and J. M. Walton (eds.), *Amid Our Troubles: Irish Versions of Greek Tragedy*, 181–97, London, 2002.
Vermeule, E., 'The Boston Oresteia Krater', *American Journal of Archaeology*, 70 (1966), 1–22.
West, M. L., 'The Parodos of the *Agamemnon*', *Classical Quarterly*, 29 (1979), 1–6.
West, M. L., *Studies in Aeschylus*, Stuttgart, 1990.
West, S., 'Aegisthus the cowardly lion: A note on Aeschylus, "Agamemnon" 1224', *Mnemosyne*, 56 (2003), 480–84.
Whallon, W., 'Why is Artemis angry?', *American Journal of Philology*, 82 (1961), 78–88.
Wilson, J. R., 'τόλμα and the meaning of τάλας', *American Journal of Philology*, 92 (1971), 292–300.
Wilson, P., 'Dikên in the *Oresteia* of Aeschylus', *Bulletin of the Institute of Classical Studies, Supplement* (2006), 187–201.
Winnington-Ingram, R. P., 'Clytemnestra and the vote of Athena', *Journal of Hellenic Studies*, 68 (1948), 130–47.
Winnington-Ingram, R. P., *Studies in Aeschylus*, Cambridge, 1980.
Wrigley, A., 'Aeschylus' *Agamemnon* on BBC Radio, 1946–1976', *International Journal of the Classical Tradition*, 12.2 (2005), 216–44.
Wyles, R., *Costume in Greek Tragedy*, London, 2011.
Younger, J. G., 'The Mycenae-Vapheio Lion Group', *American Journal of Archaeology*, 82 (1978), 285–99.
Zeitlin, F., 'The motif of corrupted sacrifice in Aeschylus' *Oresteia*', *Transactions of the American Philological Association*, 96 (1965), 463–508.
Zeitlin, F., 'Postscript to sacrificial imagery in the *Oresteia* (*Ag.* 1235–7)', *Transactions of the American Philological Association*, 97 (1966), 645–53.
Zeitlin, F., 'The dynamics of misogyny: Myth and mythmaking in the *Oresteia* of Aeschylus', *Arethusa*, 11 (1978), 149–84

Index

#MeToo 154

Achilles 21, 29, 31, 34, 63
Acropolis (Athenian) 3, 6, 76, 78, 149
Actors of Dionysus 161
adultery 15, 34, 62, 115
Aegean 34, 119, 123, 127
Aegisthus 2–5, 9, 14, 17–22, 24–6, 40, 44, 49, 51, 56, 59, 63–4, 78, 84, 95–7, 100, 116, 124, 138, 148, 157–8, 163–5, 167, 171–2
Aerope 2, 15, 24
Aeschylus 1–2, 5–11, 13–15, 17, 19–21, 24–6, 29, 39–42, 44–6, 49, 52, 54–5, 59–60, 66, 69–71, 78, 90, 98, 101, 105, 109, 119, 122–4, 131, 135–7, 139, 143–8, 152, 154–9, 161–8, 170, 172
Agamemnon 1, 4–9, 11, 13–17, 19, 21, 23, 25, 29, 35, 39–40, 42–3, 45–6, 63, 69–75, 77–9, 82, 85, 89, 101, 105–7, 115–16, 119, 122–4, 130, 136–43, 147–50, 152, 155–9, 161–2, 165, 168, 172
Choephoroi 4–6, 14, 17, 29, 51, 56, 63, 65, 75, 83, 101, 121, 128, 137–8
Eumenides 4–8, 1415, 19, 46–7, 75, 77–8, 112, 116, 121, 130, 131, 137–8
Libation Bearers, see *Choephoroi*
Oresteia 1, 3–6, 14–15, 17–19, 29, 35, 37, 65–6, 77, 80, 107, 111, 137, 147, 155, 161, 165, 167
Persae 6, 39–43, 45–6, 136, 150
Persians, see Aeschylus, *Persae*
Prometheus Bound 136
Proteus 4, 44
Suppliants 137
Seven Against Thebes 137
Agamemnon 1–5, 8, 10, 16–26, 29–37, 39–47, 49–57, 59–61, 63–6, 72–5, 78–84, 89–101, 106–7, 109–16, 119–24, 125–31, 136, 138, 140–1, 143, 146–9, 151–5, 157–9, 163–72
Agias, *Nostoi* 39
Ajax (Lesser) 39, 82, 154
alastōr 24, 62, 64, 97
Alcmaeonids 18
Alexopoulou, Marigo 39
Aphrodite 16, 18, 93
Apollo 3–4, 8, 10, 19, 52–3, 55, 59–60, 62–3, 65–6, 80, 84, 90–1, 95, 138, 142, 144, 154, 164, 171
Areopagus 3, 5, 47
Arete 40
Argolid 2
Argos 1, 15, 17, 20, 23–4, 26, 30–1, 36, 42, 47, 55, 63, 78–9, 82, 84, 91, 105, 119–21, 123–4, 126, 129, 141–2, 144, 153, 163–4, 168–9
Aristophanes, *Birds* 26
Plutus 44
Aristotle 8, 136
Artemis 3–4, 17, 22–3, 29–32, 36, 80, 89, 91–3, 98–100, 129, 146, 151, 177, 179
Atē 64, 93, 95–6, 105, 108
Athena 3–4, 19, 44, 51, 85, 121–2, 130, 138, 154
Athens 1, 3–4, 8, 14, 18, 25, 33, 46–7, 75, 78, 121–2, 124, 130–1, 138, 149–50, 161
Atossa 44, 46
Atreidae 3, 30, 32, 82, 98–9, 137, 143–6

Atreus 2–3, 14, 20, 21, 23–4, 52, 62,
    81, 95, 97–101, 115, 130, 153,
    162–3, 171
Aulis 3, 29–32, 35–6, 41, 52–3, 63, 72,
    80–1, 91, 123, 128, 140, 146, 150

bath, Agamemnon's murder in 3, 8,
    23, 42, 45–6, 58, 61, 74, 157–8,
    171
beacon speech 42, 57, 123–4, 129
Berkoff, Steven 162–5, 168
    Agamemnon 162–5
    Greek 162
Bilgames and the Netherworld 16
bitch, *see* dog/bitch
Boeotia 29, 123
bride 3, 15, 26, 45, 70, 72–3, 100,
    141–2, 154
bridegroom 45, 73
Briseis 34

Calchas 3–4, 17, 29–32, 35–6, 52,
    80–1, 84, 91–2, 98, 146, 151
Calypso 43
cannibalism 2, 13, 15, 17, 20–2, 25–6,
    163
Carthaginians 23
Cassandra 6, 8–10, 13–15, 17–18, 20,
    22–3, 25, 44–5, 49–56, 58–63,
    65–6, 73–5, 82–4, 94, 100,
    115–16, 130, 137–8, 141–3,
    149, 151, 153–9, 163–4, 168,
    170–1
child/children 1–3, 8, 13–17, 19–26,
    30, 51–2, 56, 62, 79, 91, 99, 101,
    108, 115, 138–9, 143, 155, 157,
    162–3, 165–6
Chorus (in *Agamemnon*) 8–10,
    13–15, 17, 19–20, 22–5, 30–1,
    35–6, 41–4, 49–52, 54, 56–65,
    77–85, 89–100, 105–6, 112,
    120, 122–3, 125–9, 137–41,
    143–4, 146–7, 152, 157
Cilissa 5
Citizens Theatre group, Glasgow 167

civil war 17, 121, 158
civilization/civilizing 4–5, 14, 21, 23, 46
Cleisthenes 18
Clytaemestra, *see* Clytemnestra
Clytemnestra 1–9, 14–19, 21–2, 24–6,
    29, 36–7, 40–3, 45–6, 49–61,
    63–6, 73–4, 78–9, 82–4, 89,
    91–8, 100, 105–7, 112, 119–31,
    137–8, 140–2, 144, 148–9, 151,
    153–4, 157–9, 161, 163–5,
    168–71
coffin 46
Conacher, D. J. 64
court of law 3–5, 14, 19, 75
Cronos 16–17, 20–1
Cyclopes 16, 21
Cylon 18
Cynegirus 149

daimon 17–18, 62, 64, 89–90, 94, 97,
    100, 120, 122
Darius 41, 46
Deianeira 43, 46
Delphi 3–4, 8, 20, 46, 59
Demeter 2, 20
democracy 14, 18, 26, 166
Diomedes 39
Dionysus 4, 76, 106, 124
Dionysus, Theatre of 6, 45
Dodds, E. R. 106, 157
dog/bitch 7, 56, 137, 140–2, 163
Dokimasia Painter 46

eagle(s) 6, 15, 22–3, 25, 30, 80, 91, 129,
    145–6, 151
ekkuklēma 8
Electra 3–5, 29, 39–40, 63, 157–8,
    168–9, 171–2
Eleusinian Mysteries 71, 75
Eleusis 5, 124
Eleutherae 124
Eliot, George 13
Enkidu 16
Erinys/Erinyes 3–6, 13–19, 26, 47, 56,
    62, 64, 85

Eris 94, 98
erōs 18
Euboea 3, 123
Eumaeus 43–4
Eumenides 4, 130–1
Euripides 39, 54, 135
  Andromache 39–40, 45
  Bacchae 123–4
  Electra 39, 63, 165
  Hecuba 54
  Heracles 39
  Iphigenia at Aulis 31, 55, 72, 168
  Phoenician Women 72
  Trojan Women 55
Euripus 32
Eurylochus 41
Evans, Michael 9–10

fabrics on which Agamemnon walks 8, 44–5, 50, 52–3, 63, 66, 89, 94, 100, 107, 109–10, 112, 116, 119, 164, 171
Fagles, Robert 165
Farber, Yael, *Molora* 161, 165–7
Fate 89–91, 95, 97, 100
fire speech, *see* beacon speech
first stasimon 43, 93, 105–6, 109, 112–15
First World War 156–7
Foley, Helene P. 67
Fraenkel, Eduard 9, 89–90
Fury/Furies 1, 3–4, 52, 64, 75–6, 89–90, 96, 98, 112–13, 115, 121, 130, 153, 162, 171

Gaia 15–16
games (athletic) 9, 44
Gela 6
ghost(s) 5, 13, 22, 46, 162, 168, 172
Giants 17
Gielgud, Val 157
Good Friday Agreement 156

Hades 20, 54
Hall, Peter 161

hare 22–3, 30, 80, 89, 91, 99, 129, 146, 151
Harris, Zinnie, *This Restless House* 167–71
Heaney, Seamus 157, 159
  'Mycenae Outlook' poems 150, 155–7
Hector 21
Hecuba 54
Helen 2–4, 15, 26, 41, 72–3, 89–90, 93–4, 96, 98, 100–1, 112–13, 138–9, 161
Hell 94, 157
Hephaestus 123
Hera 20
Heracles 43, 46
Herald 8, 42–5, 51, 58, 60, 82–3, 93–4, 106–7, 114, 126–8, 131, 149, 152–3, 155, 157, 164, 167
Hesiod 15, 17–18, 20
  Theogony 13–16
  Works and Days 21, 105, 108
Hestia 20
Homer 39, 41, 60–1, 74, 89, 108, 136, 144–8
  Iliad 145
  Odyssey 39, 41, 147
House of Atreus 2, 4, 17, 20, 24, 52–3, 56, 58, 60, 62, 64–6, 83, 89, 97, 100–1, 106–7, 114, 121–2, 141–2, 162–3, 167
hubris/hybris 24, 52–3, 63, 94, 100, 105, 107–15
Hymn to Zeus 30, 91, 93, 140, 146

incest 15, 34
initiation 5, 71, 75
Iphigeneia, *see* Iphigenia
Iphigenia 3–4, 15, 17–19, 22–4, 29–31, 33, 35–6, 51–2, 54–5, 63, 72, 89, 91–3, 99–101, 112, 123, 128–30, 138, 140, 144, 146–7, 149–53, 157–8, 168–9, 171–2

Iraq 158-9
Ithaca 34, 40, 42-6
Itys 25

jury 4, 130, 138
justice 1, 5, 14, 16, 26, 64, 78-9, 81-5,
    89-90, 92-4, 96-8, 100-1,
    107, 109-10, 113, 115, 122,
    137-8, 166

Kindly Ones, *see* Eumenides
Kingsmill massacre 158
Knox, Bernard 139
Koun, Karolos 161
Kubrick, Stanley 1

Leahy, D. M. 53
Lebeck, Anne 52
Lemnos 123
lex talionis 4
Lichas 43
Life of Aeschylus 19
lion(s) 25-6, 113, 138-9, 144, 157
lion cub 22, 26, 139, 142
Lloyd-Jones, Hugh 33-4, 99
Lord, A. B. 39

MacNeice, Louis 150, 156-7, 159
    Agamemnon 156-7, 159
Marathon (Battle of) 5-6, 149
marriage 29, 35, 62, 70-3, 75, 154
masks 7
Medda, Enrico 44
Megacles 18
Menelaus 2-3, 30-3, 39, 42, 44, 80, 83,
    90-1, 94, 98, 111, 127, 129, 151-2
Mēnis, *see* Wrath
Mesopotamia 16
metaphor(s) 13, 23-4, 35, 55, 65, 101,
    108, 112, 125, 128, 135-6, 154
Mnouchkine, Ariane 161
Moira, *see* Fate
Mount
    Aegalio 124
    Agiolias 124

Arachnaion 124
Ida 42, 123-4, 127, 129
Kithairon 123
Makistos 123
Messapium 123
Profitis Ilias 124
Zara 124
murder 1, 3-4, 8, 13, 15-20, 22, 24-5,
    29, 34, 37, 39, 42, 45-6, 49,
    51-2, 54-5, 59-61, 63-5, 75,
    81, 84, 91-3, 95-7, 99-101,
    115, 120-1, 128, 130-1, 136-9,
    141-3, 147, 149-50, 153,
    158-9, 161, 163, 165-7
Mycenae 2-3, 124

Nausicaa 46
Nazi Germany 157
Necessity 35, 41, 89, 92, 99
Nestor 39, 42
net used to trap Agamemnon 3, 8, 10,
    45, 56, 58, 61-2, 74, 93, 98, 125,
    158
Northern Ireland 155, 158
nostos poetry 39-44

O'Neill, Eugene, *Mourning Becomes
    Electra* 161
omen 22-3, 30, 34, 80, 82, 91, 129,
    150-1
oracle 2, 4, 58, 59, 73
Orestes 3-6, 14, 18, 24, 44, 46-7, 51,
    56, 75, 77-8, 84, 121-2, 128,
    130, 138, 148, 157-8, 165-7
orkhēstra 7
Ouranos 15-17, 20

Page, Denys 35
Pan 90
Paris 3, 26, 33, 35-6, 52, 65, 73, 91,
    93-4, 98, 111, 113-14, 116, 123,
    126, 144, 163
parodos (choral song) 7, 29, 41, 72, 77,
    79, 83-4, 112, 123, 128, 143-7
Pelopia 2

Peloponnese 15
Pelops 2, 17, 52, 97
Penelope 34, 40–1, 43, 46, 56, 61, 144
Peradotto, John, J. 99
Pericles 6, 18
Persia 19
Persians 5–6, 149–50
Persuasion 90–1, 93, 111–12, 115
Phaeacians 42, 45
Phemius 39
Phocis 3, 63
phthonos 107, 116
Pindar 9, 17, 44
Plataea, Battle of 149–50
Pleisthenes 2, 17
Pleisthenids 18
Polymestor, 54
Polyphemus 41
Poseidon 20
Procne 25–6, 62
prologue 7, 25, 41, 75, 95
prophecy 52–3, 58, 63, 65–6, 95, 146, 154
prophet/ess 3, 8, 29–30, 45, 52–3, 59–60, 65–6, 142, 146, 149, 151, 153
Pygmies 145–7
Pylades 6, 51, 84

Raikes, Raymond 157
rape 2, 54, 82, 149, 153–5
Redfield, James 129
revenge, *see* vengeance
Rhea 20
ritual 63, 69–76, 150
Ruin 89–90, 93, 95, 97, 108, 111, 114
  see also Atē

sacrifice 3–4, 17–19, 22–4, 29–37, 41, 51–2, 57, 70, 72–3, 75–6, 81, 89, 91–3, 96–101, 112, 123, 128, 130, 140–1, 146, 149–51, 153, 157–8, 168, 170
Salamis, Battle of 6, 40, 149
Scheria 40, 46
Seaford, Richard 119, 122

second *stasimon* 94, 107, 109, 112–15
Second World War 156–7
Seneca 21, 162
  Agamemnon 161–2
  Thyestes 21, 162
Shining, The 1
shroud 46, 74
Sicily 1, 6
simile(s) 15, 135–48
skēne 7–8, 45
Solon 94, 105, 107–8, 110–11, 115
Solon, *Elegy to the Muses* 111, 115
Sophocles 6, 45, 135
  Electra 39, 165
  Oedipus Tyrannus 123, 162
  Tereus 25
  Trachiniae 39, 45
Sparta 2–3, 33
Stasis, *see* civil war
Stein, Peter 161
Stesichorus, *Nostoi* 39
Strymon 43
Stuttard, David 74, 138, 161
Syria 158–9

taboo 15
Tantalus 2, 17, 97, 162
Taplin, Oliver 39
Tasmisu 16
Telemachus 39, 42–6, 145
Tereus 25, 62
theatron 7
Thebes 150
Theoclymenus 45
third *stasimon* 112, 138
Thomas, Oliver 45
Thyestes 2–3, 8, 13, 15, 19–21, 23–4, 52, 56, 59, 62, 84, 95, 97–101, 115, 130, 138, 143, 153, 162–3
Tigris 16
Tisis, see vengeance
Titans 17
Tóibín, Colm 157–9
  Brooklyn 157
  House of Names 150, 157–9

trial 4–5, 96, 121, 138
Trojan horse 129
Trojan War 1, 39, 52, 78–9, 83, 93, 98, 123–4, 149, 157, 161–2, 164
Troy 3, 8, 10, 14, 22, 25–6, 29–31, 36–7, 39, 41–5, 51, 53–9, 62–3, 65, 72–3, 75, 79, 81–2, 90–4, 96, 98–101, 105–6, 110–14, 122–31, 138, 141–3, 145, 149, 151–4, 163–4, 168–9, 171
Truth and Reconciliation Commission 165

vengeance 1–4, 15–18, 20, 24, 33, 35, 37, 52, 54–5, 60, 62, 64, 75, 79, 89–90, 95, 97, 100–1, 107, 113, 115, 121–2, 128, 130–1, 138, 144, 149, 151, 161–3, 167–8, 171

Vermeule, Emily 46
vulture(s) 143–6

Watchman 4–5, 7, 25, 40–1, 51, 64–5, 75, 79, 90, 95, 123, 156, 163, 167–9, 171
Wedding, *see* marriage
Wilson, Peter 137
Wrath 17, 83, 91, 94, 98, 112, 151
  see also Mēnis

Xerxes 41–4, 46

Zeitlin, Froma 90, 138
Zeus 2, 17, 20, 30, 34–7, 63–4, 77–85, 89–101, 109–10, 126, 140, 143–4, 146

www.ingramcontent.com/pod-product-compliance
Lightning Source LLC
Chambersburg PA
CBHW072108010526
44111CB00037B/2040